THE PICTS
AND THEIR
SYMBOLS

W.A. CUMMINS

SUTTON PUBLISHING

First published in the United Kingdom in 1999 by
Sutton Publishing Limited · Phoenix Mill
Thrupp · Stroud · Gloucestershire · GL5 2BU

British Library Cataloguing in Publication Data
A catalogue record for this book is available from the British Library

ISBN 0-7509-2207-9

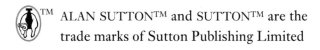 ᵀᴹ ALAN SUTTONᵀᴹ and SUTTONᵀᴹ are the trade marks of Sutton Publishing Limited

Typeset in 11/15pt Ehrhardt.
Typesetting and origination by
Sutton Publishing Limited.
Printed in Great Britain by
Butler & Tanner, Frome, Somerset.

Contents

Acknowledgements

My greatest debt is to those two giants of Pictish studies, J. Romilly Allen and Joseph Anderson, whose 1903 classic, *The Early Christian Monuments of Scotland* (ECMS), has recently been reprinted by the Pinkfoot Press. They recorded and illustrated hundreds of stones, each carefully located in relation to the nearest railway station – how times have changed! Two modern works, also published by the Pinkfoot Press, have been indispensable. Alastair Mack's *Field Guide to the Pictish Symbol Stones*, including all those found since 1903, gives their original find spots and present location (many are now in museums) together with six-figure National Grid references. Finally, *A Pictish Panorama*, published for the Pictish Arts Society, contains a comprehensive bibliography of Pictish studies edited by J.R.F. Burt.

On a more personal note, my family have given support and encouragement throughout the preparation of this book. Often more confident of the outcome than I was myself, Judy and Tig have listened to problems, taken an interest in progress, and made helpful suggestions. What would I do without them?

Acknowledgements for the reproduction of photographs are due to the following: pp. 19, 70, 71, 195, Historic Scotland: Crown copyright reserved; pp. 35, 36, 61, 82, 83, 84, 92, 144, 182, National Museums of Scotland: copyright reserved; pp. 37, 38, 43, 63, 67, 110, 119, 189, Royal Commission on the Ancient and Historical Monuments of Scotland: Crown copyright reserved; pp. 41, 42, 106, 109, 180, 188, Tom Gray: copyright reserved (42 and 180 first published in Elizabeth Sutherland, *In Search of the Picts*); p. 113, Perth Museum and Art Gallery, Perth and Kinross Council, Scotland, copyright reserved; p. 149, The British Library: copyright reserved; p. 155, The City of Bayeux, copyright reserved; p. 198, Dr S.J. Plunkett, copyright reserved. All other photographs are by the author. Line drawings of symbol stones and individual symbols are based on the illustrations in ECMS. The heraldic drawings on p. 26 are from Fox Davies, *A Complete Guide to Heraldry*. The illustrations of stone discs from Shetland, brought together on p. 173, are from original publications in the *Proceedings of the Society of Antiquaries of Scotland* for 1883, 1907 and 1934. All other line drawings and pedigrees are by the author.

CHAPTER 1
Three Stones by the Roadside

Throughout the Highland Zone of Britain, standing stones are among the most familiar and least understood of prehistoric monuments. Unless they are directly associated with burials, archaeological contexts are almost entirely lacking. Records from other places and other times suggest that there may have been various reasons for erecting such stones. In the Book of Genesis[1] we read that Jacob took a great stone and set it up as a sacred pillar. Later, when the Israelites reached the promised land and Joshua had the task of dividing it up, a memorial stone – the stone of Bohan son of Reuben – was used as one of the markers defining the boundary between the tribes of Judah and Benjamin.[2] After a decisive victory against the Philistines, Samuel set up a standing stone and, acknowledging God's part in his success, called it Ebenezer, which means 'stone of help'.[3] In Madagascar in 1797, when the King of Ambohimanga married the Queen of Ambohidratrima, a huge stone was set up, involving two months of hard labour.[4] In 1960 standing stones were set up all over Madagascar to celebrate independence from French colonial rule.[5] What could we learn of any of these stones without the benefit of the historical record?

Prehistory gave way gradually to history in the centuries following the Roman occupation of southern Britain. The stones that were set up during these Dark Ages differed from prehistoric standing stones in one important respect: they carried inscriptions. In the Celtic fringes of southern Britain, particularly in Wales and Cornwall, closest to the influence of Roman civilization, the inscriptions were in Latin and we can read them. Across the sea in Ireland, never invaded by the Roman legions, the inscriptions were in the Irish language and executed in the highly individual Irish script known as ogham. The key to this script was preserved in folk memory, as well as being set down in early manuscripts such as the *Book of Ballymote*. The interpretation of these Irish inscriptions is confirmed by a number of bilingual Latin and Irish inscriptions in Wales. In Scotland the message on the stones was presented in the form of

Three stones by the roadside: Aberlemno, looking up the road (south-west) towards the school. Aberlemno 1 is nearest the camera, Aberlemno 3 furthest away.

symbols. At the time they were carved, these symbols conveyed a meaning that could be read and understood anywhere from the Firth of Forth to John o'Groats, and even beyond the sea in Orkney, Shetland and the Western Isles. Unfortunately, like the Pictish language itself, the meaning of the symbols has been lost, almost without trace.

Three stones, which stand side by side a little way down the road from the village school at Aberlemno, provide a convenient starting point for the study of Pictish symbols. The middle one is a simple unadorned, presumably prehistoric,[6] standing stone. The one furthest from the school, leaning heavily to one side like the Heel Stone at Stonehenge, bears incised symbols on the side facing the road. Reading from the top downwards, the first symbol is a wonderfully sinuous serpent; the next a geometrical design known as a double disc and Z-rod; then, side by side, a mirror and a comb. Such stones are known as Class I Pictish symbol stones. The third stone is a tall, well-shaped, rectangular monolith displaying a huge ringed cross, carved in relief. The cross is a symbol that no one

Prehistoric standing stone: Aberlemno.

Class I symbol stone: Aberlemno 1.

Class II symbol stone: Aberlemno 3 (front).

can fail to recognize, and tells us that this particular stone was erected some time after the arrival of Christianity in this part of Scotland. The back of this 'cross slab', facing away from the road, is covered from top to bottom with carvings in relief. At the top, above a lively hunting scene, are two geometrical symbols, a crescent and V-rod and a double disc and Z-rod. Such cross slabs are referred to as Class II Pictish symbol stones.

Since the publication of *The Problem of the Picts* in 1956,[7] there have been three major attempts to crack the code of the Pictish symbols. The first was by Charles Thomas, in the *Archaeological Journal* for 1963; the second by Anthony Jackson, in his book, *The Symbol Stones of Scotland*, published in 1984; and the third by Ross Samson, in the *Journal of the British Archaeological Association* for 1992. What do these three have to say about the roadside stones at Aberlemno?

According to Thomas's system, the Class I stone described above (Aberlemno 1) would have been set up as a memorial to a member of the Serpent Group, who was a king (double disc) and had died (Z-rod, representing a broken spear, taken to be

Class II symbol stone: Aberlemno 3 (back).

an indicator of death). The memorial was erected by a woman (mirror and comb), possibly his widow. Using the same system, the Class II stone (Aberlemno 3) would have been a memorial to an under-king (crescent) who, presumably later, became a king (double disc) and had died. The V-rod, representing a broken arrow, like the Z-rod, is taken to be an indicator of death.

According to Jackson's interpretation, Aberlemno 1 records a marriage between a man of the Double disc and Z-rod lineage and a woman of the Serpent lineage, with the mirror and comb signifying the giving of bridewealth or gifts to the bride's family. Aberlemno 3 records a marriage between a member of the Crescent and V-rod lineage and a member of the Double disc and Z-rod lineage, with no indication of the provision of bridewealth.

According to Samson's interpretation, Aberlemno 1 is a memorial to a woman (mirror and comb), whose name was a combination of the syllables represented by the two symbols. Aberlemno 3 would then be a memorial to a man (no mirror or comb) whose name had the same ending (double disc and Z-rod) as the name of the woman commemorated on Aberlemno 1.

The only point of agreement between these three interpretations is that the mirror and comb are considered to be different in character from all the other symbols and somehow connected with women. Jackson makes the interesting point that the number of mirror and comb symbols is moderate on Class I stones but very low on Class II stones. He suggested that 'either bridewealth was frowned upon by Christians or else it was no longer relevant in the new tribal hierarchy'. On Thomas's system, this fall in the number of mirror and comb symbols would mean that fewer women were raising stones to the memory of their deceased husbands, or perhaps that they no longer felt it necessary to record their action. On Samson's interpretation, it would seem that fewer women were being commemorated on symbol stones, or had their sex become implicit in the names spelled out by the symbols? Perhaps the mirror and comb symbols have nothing to do with gender at all. As Samson pointed out, though mirrors are rare in the archaeological record, combs are common and are found associated with burials of either sex and any age.

Thomas's 'groups' and Jackson's 'lineages' have a good deal in common, though apparently inscribed on the symbol stones for different reasons. These groups and lineages resemble the Scottish clans of today and their symbols might be compared to clan badges. Thomas and Jackson were both interested in relating symbols to the possible historical divisions of the Pictish kingdom. Thomas, who believed that the animal symbols (serpent, eagle, goose, fish, boar, etc.) represented groups, found that they 'possessed no demonstrable territorial value at all'. Jackson, on the other hand, believed that all the symbols (apart from the mirror and comb) represented lineages. He considered that the animal symbols represented the various lineages of the Southern Picts and the geometric designs belonged to the Northern Picts. He drew up a series of tables to show that specific pairs of symbols had a meaningful geographical distribution which could be related to the divisions of the Pictish kingdom. His demonstration is not easy to follow, but would appear to contradict the observations of Thomas. Do any of the symbols show a significant regional distribution pattern?

Thomas alone gives the Z–rods and the V–rods a special meaning as a supplement to the symbols with which they are associated. Thus the double disc represents a king, whereas the double disc and Z-rod represents a dead king. The curious aspect of this interpretation is that so few symbols have these indicators of 'the dead state', as Thomas calls it. The crescent is the only symbol to be graced with a V-rod. Z-rods are only found on three symbols: the double disc, the serpent and the 'notched rectangle' symbol. Furthermore if the serpent, like other animal symbols, is supposed to represent a group, what does the serpent and Z-rod represent – an extinct group? Thomas, somewhat illogically, made this symbol a special case and supposed that it represented a chief magician or *magus*, thus weakening his case for the Z-rod as an indicator of the dead state. For Jackson and Samson the double disc and Z-rod is a different symbol from the plain double disc and represents either a different lineage (Jackson) or a different syllable (Samson).

Samson agrees with Thomas that the symbol stones are memorials to the dead but, in contrast to both Thomas and Jackson, does not consider that any of the symbols are related to groups, lineages or clans. For him, the symbols combine to spell out Pictish names. But what names? This should surely be the beginning of the investigation rather than the end. It is as if Michael Ventris, in his interpretation of the Minoan Linear B script[8] had reached the conclusion that it was syllabic and left it at that: never went on to decipher it; never transliterated a single word; never made the startling discovery that the language of the scripts was Greek.

These are what one might call secular interpretations of the symbols. It is, however, quite widely held that the symbols have a religious rather than a purely secular significance. Two recent books serve to illustrate this possibility. The first is *The Symbolism of the Pictish Stones in Scotland* by Inga Gilbert, published in 1995; and the second, *The Message of Scotland's Symbol Stones* by Edward Peterson, published in 1996.

According to Gilbert the serpent on Aberlemno 1 represents the snake goddess. The double disc and Z-rod is a compound symbol. The two discs represent An, the god of heaven, and Ki, the god of earth, linked together by Enlil, the god of air and atmosphere. These are crossed by Adad, a weather god symbolized by the rod of lightning and the thunderbolt, who is also the Mesopotamian god of war. The mirror as a sun disc represents the Great Goddess (but it may be a gong rather than a mirror) and the comb may represent a warrior rather than a lady. The crescent and V-rod, on Aberlemno 3, represents Sin, the moon god. The terminals of the V-rod crossing the image of the crescent moon are said to be stylized images of axe-heads. Below this, we have the double disc and Z-rod, representing (as above) the gods An, Ki, Enlil and Adad. The names applied to all these gods are those employed in Mesopotamian mythology.

Peterson considers that the serpent on Aberlemno 1 was probably the totemic symbol of 'the Pictish serpent tribes'. The double disc (viewed as two pairs of concentric stone circles joined by an avenue) is believed to be a symbol of prehistoric and druidic sun worship. Like Thomas, Peterson considers the Z-rod (identified as a broken lance) to be a symbol in its own right, added to the double disc to indicate 'the tribal transfer and dedication of the Druid temple to a Christian Church'. The crescent on Aberlemno 3 is a symbol of moon worship, but is crossed by a V-rod (seen as a broken arrow) indicating that 'the Christian faith had been accepted at the Druid's temple'. According to Peterson, the mirror is another representation of a stone circle with an avenue leading to a smaller cairn and therefore is presumably connected, like the double disc, with sun worship. But then he points out that the early Christian missionaries could have used the mirror symbol, without any alteration, for their own purposes. He quotes from St Paul's first letter to the Corinthians: 'Now we see only puzzling reflections in a mirror, but then we shall see face to face,' and from a letter of Pope Gregory the Great: 'The Holy Bible is like a mirror before our mind's eye.' They could have, but did they? Peterson says that 'the comb represents a cairn and was referred to by the holy men as a comb to portray the cleansing of the old pagan tribal beliefs and customs'.

We have on offer several different interpretations of the Pictish symbols. By the nature of things, they cannot all be right and it is perfectly possible that they are all wrong. They do not carry conviction because not one of them can be derived from the symbol stones themselves. Is there any real evidence, for example, that the animal symbols represent groups or clans, or that the object (non-animal) symbols denote rank or status? Absolutely none! These are ideas which Thomas applied *to* the symbols, not conclusions which he derived *from* them. And the same applies with equal force to Jackson's lineages, to Samson's syllabic themes or name components and to the various religious suggestions of Gilbert and Peterson.

Why should it be so difficult to find a convincing interpretation of the Pictish symbols? Part of the answer may lie in the extreme brevity of the 'texts', which seldom contain more than four symbols. Presumably the message they were trying to get across was a short and simple one and it would help if we knew what that message was likely to be. However, in view of the past history of Pictish symbol studies, it would be a grave mistake to start by making assumptions about the nature of the texts. The analysis must start with what can be deduced from the symbol stones themselves. Katherine Forsyth attempted just that in a recent paper, in which she discussed the possibility that the symbols might be a system of writing.[9] No specific interpretations emerged and we are left with the rather forbidding prophecy that 'a comprehensive study of the spatial, chronological and contextual distribution of symbols individually and in combination, using the techniques of multivariate statistics, would produce a number of insights, particularly if the results were combined with analysis of comparative writing systems'.

There are over thirty different Pictish symbols but no one can say exactly how many there are. Bird symbols, for example, identified as eagles by one scholar (one symbol: eagle), may be subdivided by another so that some are identified as eagles and others as geese (two symbols: eagle and goose). Only the Picts themselves could tell us whether the differences were really significant in terms of meaning, or whether they represented artistic or ornithological licence. In Egyptian hieroglyphs there were many different bird symbols, some alphabetic and some syllabic.[10] Among the alphabetic hieroglyphs, the eagle represented the letter *a*, the owl *m*, and the chick *u*. There were also a great number of syllabic hieroglyphs including: vulture – *mut* or *ner*; ibis – *tehuti*; feeding ibis – *qem*; goose – *sa*; duck – *aq*; flying duck – *pa*; and so on. By analogy with these Egyptian hieroglyphs we might suppose that specific differences among Pictish bird symbols should be significant, and the same argument could be extended to other Pictish symbols (animal and geometrical). There is of course no direct connection between the Egyptian hieroglyphs and the Pictish symbols and this argument by analogy simply suggests that we should perhaps err in the direction of a larger, rather than a smaller number of symbols.

Interpretation of the Egyptian hieroglyphics was made possible by the discovery of the famous Rosetta Stone in 1799. The text on this stone is repeated in three different scripts: first in traditional Egyptian hieroglyphs, then in the relatively modern Egyptian Demotic script, and finally in Greek. Ptolemy was the only name mentioned in the Greek text and could easily be picked out in the hieroglyphs because one particular sequence of symbols (and no others) was contained in an oval outline known as a *cartouche*. The discovery of another bilingual inscription, on the island of Philae in 1815, was particularly timely. The text, in Egyptian hieroglyphs and Greek, contained two names, one of which happened to be Ptolemy. The other was Cleopatra, a name which has several letters in common with Ptolemy. From then on it was only a matter of time and careful scholarship before Egyptian hieroglyphic texts could be read for the first time in about fifteen hundred years. At this point you may be excused for saying 'So what? This would be fine if we had a Pictish equivalent of the Rosetta Stone.'

But we *do* have such a stone. Indeed we have several such stones. Why then have they not been the starting point for every interpretation ever attempted of the Pictish symbols? The answer is simple. All but one of them involve inscriptions in the Irish ogham script and ogham inscriptions in Scotland are generally incomplete, sometimes illegible and widely considered to be unintelligible. The remaining 'Pictish Rosetta Stone' is the well-known Drosten Stone, in the St Vigean's Museum near Arbroath, which has an incomplete inscription in Hiberno-Saxon lettering.

CHAPTER 2
Symbols, Pictures and Stories

Many of the Pictish symbols, like the crescent and V-rod or the double disc and Z-rod on Aberlemno 3, are abstract designs. Others, such as the serpent on Aberlemno 1, are clearly recognizable pictures of more or less familiar subjects. A picture of a snake may be just that or, like the Egyptian hieroglyphic birds and beasts, it may also be a symbol representing something else. The variety of animals, both real and imaginary, represented on Class II symbol stones is far greater than on Class I stones. On some such stones they are shown individually, occasionally set in what one might call picture frames; on others they form part of larger, more complex pictures. On these cross slabs we see the Pictish artist at work, seemingly determined to fill all the available space on both sides of the stone.

The front of each cross slab is dominated by the great Christian cross, decorated by a great variety of complex and beautifully executed interlace patterns. The cross leaves four spaces to be filled: two square ones on either side above the arms of the cross, and two tall rectangular ones flanking the shaft of the cross. On the Dunfallandy stone these spaces are occupied by ten animal pictures, each in its individual panel and ranging from a perfectly realistic deer to a monster, with two legs and a fish's tail, biting at the rear end of a disappearing human figure. On the Aberlemno Church cross slab (Aberlemno 2), the top two spaces are occupied by individual animals, while the side spaces are filled with wonderfully intertwined serpentine creatures. These animal pictures, whether individual or interlaced, are quite distinct from the symbols on the Class I stones and may or may not themselves by symbols.

The reverse side of a cross slab gave the Pictish artist much more freedom. He started, so to speak, with a clean sheet and was not constrained by small or narrow spaces. Here he was able to draw complete pictures. Hunting scenes, such as that on the back of Aberlemno 3, were popular and probably give an insight into contemporary Pictish sport. Other aspects of Pictish life are represented by

Aberlemno 2: front. Note the non-symbol animals above the arms of the cross.

pictures of (elderly) people sitting in chairs, noblemen riding well-groomed horses, musicians performing on a variety of instruments, and priests or monks in their distinctive clothing. These stones are a lasting memorial to the artistic ability of the Pictish sculptors of more than a thousand years ago. They are also a valuable source of information on Pictish life.

The contrast between the Class I and Class II symbol stones could hardly be greater. There is no transition, no evolution, no development from one to the other. There were Class I stones. Then there were Class II stones, apparently fully formed at birth. This is a phenomenon of what has aptly been called *The Age of Migrating Ideas*.[1] As far as the Picts were concerned this followed a long period of relative isolation and cultural stagnation.

The Picts occupied a large part of eastern Scotland, from the Pentland Firth down to the Forth–Clyde line. Bounded to the north and east by the sea, they were separated from the western coastal strip by a range of almost impenetrable mountains known to early writers as 'the Spine of Britain'. To the south the boundary was not so much physical as political and military. During the Roman occupation of southern Britain the Antonine Wall marked the boundary between the Picts (and proto-Picts) to the north and the more or less Romanized Britons to the south. It was in this relatively isolated environment that the distinctive culture and language of the Picts evolved.

The Roman occupation of southern Britain came to an end early in the fifth century. The administration collapsed, the buildings fell into disrepair and the people went in fear of barbarian raids. But in spite of this general devastation the Christian religion, which had taken root in the second half of the previous century, flourished and spread. St Patrick carried it across the sea to Ireland, and his mission was so successful that within a few generations Christian missionaries were setting out from Ireland and crossing the sea in the opposite direction.

In AD 485 Darlugdach, later to become the second abbess of Kildare, established a church among the southern Picts at Abernethy, not far from Perth. In 563 St Columba arrived on Iona and established the 'base camp' from which he journeyed along the Great Glen to convert the northern Picts beyond the mountains. Then in 633 Oswald, King of Northumbria, who had become a Christian during his years of exile among the Picts and Scots, sent to Iona for a bishop to instruct his people in the new religion. Aidan answered the call and founded his church on the tidal island of Lindisfarne. From Patrick to Aidan, a period of some two hundred years, the Christian message had been spreading in a clockwise direction round the British Isles.

Meanwhile a completely independent Christian mission was approaching Northumbria from the south. St Augustine had been sent from Rome on a mission to convert the English and, through the good offices of Edwin, King of Kent, had founded his church at Canterbury where he was joined a few years later by Paulinus, another Roman priest. Paulinus moved northwards in 625, became Bishop of York, and set out to convert the people of Northumbria.

The eventual meeting of the two missions ought to have been the occasion for a happy reunion. It was not. The Celtic Church of Ireland, Iona and Lindisfarne had been expanding and evolving in effective isolation from the Roman church for two hundred years. There were disagreements between them on how to calculate the date of Easter and differences in the style of tonsure worn by the priests. These differences may seem relatively unimportant to us now, but at the time they were of fundamental importance and both sides were set in their ways and convinced that they were right. As far as each was concerned, things had always been done their way, from time immemorial. King Oswy, Oswald's younger brother and successor, realized that the matter had to be settled once and for all. A synod was convened at Whitby in 664 and a heated debate took place with neither side prepared to make any concessions. With the church incapable of reaching a conclusion, it was Oswy himself who made the final decision in favour of the Roman church. It was a political rather than a religious choice and did not resolve the differences between the two parties.

Northumbria joined the rest of England in acknowledging the supremacy of Canterbury and Rome. Colman, the third Celtic Bishop of Lindisfarne, together with other Celtic priests and many English priests trained by them, could not accept the decision of the Synod. They turned their backs on Northumbria for ever and made their way to the north, where the Picts and the Scots still looked to Iona for spiritual guidance.

For a brief period of thirty years a religious and cultural link had existed between the Northumbrian English and the Picts and the Scots, all the way from the holy island of Lindisfarne in the east to the holy island of Iona in the west. The Synod of Whitby severed that link and it was not re-established for nearly fifty years. Once again it was a king who made the decision which affected the Church throughout his kingdom. In 711 Nechtan, King of the Picts, sent messengers to Ceolfrid, Abbot of Wearmouth and Jarrow, asking his advice on how best to introduce the Roman system for calculating the date of Easter. Ceolfrid sent a detailed reply and Nechtan took immediate action.

The twin monasteries of Wearmouth (now Monkwearmouth) and Jarrow had been founded by Ceolfrid's predecessor Benedict Biscop in 674 and 681 respectively. Born in Northumbria about 628, Benedict was one of the most remarkable men of his age. He made in all five pilgrimages to Rome, travelling overland through France and then by sea from Marseilles to Rome. He spent two years (665–7) in the famous monastery on Lerins, a little offshore Mediterranean island, not far from Cannes, and a year (669) as Abbot of St Augustine's Abbey, just outside Canterbury. On his last two visits to Rome he purchased the books which were to form the nucleus of the libraries at Wearmouth and Jarrow. From the outset these two foundations were destined to be centres of learning as well as of religious observance.

One of the first and probably the greatest scholar to benefit from Benedict Biscop's foundations was the Venerable Bede, the Father of English History, who spent most of his life at Jarrow. In his *Ecclesiastical History of the English People*,[2] written in 731, Bede rejoiced in the fact that the four nations of Britain – the English, the British, the Irish (*Scotti*) and the Picts – each with its own language, were all united by a fifth language: Latin, the universal language of the Roman Church. And this was equally true on the continent. Benedict Biscop and others like him travelled widely on the continent, and the experience they brought back enriched the culture of their native land.

Nechtan's correspondence with Ceolfrid achieved much more than settling their differences over the date of Easter; much more indeed than standardizing the priestly haircut. It enabled the Picts to make their own distinctive contribution to what has become known as Insular art. This may have resulted from Nechtan's final request, which was for Northumbrian architects to build him a stone church in the Roman style. No trace of this stone church has been preserved and we do not even know where it was built. We do, however, know something about the monasteries of Wearmouth and Jarrow, upon which it was likely to have been modelled.

The western entrance to Benedict Biscop's church at Monkwearmouth is still standing to a height of 2 metres. Carved on the flat surface of the lower part of the door jambs are strange beasts with long narrow ribbon-like bodies, two on each side. They have narrow heads with long beaks, and fish tails. Their beaks are interlocked and their long limbless bodies slide down opposite sides of the stones, meet at the bottom, and rise intertwined up the middle.[3] Zoomorphic interlace, executed so brilliantly on Anglo-Saxon metalwork, had become part of the sculptor's repertoire.

More formal interlace patterns were also to be seen inside the church at Monkwearmouth and fragments have been recovered in excavations.[4] One of the most interesting is part of a band of interlace about 12 centimetres wide and bounded on either side by roll moulding. This may have been part of a pilaster.

Graves of the priests were marked by inscribed cross slabs on which the crosses stand out in relief. One complete cross slab is known from Monkwearmouth and several more or less fragmentary ones from Jarrow.[5] The crosses are generally undecorated, though most are outlined by a raised moulding. These Northumbrian cross slabs are carved on one face only, as also are some of the earlier Class II symbol stones. The crosses may be flanked by inscriptions, as on the Herebericht stone (Monkwearmouth 5): HIC IN SEPVLCRO REQVIESCIT CORPORE HEREBERICHT PRB (Here in the tomb rests Herebericht the priest in the body).

One of the most unusual features of Benedict Biscop's monastery at Wearmouth must have been the pictures which adorned the walls. No trace of these survives today, but we know of their existence from Bede's *Lives of the Abbots*. There were pictures of the Virgin Mary and the Apostles in the chancel area, scenes from the Gospel story on the south wall and scenes from the Apocalypse on the north wall. These pictures, or small 'patterns' from which they could be copied, were brought by Benedict from Rome.[6]

All the components necessary for the development of Class II Pictish stones were available in the monasteries of St Peter at Wearmouth and St Paul at Jarrow when Nechtan sent his messengers to consult their abbot, Ceolfrid. It was no accident that Nechtan chose to consult Ceolfrid. From the time of their foundation by Benedict Biscop, the reputation of these two monasteries, with their libraries and the scholarship based on them, had spread far and wide. Bede himself, now nearly forty years old and in his prime, had been writing commentaries on the various books of the Bible since he was thirty, and these were much in demand by preachers at home and overseas. If these Northumbrian monasteries did indeed provide the inspiration for the Class II Pictish symbol stones, two conclusions may be drawn.

Any symbols or pictures appearing for the first time on Class II stones cannot be presumed to be of native Pictish origin. Such images – like the zoomorphic interlacing, the geometrical interlace patterns, the cross in relief and the concept of narrative pictures – could have been introduced via Northumbria, from as far afield as Rome or as close as eastern England. The symbols on the Class I stones, most of which are also found on Class II stones, are the only ones we can accept without reservation as genuine native Pictish symbols developed before the Age of

Migrating Ideas. The distribution of Class I symbol stones is quite restricted. They are mostly found in eastern mainland Scotland, north of the Forth–Clyde line, with a sprinkling in Orkney, Shetland and the Hebrides, all accessible by sea and closer to the mainland Picts than to anyone else.

The fact that the Class II symbol stones, with their prominent decorated crosses, are quite clearly Christian does not mean that the Class I stones are therefore either pre-Christian or non-Christian. Indeed there is no reason to suppose that they have any religious significance at all. Rather the contrary. Let us suppose, for the sake of argument, that the designs on the Class I stones are pagan religious symbols. Why then did the Picts continue to erect such prominent monuments throughout the seventh century, after they had been converted to Christianity? You may perhaps question the completeness of their conversion or the dating of it, but the Class II stones are more difficult to explain away. Why did the Picts continue to carve these supposedly pagan symbols on their Christian Class II stones? It is much more likely that the Pictish symbols had no religious connotation at all.

These conclusions are rather negative and it is perfectly possible that a pre-Christian native Pictish symbol or traditional story *might* be represented on a Class II stone, though it would be difficult to prove it. The Cossans stone, for example, has a representation of six men in a boat. Is this one of the longboats conveying the legendary ancestors of the Picts from Scythia to Ireland and thence to Scotland, where they settled with their Irish wives? Or is it just a fishing boat, the marine equivalent of the hunting scene on Aberlemno 3? In attempts to solve such problems, quite small clues have sometimes assumed mammoth proportions. The St Andrews sarcophagus provides an interesting example.

Found in 1833 during grave-digging near St Rule's Tower, the oldest surviving building in the St Andrews Cathedral complex, the front panel of the sarcophagus is considered to be one of the finest examples of Pictish sculpture. Viewing the panel from right to left, we begin with a burly individual occupying the full height of the panel, with a sword at his side, engaged in single combat with a lion. A little to the left, in the upper part of the panel, the same man is riding rather a small horse. The lion is rearing up in front of him and he is preparing to ward it off with a sword, while at the same time bearing a falcon on his left hand. In the lower part of the panel, the man is out hunting on foot, armed with a spear. Ahead of him his dog is following some wild animals. Various other animals fill in the gaps in the design. Who is this man, engaged in such desperate combat with the lion?

The St Andrews sarcophagus: the main pictorial panel. (Photo: Historic Scotland)

The main clue to his identity is that St Andrews Cathedral was, from the time of its foundation, one of the most important Christian centres in the whole country. It is therefore likely that the lion fighter is to be identified somewhere in the Bible. He is not Daniel in the lions' den. Daniel did not have to fight the lions because an angel came and shut their mouths. The general opinion is that he is King David who, before his encounter with Goliath, had already released one of his father's sheep from the mouth of a lion and then killed the lion. And, as if to confirm this identification, there is a rather happy looking sheep at the top of the panel, protected from the lion on both sides by two views of his rescuer.

This identification has been generally accepted,[7] though Inga Gilbert, in her recent book,[8] tells us that it 'has always been wrongly interpreted'. The real story on this panel, she says, 'is that of the great epic hero Gilgamesh, the ruler and "shepherd king" of the ancient town of Uruk in southern Mesopotamia'. Gilgamesh, part god and part human, with his friend and servant Enkidu, set out against all the omens to kill the giant watchman of the cedar forest, an evil spirit called Humbaba. But Humbaba was also a nature divinity and his killing angered the gods, who decided that Enkidu must die as a punishment. For Gilgamesh the punishment seems to have been the loss of his beloved companion. He goes off on a long journey by himself in search of immortality. High up in a mountain pass he comes across some lions in the moonlight and kills them. Eventually, after many more adventures, Gilgamesh returns to his kingdom and his mortal state. Why should such a story from middle eastern mythology have been displayed so prominently on a sarcophagus in Christian St Andrews?

Gilbert has two answers to this question, one historical and the other art-historical. Bede, she tells us, *states* that 'Picts from Scythia put to sea in a few longships and were driven by storms around the coasts of Britain.' So, 'Let us trust him in this as in other historical matters, and start our investigation with the Scythians.' In the book which follows, middle eastern sources are proposed for a wide variety of Pictish symbols and Class II sculpture. Unfortunately the clue on which these interpretations are based is not as good as it appears. What Bede actually said was, '*It is said that* some Picts from Scythia put to sea in a few longships and were driven by storms around the coasts of Britain.' Bede is simply reporting the legend about the origin of the Picts as he had heard it. His report adds absolutely no authority to the story and it remains no more than a legend.

The art-historical argument is that the front panel of the sarcophagus belongs stylistically 'to the Greek–Scythian world of the 5th to 4th centuries BC'. How and when did such an art style come to be emulated in Scotland? Even if we were to accept the legend of the Picts coming from Scythia as historical fact, we can hardly believe that they brought with them not only the story of Gilgamesh but also a knowledge of the art style in which that story was to be portrayed – a knowledge that was to lie dormant for centuries until they acquired the necessary skills to carve it in stone. But, if that is not how it happened, we are back to the Age of Migrating Ideas and the introduction or evolution of this style some time after the beginning of the eighth century.

This question of the identity of the man grappling with the lion on the St Andrews sarcophagus may seem rather far removed from the study of Pictish symbols, but there is what we might call a moral to the story. What you get out of a picture or a symbol depends very much on what you put in. In this particular example, if you put in Scythians you might get Gilgamesh, whereas if you put in Christianity and the Bible you will probably get David. Some writers have attempted to identify Pictish symbols in terms of Roman artefacts,[9] others in terms of prehistoric sites of one sort or another.[10] Not surprisingly they come up with different and, it has to be admitted, equally unconvincing answers.

The term 'Pictish symbol' is generally restricted to those designs that are represented on the Class I symbol stones, but they also provide a sense of continuity by being represented on Class II symbol stones. The use of these symbols was well established among the Picts before the beginning of the eighth century. They were quite definitely not a product of the Age of Migrating Ideas, nor did they show the slightest migratory tendency themselves once the routes were open. They were Pictish in origin and remained uniquely Pictish to the end. These are the symbols whose interpretation will be attempted in the chapters which follow.

CHAPTER 3
The Pictish Symbols

The Pictish symbols were divided by Thomas into animal symbols and object symbols, though the identification of the objects was sometimes very obscure. Jackson preferred to think of the non-animal symbols as geometrical. He also believed that 'symbols are simply devices to represent something *other* than that which their actual appearances suggest', so that 'all attempts to link the Pictish symbols with comparable artefacts from the past are a monumental waste of time'.[1] This is surely not true. Symbols, if they are to be of any general use, must be easy to read and remember.

Some years ago I was looking at a geological map of Japan, on which all the lettering was in Japanese except for the key to the colours representing the geological periods, which was duplicated in English:

Upper Cretaceous
Middle Cretaceous
Lower Cretaceous
Upper Jurassic
Middle Jurassic
Lower Jurassic

The Japanese version of the geological periods, Jurassic and Cretaceous, was spelled out in Japanese syllabic characters, but what struck me immediately was that the word for 'middle' was represented by a single geometrical character which was so simple and meaningful that I have never forgotten it. It was a rectangle, elongated horizontally, with a vertical line through the middle. I have no idea what the Japanese word for middle sounds like, but I can read that symbol straight into its English language equivalent without any need for translation.

Among the predominantly syllabic characters of the Minoan Linear B script, some words are still represented by recognizable but simplified pictures (ideograms). Thus 'woman' is represented by a figure in a full-length dress, 'horse' by a horse's head, 'cup' by a picture of a cup, and so on. Egyptian hieroglyphic characters may be used to represent complete words, as well as syllables and letters. Thus the feeding ibis, with its head lowered, searching the mud for food, represents the verb 'to find' as well as the syllable *qem*, and the flying duck represents the verb 'to fly' as well as the syllable *pa*.

Medieval heraldry provides another example of the interpretation of symbols. Imagine yourself back in the late thirteenth century watching a knight in full armour advancing towards you. Who is he? His shield is red with three gold-coloured fishes arranged vertically, side by side, with their heads at the top. Is his name Fish? As he draws closer you see that the fish are not just any old fish, but quite definitely pike. Is his name Pike? You have never heard of a thirteenth-century knight of that name. Who then? The problem is that you are thinking in English. Had you really been a contemporary knight, you would have known at once that this was Sir Geoffrey de Lucy, whose arms were *Gules [red], three lucies haurient or [gold]*. A lucy (old French *luz*) is a pike. So long as you are thinking in the right language, Sir Geoffrey's arms are a pun on his name (canting arms) and this makes them easy to remember. It is also worth noting that had these fish been *naiant* (swimming) instead of *haurient* (on end, as if coming up for air), and had the fish and background been a different colour, we might have been gazing at a knight of Pikeworth, whose arms were *Argent [silver], three pikes naiant gules*. The man himself may well have been quite invisible, totally encased in armour and with his vizor down. A correct reading of the symbols on his shield could have been important.

Only a small proportion of medieval coats of arms made such direct reference to the name of the individual or his family (his lineage). Animals, particularly lions, were popular, and these were probably intended to represent bravery or prowess on the battlefield. Many early coats of arms made use of simple geometrical designs which bore no resemblance to any real object and whose only virtue was that they were easy to recognize. Examples of such geometrical heraldic symbols are: the chevron (point upwards), the fess (horizontal band across the middle of the shield), the chief (horizontal band across the top of the shield), the bend (diagonal band across shield), annulets (rings), crescents, crosses, lozenges and mullets (star shapes), all capable of variation in detail.

From the examples given above and in the last chapter, it is clear that if symbols are syllabic or alphabetic, no amount of analysis of an individual symbol will reveal its phonetic value. If, on the other hand, they represent complete words, it is possible that their meaning may still be readable. On the other hand, if a word symbol is purely geometrical, it is unlikely to yield up its secrets. With these points in mind, we may embark on a description of the Pictish symbols.

Anticipating discussion in the next chapter, Pictish symbols may be divided into two types: pair-forming symbols, which provide the main symbol texts, and supplementary symbols, which supply additional information but never appear by themselves. Most of the pair-forming symbols are abstract or geometrical designs, which may or may not be representations of real objects. A smaller number are more or less easily recognizable animals. The symbol nomenclature used here follows that of Alastair Mack in his recent *Field Guide to the Pictish Symbol Stones*. The symbols are listed in order, from the most abundant downwards, giving their relative abundance (in brackets) as a percentage of the total number of pair-forming symbols known on Class I and Class II stones.

PAIR-FORMING SYMBOLS

The *crescent and V-rod* (19.5 per cent) is by far the most abundant of the Pictish symbols, and is also one of the most interesting. The crescent is almost certainly a representation of the moon, but a moon unlike any that we have ever seen. The new crescent moon that can be seen soon after sunset has the horns of the crescent pointing upwards and away from the sun. Three weeks later the old crescent moon can be seen before sunrise, also with its horns pointing upwards and away from the sun. If we imagine the new moon following the sun through the night until morning, it will rise after the sun and the horns of the crescent will be pointing downwards and away from the sun; but it will not be visible because it is too close to the much brighter sun. The Pictish crescent generally has the horns pointing downwards. It seems thus to be a representation of a theoretical moon which was known to exist but could never be observed.

Thomas thought of the V-rod, which overlies the crescent, as a broken arrow, though the angle between the two halves is generally quite clearly hinged rather than broken. It bears some resemblance to a pair of dividers in a set of geometrical instruments and its function may have been to divide the moon up into three parts, perhaps signifying the waxing moon, the 'round moon' (when it is more than half-full) and the waning moon. Such a symbol would seem to have something to do with a knowledge of astronomy and the seasons, perhaps including a special awareness of things not normally visible, or at least not generally understood. The crescent may occur without the V-rod, but is very much more abundant with it. The V-rod never occurs by itself, nor is it ever associated with any symbol other than the crescent.

The crescent and V-rod is also more than just a symbol. It may be an actual object. Only one such object survived into modern times and that has now been lost for many years. It was a crescentic bronze plaque, ornamented with a rectilinear pattern and divided into three parts by a V-rod, just as on the symbol stones. Furthermore it was itself marked on the back by two symbols, a double disc and Z-rod, and a dog's head. The fact that the symbols were on the back indicates that they were not there for display. Perhaps they were an indication of ownership, authority or identification. It was evidently an object of value to its Pictish owner and, probably in the ninth century, fell into the hands of a Viking raider called Grimkitil, who inscribed his name on it in runes. It was found in the eighteenth century in a broch at the Laws, near Monifeith.

The *double disc and Z-rod* (12.9 per cent), like the crescent and V-rod, is a composite symbol. The double disc consists of two circles, variously ornamented, linked together by a band which is often waisted. The double disc may occur without the Z-rod, though much less commonly than with it, but the Z-rod never appears by itself.[2] The Z-rod was considered by Thomas to be a broken spear but, as in the V-rod, the angles are quite clearly hinged and not broken. It seems therefore to represent a Z-shaped object or perhaps, like the zig-zag lines so graphically used in strip cartoons, what we might call a Z-shaped 'concept'.

It is possible that it represents a sudden loud noise produced by the banging together of the two discs: the clashing of cymbals. It is also possible that it represents a flash of lightning between two thunderclouds. This is pure guesswork, but there has to be some reason why the Z-rod is associated with three basic symbols and not with all the others.

The so-called *Pictish elephant* (12.3 per cent) is the most abundant of the animal symbols and also one of the most difficult to identify. It is so stylized that, though clearly an animal, it has few diagnostic features. It is difficult to see how the delicate limbs on this beast can possibly be derived from the massive legs of an elephant. A somewhat more likely possibility is that it is a dolphin, though the down-turned head, with its chin resting on its chest, would be an impossible contortion for a real dolphin. It is perhaps not entirely irrelevant to point out that, as A.C. Fox-Davies remarked in his classic *Complete Guide to Heraldry*, 'heraldic representations of the dolphin are strangely dissimilar from the real

Problem beasts: dolphin on arms of Grauff von Dälffin (left), heraldic dolphin (top right), Pictish elephant (bottom right).

animal'. One truly remarkable dolphin appears on the arms of the Count von Dälffin' (canting arms again). This creature has a long curved trunk, exactly like the trunk of an elephant! However, we know that it is intended as a dolphin because the arms are blazoned *Argent, a dolphin azure within a bordure compony of the first and second.*[3]

The *double disc* (4.8 per cent) requires little further comment (see double disc and Z-rod above). A few double disc symbols have a 'bite' taken out of opposite sides of the two discs. It has been suggested that such notches, which also occur on a few other symbols, might modify the meaning of the symbol they affect.[4] On the other hand, since notches, like Z-rods, only occur on very few symbols, the notched symbols may in fact be quite separate symbols.

The *horseshoe* (4.5 per cent) is a purely descriptive name given to a rather variable group of symbols, for which the *arch* is an alternative name. Perhaps they should be two different symbols, with the horseshoe being curved through more than a semicircle and the arch consisting of a semicircular portion resting on vertical supports. Thomas suggested that this symbol might represent an oblique view of a partly open hinged bronze collar, though this interpretation could hardly be

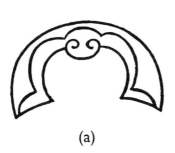
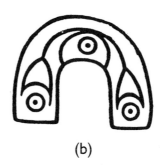

(a)   (b)

Problem symbols: (a) horseshoe, (b) arch. Are they variations of one symbol or are they two different symbols?

applied to the arch-like members of the group, and the innocent outsider might be pardoned for wondering why anyone should choose to draw such a difficult subject for a symbol. The horseshoe also bears some resemblance to the silver sword chapes from the St Ninian's Isle treasure. The difficulty with this comparison is that the inner and outer curves of the horseshoe-like members of the group are not concentric, so that they are thin at the top and wider along the sides. There is no obvious reason why the symbol has to represent any actual artefact.

The *mirror case* (4.5 per cent) is another purely descriptive name and there is no evidence that Pictish mirrors were ever kept in cases. It consists of a circle, variously ornamented, supported on a small rectangle. The whole symbol resembles a double disc symbol with one disc removed. As in the double disc, the 'rectangle' is sometimes waisted and may also be notched at the base, so that it seems to stand on two legs. This symbol has been likened, on the one hand, to certain figures in Bronze Age 'cup-and-ring' rock art and, on the other, to the handle of a Roman *patera* or skillet. It is possible that more than one symbol type is included under the general heading of 'mirror case'. Allen and Anderson, in their classic *Early Christian Monuments of Scotland* (generally abbreviated to ECMS) have a *circular disc and rectangle* and a *circular disc and rectangle with square indentation*. The rather cumbersome terminology may be one reason why these two groups have generally been merged together. There is also a possible confusion between some members of this group and the *tuning fork* symbol described below.

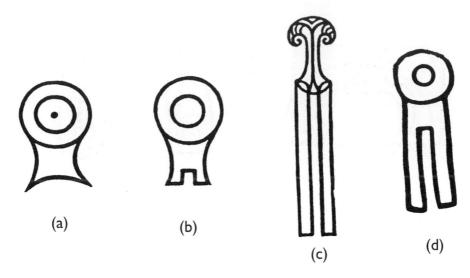

Problem symbols: (a) mirror case, (b) notched mirror case, (c) tuning fork, (d) unidentified symbol: is it a notched mirror case with 'long legs'; is it a ring-headed tuning fork; or is it an otherwise unknown symbol?

The *fish* (4.1 per cent) is generally well drawn and identifiable as a salmon. The salmon may be swimming horizontally to the right or to the left, upwards in either direction, or indeed straight up. Whether these differences have any significance in terms of meaning, or whether they are to some extent controlled by the shape of the available space or the texture of the rock is not certain.

The *rectangle* (3.8 per cent) has its long axis horizontal and about half as long again as the vertical axis. The internal ornament sometimes suggests that this symbol represents an envelope-shaped container for something.

The *eagle* (3.4 per cent), formerly grouped together with other bird symbols now identified as geese, is easily recognized, when complete, by the vicious hooked beak. A supposed eagle on the Knowe of Burrian stone in Kirkwall Museum, Orkney, has a long sharp beak without a sign of the characteristic eagle hook. Perhaps this bird is a raven and not an eagle at all.

The *serpent and Z-rod* (3.2 per cent) consists of a serpent, with all three limbs of its S-shaped body crossed by the middle limb of the Z-rod. The middle limb of the Z-rod may be drawn entirely over or under the serpent, or it may be

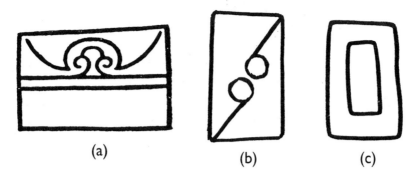

(a)   (b)   (c)

Problem symbols: (a) rectangle (normal pair-forming symbol type), (b) rectangle in Sliding Cave, East Wemyss, (c) rectangle in Covesea Cave (shows some resemblance to double-sided comb, but absence of mirrors makes this identification unlikely). To what extent are the cave rectangles related to those on the symbol stones?

interwoven (over and under). On this symbol the Z-rod could hardly represent a flash of lightning but, by an extension of the same concept, it might represent the sudden movement of the serpent as it strikes at its prey.

On a Class II stone at Logierait, in Perthshire, is a symbol which has been classified as a serpent and Z-rod, but is sufficiently unlike any other Pictish symbol that it might be given separate symbol status. The serpent on this stone has an extra curve beyond the usual S-shape and is intertwined with an absolutely straight rod, rather thicker than the usual Z-rod, but with similar floreated terminals.

The *triple disc* (3.0 per cent) consists of a large central circle or disc, flanked by two smaller circles. There is sometimes a straight rod passing through the lateral circles and over the central one. The triple disc on the Glamis manse stone (Glamis 2) shows the lateral circles very clearly as hinged rings so that the symbol can definitely be identified as a metal cauldron viewed from above. A lateral view of such a cauldron, suspended by a rod through the two rings, is shown on the same stone, on the opposite side of the cross shaft. Such a definite identification of a non-animal pair-forming symbol is quite exceptional.

The *divided rectangle and Z-rod* (2.8 per cent) is the third and last symbol to display the Z-rod. Above the divided part of the rectangle, there are generally two circles connecting with the outside world via a short passage, one on each side. The divided rectangle has been compared to a stalled chambered cairn in plan view. It has also been interpreted as a highly stylized vertical view of a light war chariot, drawn by two ponies. Finally, it has been derived from a series of fourth-century Roman 'camp-gate' coins. It seems that we can choose from a Neolithic model,[5] an Iron Age (possibly more or less contemporary) model[6] or a Roman model.[7] It is clear that we are dealing with a stylized figure, possibly so far removed from its original source as to have become almost abstract. Taking the addition of the Z-rod into consideration, the complete symbol might represent the sudden destruction of a Roman town or principal building by Pictish raiders in the fifth century or possibly some memorable victory won by a chariot charge.

The *serpent* (2.0 per cent) is much less abundant without the Z-rod than with it. It is generally S-shaped, as with the Z-rod, but there is one example of a serpent extended horizontally and only slightly wavy. This is so different from the standard serpent, with or without the Z-rod, that it should perhaps be treated as a separate symbol.

The *tuning fork* (1.8 per cent) was formerly known by the rather cumbersome description of 'notched rectangle and curved end'. Tuning fork is easier to remember and conjures up an image without implying a functional identification. It bears some resemblance to the narrower examples of the divided rectangle described above (with Z-rod) and, like them, has been compared to the plan view of a stalled chambered cairn. By comparison with the divided rectangle, it has been compressed laterally and stretched out vertically, so that the notch, or gate, has become a long narrow gap between two equally long and narrow bars. The resultant 'tuning fork' has been provided with a handle, which has been likened to the hilt of a sword. Thomas identified this symbol as a broken sword and linked it with the V-rod and Z-rod as an indication of the dead state, though how a break could possibly split the blade lengthwise into two quite distinct and equal rectangular halves was not explained. The 'hilt' of the 'sword' has also been compared to a ram's head with its distinctive curved horns. Attempts to link this symbol to actual objects seem doomed to failure.

The so-called *flower* (1.8 per cent) bears little resemblance to any real flower, though a recent suggestion that it should be rotated through 90 degrees anti-clockwise and become a whale, with its mouth wide open,[8] seems even less likely. With this marine image in mind, it might perhaps represent a wave breaking on the shore. There is no obvious model for this symbol and it may be purely abstract.

The *disc* (1.8 per cent) is characterized by having three smaller circles symmetrically arranged within it. No convincing model has been proposed for this symbol and it is probably an abstract geometrical design.

The *crescent* (1.6 per cent) requires little further comment (see crescent and V-rod above). There is one example of a crescent with a notch in the middle of the concave curve.

The *divided rectangle* (1.4 per cent) requires no further comment (see divided rectangle and Z-rod above).

The *step* (1.4 per cent) consists of two rectangles joined together and offset to produce the step-like effect. One example has handles on the free ends of the rectangles, resembling the hilt of the supposed broken sword in the tuning fork symbol, described above. Perhaps this should be treated as a separate symbol, the *stepped rectangle with curved ends* of ECMS. Also included as a step symbol by Mack is the *L-shaped rectangular figure* of ECMS, known more recently as the *Don terret*.

The *deer's head* (1.4 per cent), cut off above the shoulders, has the neck upright and the nose pointing horizontally to the right or left, as if sniffing the air. One rather different deer's head symbol, very delicately drawn, has the nose pointing downwards, rather in the style of the 'Pictish elephant' symbol.

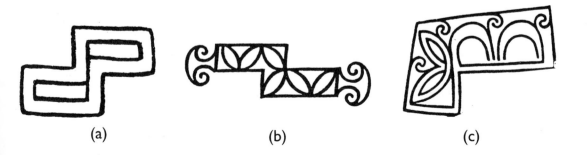

(a)   (b)   (c)

Problem symbols: (a) step, (b) step with handles, (c) L-shaped figure (Don terret). How many symbol types do these represent?

The *triple oval* (1.1 per cent) consists of three narrow oval shapes joined together side by side.

The *ogee* (1.1 per cent), also known as the *S-shaped figure*, is interesting because it can be derived from the horseshoe by taking the left half and rotating it through 180 degrees about its apex. Included here is a unique symbol described by Mack as 'rather like a double snap-hook'. This last is considered by others as a separate symbol.

The *fish monster* (0.9 per cent), with its upright posture, forward-looking head and coiled tail, bears some resemblance to a rather solid looking sea-horse. On three Class II symbol stones pairs of these fish monsters face each other above a pair of other symbols. On these stones they seem to have an ornamental rather than symbolic function. They also appear, together with many other more or less fantastic creatures, around the cross on Class II stones. One fish monster that is so unlike all the others that it should perhaps be treated as a separate symbol occurs on a Class I stone at Upper Manbeen, near Elgin. It is swimming horizontally and looks like a perfectly ordinary fish except that it has the head and ears of a land mammal.

The *double crescent* (0.9 per cent) consists of two crescents joined together back to back.

The *goose* (0.7 per cent), distinguished by its heavy body and long neck, is represented in two distinct forms. One has the head up, facing to the front, as if on the alert. The other has the head bent round over the back, almost in sleeping posture. These may be two distinct symbols.

The *boar* (0.7 per cent) is a rare life-like animal symbol.

The *beast* (0.5 per cent) is a representation of an unidentified land animal.

The *twin discs* (0.5 per cent) are much closer together than in the more familiar double disc (with or without the Z-rod) and lack the connecting band.

The *helmet* (0.2 per cent) is a rather more suitable name for a symbol formerly known as the *bow and arrow*. Only one example is known.

The *dog's head* (0.2 per cent), cut off at chest level, shows enough of the body to reveal a pair of small flippers. These and the small ears suggest that it might be a seal. However, like the Pictish elephant, the head is bent forward in a manner which would be quite impossible for a real seal. So much of the body is shown that in heraldic terms it would be not a dog's head but a demi-dog.

The *stag* (0.2 per cent) is a life-like representation of a familiar member of the local fauna.

The *wolf* (0.2 per cent): another life-like animal symbol.

The *horse* (0.2 per cent): another life-like animal symbol.

The *bull's head* (0.2 per cent), unlike the deer's head and dog's head symbols, is shown full face.

The *square* (0.2 per cent) is an approximately square figure with double outline and curved angles. At two opposite corners there is an outward extension of the figure, and, at the other two corners a similar inward extension.

The so-called *horseshoe and V-rod* (0.2 per cent) is an arch, of which the upper part is separated from the lower by a double V-shaped line, quite unlike the V- and Z-rods associated with some other symbols. It is the only one of its type.

SUPPLEMENTARY SYMBOLS

The *mirror* (12.0 per cent) is a straightforward pictorial representation of a circular mirror with a handle. So well are these mirrors drawn that it is possible to study the typology of their handles and compare them with the rare Celtic and Romano-British mirrors of the first few centuries AD.[9] Those on Class II stones are quite different from the Class I mirrors and this is probably due to Northumbrian influence, though I have been unable to locate any examples of Anglo-Saxon mirrors for comparison. The mirror symbol may represent nothing more than itself, or it may represent something associated with its function, such as a reflection. In view of its frequent association with a comb, it probably represents something to do with looking into the mirror to improve one's appearance.

The *comb* (7.1 per cent), like the mirror, is a straightforward pictorial representation of a familiar domestic object. As with the mirror, the combs are often so well drawn that their typology can be compared with that of combs from Pictish and related archaeological contexts.[10] The comb is never found without the mirror and their association has been commented on above.

The *hammer* (0.65 per cent), *anvil* (0.65 per cent), and *pincers* or *tongs* (0.4 per cent), though rare, occur together and indicate something to do with metal-working. There are also *shears* (0.2 per cent), as used in sheep-shearing, and a *crosier* (0.2 per cent), which looks just like a walking stick, but is identifiable by its association with a priest in a peaked hood, perhaps a bishop or an abbot.

The total number of symbols detailed above is about forty-five, depending on how closely some of them are defined. Even excluding the mirror and comb, and the hammer, anvil, tongs, shears and crosier, as Jackson does, there seems little justification for his clearly stated and apparently crucial assumption that there are exactly twenty-eight pair-forming symbols.[11] Mack lists thirty-six pair-forming symbols but, as has been shown above, this list is a fairly restricted one. There are other symbols, which are not mentioned above because they have not (yet) been found on symbol stones. An expanded list of Pictish symbols can be found in Appendix 1.

CHAPTER 4
Symbols for What?

One of the most striking things about the Pictish symbols is that, compared with Egyptian hieroglyphs for example, they are used so sparingly. Stones with more than four symbols on them are extremely rare and more often than not are the result of re-use rather than a longer than usual 'text'. A particularly interesting example of re-use is provided by a Class I stone from Easterton of Roseisle, Moray, now in the National Museum of Antiquities. There are six symbols on this stone, but these belong to two quite distinct texts, an earlier one of four symbols and a later one of two. On one face there is a beautifully drawn

Easterton of Roseisle: back, with later symbols the right way up. (Photo: National Museums of Scotland)

Easterton of Roseisle: front, with early symbols upside down. (Photo: National Museums of Scotland)

goose above a salmon. The other, earlier, face displays, from the top downwards, a mirror and comb, a crescent and V-rod, and a crescent. The mirror has its handle uppermost, both crescents are concave upwards, and the mirror and comb are at the top instead of the bottom of the sequence. The whole thing is upside down. When the monumental mason was commissioned to carve the goose and salmon, he had the stone uprooted and laid face down on the ground so that he could work on the free face. Did he not realize till too late that the top of the stone, as originally designed, would now be at the bottom? There is an alternative explanation. This stone was found in position as part of the wall of a long cist (presumably a burial, though no human bones were found in it). 'It lay on its narrow edge, with its longest dimension horizontal and the side with the crescent and V-shaped rod on it facing towards the inside.'[1] The fact that the second set of symbols were in almost mint condition suggests that they had never been exposed to the ravages of a northern winter, and had therefore been carved for use in the long cist where they were found. In this case, they were never intended for public display and there was no right or wrong way up.

Glamis 2: back, showing Class I symbols. (Photo: Royal Commission on Ancient and Historical Monuments of Scotland)

Glamis 2: front, showing Class II cross and symbols. (Photo: Royal Commission on Ancient and Historical Monuments of Scotland)

Another interesting example of re-use is Glamis 2. One face was carved in the Class I style, and shows a serpent above a fish and a mirror. The other side has a Class II cross carved in relief and, in the space beneath the right arm of the cross, two symbols: a deer's head and a triple disc. There are five symbols on the stone, but they belong to two texts: an earlier (Class I) text of three symbols and a later (Class II) text of two symbols. Our attention should therefore be directed at the number of symbols in an individual text rather than the number of symbols on a stone.

Many of the surviving Pictish symbol stones are broken or fragmentary and may show incomplete symbol texts. For statistical purposes, therefore, it is necessary to exclude such damaged stones. The sample considered below consists of ninety-seven symbol texts on ninety-four complete stones, both Class I and Class II, on which the symbols are clearly legible. The statistics for the number of symbols per text are as follows:

1 symbol	6
2 symbols	56
3 symbols	11
4 symbols	20
5 symbols	1
6 symbols	1
7 symbols	1
8 symbols	1

Only four out of ninety-seven have more than four symbols and more than half the sample have two symbols only. These figures are even more remarkable when we take into account the behaviour of two of the commonest symbols, the mirror and the comb. These two symbols are so closely associated that they are often treated together as a single symbol. The mirror may occur without the comb, but the comb never appears without the mirror. When both are present, they are always drawn together at the end (bottom) of the text, a position also invariably occupied by the mirror when it is shown without the comb. It is as if the mirror and comb conveyed a meaning that was so widely understood that it could be represented quite satisfactorily by the mirror alone. It is clear that, whatever these symbols meant, it was something quite different from all the other symbols. With this in mind, we can now rearrange the statistics for the number of symbols in a text.

1 symbol	7	(including 1 with mirror and comb)
2 symbols	82	(including 18 with mirror and comb, 8 with mirror)
3 symbols	3	(including 1 with mirror and comb)
4 symbols	2	
5 symbols	0	
6 symbols	1	
7 symbols	1	
8 symbols	1	

A simple pair of symbols, with or without the mirror and comb, is by far the most frequent form of text on the Pictish stones. Indeed, so general is this arrangement that Jackson used it as a criterion for defining a symbol as 'a design that combines more than once with another design, in a pair'.[2] On this basis he excluded several very realistic object symbols – hammer, tongs, anvil, shears, crosier – from his limited repertoire of 'true symbols'. Possibly these, like the mirror and comb, belong to a different category from the main line pair-forming symbols.

The fact that most of the symbol texts consist of a pair of symbols must not be allowed to take on the aura of a law of Pictish symbol writing. A significant minority of texts, even on undamaged stones, consists of one symbol only. Furthermore, not all the texts with more than two symbols can be broken down into pairs. Paired-symbol texts may be dominant, but they are certainly not universal.

On the evidence of the stones themselves, we are able to distinguish the pair-forming symbols (Jackson's true symbols) from the mirror and comb (and possibly other realistic object symbols), as conveying different sorts of meaning, but it is not immediately obvious what these meanings might be. The clue comes from the Class II symbol stones which display a range of pictorial information in addition to the symbols themselves.

The Kirriemuir Class II stone (Kirriemuir 2) has, in effect, two pictures, partly overlapping to fit them into the confines of the available space. In the upper picture a man on horseback, almost stationary, carries a spear in his right hand. The lower picture is a hunting scene in which a man on horseback, a stag, and a hound are all caught in motion as they speed to the right. Judging by his beard and distinctive hair-style, the huntsman is probably the same man; he has his right arm raised, ready to plunge his spear into the flank of the stricken stag. The only symbol on this stone, a rather crudely drawn double disc and Z-rod, is placed immediately behind the upper man, so close that it is crossed by his spear.

Kirriemuir 2: symbol associated with equestrian portrait. (Photo: Tom Gray)

The symbol belongs to the man, just as the coat of arms on his shield belongs to the knight on a medieval brass.

The Dunfallandy stone is unusual in showing eight symbols and three figures. At the top two seated figures face each other with a small cross between them. Below them is a single figure on horseback. The two seated figures have been variously identified as St Paul and St Anthony in the wilderness, and Moses and Elias. Each figure has his or her own symbols and there can be no question about which symbols belong to which figure. The seated figure on the left has a Pictish elephant, with the possibility of another symbol having been lost. The seated figure on the right has a double disc above a crescent and V-rod, and the figure on horseback has a crescent and V-rod above a Pictish elephant. A symbol or pair of symbols securely attached to each individual figure must have enabled these figures to be identified. The purpose of the symbols is analogous, if not exactly identical, to that of medieval heraldry. The other interesting feature of the Dunfallandy stone is the presence of three realistic object symbols – the hammer,

Dunfallandy: symbols associated with individual portraits. (Photo: Tom Gray)

anvil and tongs – and their position right at the bottom of the picture, exactly the position so often occupied by the mirror and comb. This confirms the suggestion made above that these symbols are different in character from the regular pair-forming symbols.

The Golspie stone, like the Dunfallandy stone, has a larger than usual number of symbols. Jackson finds eight symbols on this stone, which he treats as four pairs: a rectangle above a Pictish elephant; a dog above a fish; a 'flower' above a crescent and V-rod; and a double disc above a serpent. In the midst of these symbols is a fierce-looking man armed with an axe in his right hand and a dagger in his left. He is confronting the dog, axe to snout, and if the fish rose a little higher it would be in serious danger from the knife. It has been suggested that the man is a pagan Pict confronting Christianity in the form of the lion of St Mark and the fish as a symbol of Christianity. But the stone is not a pagan stone; it is a Christian cross slab. This man is certainly a Pictish warrior, but not a pagan one. The dog may perhaps be a lion but, either way, it is a Pictish symbol, as is the

Golspie stone (Craigton 2): symbols associated with portrait. Ogham inscription visible on the right side. (Photo: Royal Commission on Ancient and Historical Monuments of Scotland)

fish. There is only one genuine pair of symbols on this stone – the rectangle and the Pictish elephant above the man's head. These are larger and more impressive than all the other symbols and must be his own personal symbols.

Beneath the dog and the fish, the remaining symbols on the Golspie stone are packed into the available space with little regard for order. The man is marching forward – almost goose-stepping – through them and trampling them underfoot. If the symbols above the man's head represent him personally, then the jumble of symbols through which he is marching must represent other individuals, probably his defeated (Pictish) enemies. The serpent, at the bottom of the heap, is not really a serpent at all, but two intertwined serpentine sea-beasts, each biting the other's fish-like tail. The man was probably a local hero in the Pictish civil wars of the eighth century.

The relationship between a man and his symbols on some of the Class II stones seems to indicate that the symbols are in some way serving to identify the man, most likely by providing him with a name. If they do indeed represent his name, they can do so in two distinct ways. They may combine to spell out a single name, as suggested by Samson; or each symbol may represent a complete name, in which case we are mainly concerned with what a biologist might call binomial classification. Is there any way in which we can distinguish between these two possibilities?

The answer to this question depends on whether the Pictish symbols are presented in a particular order or not. Paired symbols generally appear one on top of the other. Should they be read from the top downwards, like the successive lines on the pages of a book, or should they be read from the bottom upwards, like Irish ogham inscriptions? Or should they perhaps just be combined, regardless of order? Egyptian hieroglyphs could be read either from left to right, like English (or the Greek of the Rosetta stone), or from right to left, like Arabic. But you can always tell which way to read them because your eye must 'pass through' the animals, like food, from front to back. If the lions, eagles, serpents, etc., are facing to the right, you read from right to left, and *vice versa*. Apart from our natural reluctance to believe that the symbols could have been drawn in random order, the fact that the mirror and comb are invariably placed below the other symbols is strong evidence of the importance of order in the Pictish symbol texts.

With this in mind, we are now in a position to consider Samson's table of prefix and suffix 'themes' which can be combined to form most of the known Anglo-Saxon names. If we take a selection of familiar names from English history before the Norman conquest, we can easily split them into their component parts.

Alfred	*Aelf-*	*raed*
Edmund	*Ead-*	*mund*
Edward	*Ead-*	*weard*
Ethelred	*Aethel-*	*raed*
Ethelwulf	*Aethel-*	*wulf*
Redwald	*Raed-*	*weald*
Wulfstan	*Wulf-*	*stan*

In this small list, some components appear as both prefix and suffix. *Raed* appears both in Alfred and in Redwald; *wulf* both in Wulfstan and in Ethelwulf. But other components, such as *Aethel* and *Ead*, though common as prefixes, never occur as suffixes. Similarly, there are components that only occur as suffixes. An analysis of the 244 Anglo-Saxon prefix and suffix name components reveals the following statistics:

Prefix only	61 per cent
Suffix only	14 per cent
Prefix or suffix	25 per cent

Surnames, which evolved rather more recently, provide further examples of common name components. They had their origin in the extra details which became necessary to differentiate between several individuals of the same name, for example:

John son of Richard
John the miller
John of Hatton
John the red-head
John of the white house

The first of these examples is a patronymic and, in the English language, took the form 'Richard's son' which soon became Richardson. The Donaldsons, Jacksons, Johnsons, Richardsons, Robertsons, Williamsons and many others bear testimony to the importance of this construction. In the related Scandinavian languages, we have Christensen, Eriksson, Hansen, Johansson, Olafsson and Petersen (the -sen forms being Danish). The -son component of these names is invariably a suffix. It has to be so because of the grammatical rules governing the construction of the name.

Mac is the Gaelic equivalent of son, but the Gaelic equivalent of Donaldson is not Donaldmac but Macdonald. The Mac- name component, often abbreviated to Mc-, is always a prefix, hence the great gathering of the clans – Macdonald, MacGregor, McLeod, Macneil, McNicoll and others – in the middle pages of every telephone directory. The Welsh equivalent of *mac* is *map*, generally shortened to *ap*. So we have names such as ap Rees and ap Richard, which are often anglicized to Preece and Pritchard, leaving the prefix so reduced as to be almost unrecognizable. But whether the name component is Mac-, Mc-, map, ap or simply P-, the grammatical construction decrees that it must be a prefix.

Occupational surnames of the Miller type involve the syllable -er. One who mills is a miller, one who thatches, a thatcher, and so on; hence such names as Carpenter, Chandler, Fuller, Gardner, Potter, Roper and Weaver. The -er component is invariably a suffix. That is how the worker-word was derived from the work done.

We could continue this analysis to include such names as Redhead and Whitehouse, and the names of places, from which many people have derived their surnames. Wherever we look we find that, when names are made up of meaningful component parts, those are arranged in a sound grammatical order and will be entirely (or dominantly) either prefixes or suffixes. If this were not so, we would keep meeting people with names like Sonjack, Gregormac, Leodmc, Reesap, Erthatch, Headred, Housewhite and Tonhat! It seems to be a general rule that names composed of meaningful components have an ordered structure.

But what about Pictish names? Did they have an ordered structure? Surely these are the names we should be considering. This is very true, but there are problems. The available sample of Pictish names is small and almost confined to those of the kings, whose reigns are listed in the *Pictish Chronicle* and whose deaths were noted by the Irish annalists. The spelling of the names shows considerable variation, due partly to original differences between Gaelic and Pictish and partly to subsequent scribal errors. By way of an example, we may take two of the better known Pictish kings, who happen to have shared the same name – Oengus son of Fergus.

In Gaelic records, there is considerable variation in the spelling of Oengus, but absolute consistency with regard to Fergus:

Aengus	Fergus
Aongus	
Engus	
Hungus	
Oengus	

In Pictish records, the spelling of both names is variable:

Onnist	Urguist
Onuist	Urgust
Uidnuist	Urgut
Unest	UUrguist
Unuist	UUrgut
	Wirguist
	Wrguist

Both names contain the same suffix, *-us* in Gaelic or *-uist* in Pictish. This name component is nowhere found as a prefix, though it does occur as a complete name on its own in the early (prehistoric or legendary) part of the *Pictish Chronicle*. The second name has the prefix *Fer-* or *Wr-*, which also occurs in other Pictish names of which the Gaelic and Pictish forms are shown below:

Ferat	Wrad
Feredach	Wradech

This name component never occurs as a suffix, but is common as a prefix in Gaelic names, such as Ferchar, Fergal and Fergna. A Pictish name component which may occur as a prefix or a suffix is *gart*. There were several Pictish kings called Gartnait and several Scottish kings called Domangart. In so far as Pictish names can be split into recognizable components, they would seem to have the same sort of ordered structure as names in other languages.

It follows from this analysis of the ordered structure of names that, if the Pictish symbols represent name components, then a significant number of them ought to represent prefixes only, while others should represent suffixes only, and the remainder could occupy either position. If this is so, then some of the pair-forming symbols should only occupy the upper position and others only the lower position.

The symbol stones themselves give an unequivocal answer. Almost without exception, the pair-forming symbols occupy both upper and lower positions without showing any strong preference for either. The few that do occur in one position only are so rare that their preference for that position has little significance. It is quite clear from this that the individual symbols do not represent name components. They must therefore represent complete names or words. The dominant paired symbols should probably be read as what we might call forenames and surnames, though without implying anything hereditary about the surname.

CHAPTER 5
Pictish Names

The analysis of the symbols presented in the last chapter led to the conclusion that the symbols represent names. It should be possible to test this conclusion against the available samples of Pictish names. The first test is to determine how many name-words (excluding connecting words such as 'son of') were required to identify an individual Pict. The answer, at least as far as the kings are concerned, can be found in the several versions of the *Pictish Chronicle*.[1] Restricting the analysis to the more or less historical age of the Picts, between the middle of the fifth century (Drust son of Erp) and the middle of the ninth century (Kenneth mac Alpin), the statistics are as follows:

1 name	1 to 3
2 names	29 to 41
3 or 4 names	1

The variation is due to the fact that, for a variety of historical reasons, some copies of the *Pictish Chronicle* give longer lists of kings than others. This variation cannot obscure the one outstanding feature of these statistics, and that is the dominance of the two name-word form of Pictish names.

A very similar pattern emerges from an analysis of the Pictish names in the Irish Annals[2] for the same period:

1 name	7
2 names	33
3 names	3

Six out of the seven with only one name were further identified as kings of the Picts, a perfectly adequate description for a contemporary chronicler. Once again, the clear dominance of the two name-word format is demonstrated. This is entirely consistent with the conclusion of the last chapter, that most of the Pictish symbols represent names. If, as suggested, the second name is like a non-hereditary surname, the next step is to see what sort of surnames are involved.

In the same samples of Pictish names, over 90 per cent of the second names were patronymics. Most Picts were best identified as the sons of their fathers. But what of the rest? Were they known by their occupation or by some personal characteristic, or perhaps by the place where they lived? To answer these questions, we need to translate some of these second names. But they were Pictish names and Pictish is a forgotten language. Nobody has spoken it for over a thousand years. The problem seems almost insurmountable until we realize that these second names were not really names at all, but ordinary words in everyday use – words that could easily be translated into another language by a contemporary writer. There are three sources for Pictish names: the Irish annals and two quite distinct versions of the *Pictish Chronicle*. In one version of the *Pictish Chronicle*, which may conveniently be referred to as Group A, we have what seem to be Pictish forms of some names, such as Onnuist and Wrguist. In the other, Group B version, these same names appear in their Gaelic form as Oengus and Fergus. There are three main languages in which the second names may have been preserved: old Irish (the ancestor of modern Gaelic), Pictish and Latin (the language of the Church, where much of the writing might have been done). Original differences between the three sources have been compounded by scribal errors in making copies, so that we may have half a dozen or more different renderings of each name.

Gartnaich diuberr was a late prehistoric King of the Picts who may have reigned in the late fourth century. Variations in the spelling of his name in the Group A *Pictish Chronicle* are Gartnait diuperr and Gartnait duipeir. In the Group B version his name has been translated and appears as Canath dives, Garnard dives, Gauiach diues and Garnard le riche. *Dives* is the Latin for rich, and the Norman-French *le riche* is probably a translation from the Latin. *Diuberr* is presumably the Pictish word for rich, since the old Irish *saidber* is hardly a close match.

Three other examples will serve to illustrate the sort of second names (other than patronymics) by which Pictish kings were known: Galam cennaleph, who died in 580; Drest gurthinmoch, who died about 536 and Necton morbrec, who died about 506.

Galam cennaleph was the first Pictish king whose death was recorded by the Irish annalists, and they referred to him by his second name only as Cennalat or, in another copy, Cendaeladh. In the Group A *Pictish Chronicle* he is listed as Galam cennaleph or Galum cenamlapeh. *Cenn* is the old Irish word for head, and *alad* for wound. Galam was known as Galam Head-wound. Perhaps today he would have been called Scarface! *Aleph*, or something like it, was probably the Pictish equivalent of *alad*. In the Group B *Pictish Chronicle* Cennalat was listed as Talalad, variously spelt as Tagaled, Talagach, or Tagalad. This is not a translation of Cennalat, but a different name. *Tal* is the old Irish for axe. As far as the Group B *Pictish Chronicle* was concerned, Galam was known as Galam Axe-wound. The Pictish stones themselves show us that in those days there was a very real risk of suffering an axe wound. Galam's achievement was that he survived such a wound and lived to become king.

Drest gurthinmoch or Drest gurthimoth of the Group A *Pictish Chronicle*, was called Drust gernot, Drust gortinoch or Drust gocineht in the Group B *Pictish Chronicle*. *Gort* is the old Irish word for standing corn, and *moch* for early. Drust presumably had the good fortune to have a field with such a favourable combination of soil and position that his corn always ripened early.

Nechtan son of Erip was the only Pictish king to have been accorded the title 'Great'. In a Latin text giving the background to his gift of land at Abernethy to Saint Bride for the foundation of a church, he is referred to as *Nectonius magnus filius Wirp, rex omnium provinciarum Pictorum* (Necton the Great, son of Wirp, king of all the provinces of the Picts). In the Group A *Pictish Chronicle* he is known as Necton morbet son of Erip, Nectan morbrec son of Erip and Nectan mor breac son of Eirip. The *mor* component of this name means great and corresponds with the Latin (*magnus*). *Brec* is the old Irish for 'freckled', a personal epithet applied to a number of Dark Age Celtic kings. Nechtan's name, as recorded in the Group A *Pictish Chronicle*, had four components. He was Nechtan the great, Nechtan the freckled, and Nechtan son of Erip. There was no possibility of confusing him with any other Nechtan! In the Group B *Pictish Chronicle* Nechtan is known by a completely different name, variously spelt as Nethan chelemot, Netthan thelchamoth, Nectane celtaniech and Nectan celchamoch. *Cell* is the old Irish word for church, familiar in many place names such as Killarney, Kilkenny and Kilmarnock. *Moch*, as noted above, means early. Nechtan's second name of celcamoch is probably a reference to his part in the establishment of Christianity at Abernethy, in the land of the southern Picts, about eighty years before Saint Columba arrived in Iona.

Rich, head-wound, axe-wound, early cornfield, great, freckled, early church. These are not names in the sense that Gartnait, Galam, Drust and Nechtan are names. They are ordinary words, taken from the great pool of words in the unwritten Dark Age equivalent of a dictionary. They are used to give quite specific descriptions of individual Pictish kings and would not be applicable to the sons or the fathers of those kings. If we take Nechtan son of Erip as an example of a patronymic second name, Nechtan and Erip are both real names, chosen from the much smaller pool of names (not words) available for providing an identity for a newborn Pictish infant.

Returning to the problem of the Pictish symbols, let us suppose that the first name of a pair, Nechtan, for example, is represented by a symbol. How is the second name going to be represented? If the second name is a patronymic, as in the case of Nechtan son of Erip, that second name was the first name of Nechtan's father and should also be represented by a symbol, one of the set of symbols representing 'real names'. If, on the other hand, the second name was not a patronymic, the problem is somewhat different. Some of the second names are single words and some are compound words. In the case of Galam cennaleph, should we have a single symbol for the compound word cennaleph (head-wound), or should we have separate symbols for head and wound, both of which might appear in other combinations. We cannot know the answer to this question, and it may well be a question that was never asked. In either case (one symbol or two), the symbol or symbols will not come out of the same set as those representing real names. Head and wound, or head-wound, are words not names.

Pictish symbols and Pictish names both occur predominantly in pairs, and the evidence suggests that the symbol pairs represent patronymic name pairs. However, while it is true that pairs of symbols are dominant, some stones do carry a larger number. What combinations of names might be represented by such symbol texts? Necton morbrec son of Erip is not relevant in this connection, because the middle of his three names is not a 'real name'.

In the Irish annals, there are several examples of three-generation patronymics, such as Brude son of Oengus son of Fergus, who died in 736, and Talorgan son of Fergus brother of Oengus, who was killed in a battle in 750. Apart from these, the best source of comparable information comes from the great series of Dark Age inscriptions in Wales.[3] These inscriptions are nearly all in Latin and leave us in no doubt that most of them are memorials to the dead. The statistics for the number of names per inscription (excluding multiple memorials, for example to a man and his wife) are given below:

1 name	48
2 names	81
3 names	6
4 names	1

Two-name inscriptions are by far the most abundant, as are two-symbol texts on the Pictish stones, though one-name inscriptions are far more abundant than one-symbol Pictish stones. The small number of inscriptions involving more than two names may be compared with the equally small number of Pictish symbol texts involving more than two pair-forming symbols. Here the resemblance between the Pictish and the Welsh stones comes to an end. The Pictish texts, being composed of a very limited number of symbols, are very restricted in the range of meanings they can convey. The Welsh ones, written in Latin words, are far more flexible. Taking the two-name inscriptions and summarizing them in the most basic form, we find the following forms:

A son of B	64
A daughter of B	4
A wife of B	3
A mother of B	1
A of tribe B	2
A, stone erected by B	7

The three-name inscriptions include the following forms:

A cousin of B, of tribe C	1
A son of B, great grandson of C	1
A son of B, stone erected by C	2

The four-name inscription is of the form:

A wife of B, disciple of C, of tribe D

Such meanings could not possibly be conveyed by the Pictish symbol texts without separate symbols for son, daughter, father, mother, wife, cousin, grandson, etc. If such symbols did exist and were used regularly, we would expect more three-symbol texts, and one symbol in such texts (the symbol indicating relationship) would not belong to the main series of pair-forming symbols (interpreted as names).

In a nation whose kings were chosen from the female royal line, it is surprising that we know nothing about individual Pictish women, royal or otherwise. The Irish annalists mention just one Pictish woman by name – Eithni, daughter of Cinadon, whose death in 778 was recorded in the *Annals of Ulster*. Her father Cinadon, King of the Picts, had died three years earlier. Eithni was a member of the female royal line and a potential mother of a future Pictish king. She would have been a suitable wife for an ambitious young Pict anxious to better his position in the world. But she died before her potential could be realized. Perhaps Cinadon had no other daughters, and that was why her passing came to the notice of the Irish annalists.

Was the Pictish symbol system so inflexible that it was unable to cope with female memorials, or did the Picts never erect memorial stones to their mothers, wives or daughters? Or were female names, Eithni for example, sufficiently distinctive to have their own symbols which would be recognized as female, just as we would recognize Elizabeth or Margaret as being unmistakably female? In the absence of surviving Pictish female names it is impossible to answer this question.

This chapter set out to test the conclusion that the pair-forming Pictish symbols represent names, and there is good reason for making the tests as thorough as possible. As Samson truly remarked in his paper on the interpretation of the Pictish symbols, 'Nothing seems more immediately probable than that the Pictish symbols signify the name of the deceased. Yet this, the simplest and most obvious possible explanation has had no takers. Why?'[4] The reasons he came up with were that there were too few symbols to represent a reasonable range of names, and that a small number of them (the crescent and V-rod, the double disc and Z-rod, and the Pictish elephant) were far more abundant than any individual name was likely to be.

Statistics for the most common pair-forming Pictish symbols are given below. The sample of 440 symbols from which these figures are derived consists of all the pair-forming symbols listed by Mack, on both Class I and Class II stones.

Crescent and V-rod	19.5 per cent
Double disc and Z-rod	12.9
Pictish elephant	12.3
Double disc	4.8
Horseshoe	4.5
Mirror case	4.5
Fish	4.1
Rectangle	3.8
Eagle	3.4
Serpent and Z-rod	3.2
Triple disc	3.2
Divided rectangle and Z-rod	2.3
Serpent	2.0

The most notable feature of these figures is that the three most abundant symbols make up nearly half the total number listed. This implies, if the symbols do represent names, that these three names were so popular that they were used more often than all the other names put together. Is this likely? The obvious thing to do is produce comparable statistics from a sample of Pictish names.

If we now look at the names of the forty kings listed in the Group A *Pictish Chronicle*, from Drust son of Erp to the last Pictish king before Kenneth mac Alpin, we get the following statistics:

Drust	9
Talorgan	6
Brude	5
Gartnait	4
Nechtan	3
Cinioch	2
Elpin	2
Onnist	2

These are followed by seven names with only one occurrence each. In this sample at least, the most popular names were surprisingly abundant – even more so than the most popular symbols. The top three names account for exactly half the total. But there is a catch. If you look at the names of the fathers of these same kings, you would not think that they came from the same population. Drust, Brude, Gartnait and Nechtan are entirely absent and there is only one Talorgan. Not a single name is significantly either more or less abundant than any other. Why should there be such a difference between these two samples, the kings and their fathers?

The first thing to note is that the sample of fathers' names is considerably smaller than that of kings' names. There are two reasons for this. First, we do not have fathers' names for all the kings: Galam Cennaleph for example. Secondly, Pictish kings were often succeeded by their brothers. Drust son of Girom (553–558) was followed by Gartnait son of Girom (558–565) and Cailtram son of Girom (565–566): three kings but only one father. Finally, the Pictish royal family, like all other ruling dynasties throughout the ages, intermarried with neighbouring royalty. A well-known example is Brude son of Bile, the victor of the great battle of Nechtansmere in 685. His father Bile was a Briton of Strathclyde. Talorgan son of Enfret (656–660) is another. His father was Eanfrid, an exiled Northumbrian prince who lived among the Picts for many years. And there may well be others.

The list of king's names may be little more representative than that of their fathers. These were names chosen by their parents for baby boys who were possibly destined to be kings. Choosing names for a new baby is a difficult enough task for any parents, but the possibility that the baby might one day be a king must surely add an extra dimension to the problem. Looking back through the pages of history we can occasionally recognize a particularly significant choice. King Henry III of England came to the throne at the age of nine, 150 years after his great-great-great grandfather William the Conqueror defeated the English at the Battle of Hastings. He married Eleanor, daughter of Raymond Berenger IV, Count of Provence, and had two sons, Edward (later Edward I) and Edmund. He gave his sons English names, never before used by the post-Conquest Norman kings. Henry III was King of England by descent from William I, the Conqueror, but he wanted to be seen not just as King of England, but as an English king. This is clearly seen in a pedigree drawn up in 1230.[5]

King Henry, son of
King John, who was brother of the indomitable general, King Richard, who
    was son of
King Henry, whose mother was the
Empress Matilda, whose mother was
Matilda, Queen of the English, whose mother was
Margaret, Queen of the Scots, whose father was
Edward, whose father was
Edmund Ironside, whose father was
Ethelred, whose father was
Edgar the peaceful, whose father was
Edmund, whose father was
Edward the elder, whose father was
Alfred the Great

The Empress Matilda (whose first husband was the Emperor Henry V) was the daughter of Henry I and granddaughter of William the Conqueror. The pedigree quite deliberately sidesteps these two Norman kings and proceeds through the female line to Edward, the exiled son of Edmund Ironside, and through him to the long line of Kings of England and Wessex as far back as they could be traced. Henry was as much an English king as he was a Norman king, and he gave his sons distinctively English names. If this sort of consideration was involved in the naming of potential kings, how good a guide is a list of kings' names to the names in use by the population at large, or at least by the aristocracy? Fortunately, we are able to answer this question as far as the post-Conquest kings of England are concerned. If we take all the kings and all the kings' sons, from the battle of Hastings (1066) to the Battle of Bosworth (1485), a period approximately equal to that covered by the sample of Pictish kings discussed above, we have a sample of thirty-eight names, summarized in the following statistics:

Edward	8
Henry	7
Richard	6
William	4
Edmund	3
John	3
Thomas	2

These are followed by five more names with only one occurrence each. The figures are very similar to those for the Pictish kings' names. The top three names account for well over half the total. A comprehensive list of the Anglo-Norman aristocracy round about the middle of this period was published in four volumes by the Harleian Society with the title *Knights of Edward I*.[6] A sample of five hundred names from the first volume gives the following statistics:

John	18 per cent
William	16
Robert	8
Thomas	6
Henry	5
Richard	5
Hugh	3
Roger	3
Ralph	3
Nicholas	3
Walter	3
Reginald	2
Geoffrey	2
Peter	2

These were followed by fifty-two more names occurring with a frequency of less than 2 per cent each. Five of the top six names in this list (John, William, Thomas, Henry, Richard) appear in the top seven kings' names, but not in the same order. John, the most popular name among the aristocracy, makes a poor showing in the royal family. It seems that the medieval kings of England agreed with Robin Hood and popular opinion ever since, that John was a bad bet for a king, whereas Richard might well turn out to be 'an indomitable general'. Apart from the introduction of Edward in the middle of the period, the post-Conquest, pre-Tudor kings and their sons had names which were a fairly good guide to the more popular names among the aristocracy at the time. By analogy, therefore, it seems that Drust, Talorgan, Brude, Gartnait and Nechtan, the most popular names among the Pictish kings, were likely to have been equally popular among the general population, or at least among the Pictish aristocracy.

The knights of medieval England resembled the Picts of the symbol stones in several respects. They were accomplished horsemen who fought and hunted on horseback. They employed skilled craftsmen and artists to set up lasting memorials to their dead, and an important place on those memorials was taken up by their symbols, the heraldic devices known as coats of arms and generally represented on shields. There can be no reasonable doubt that the Picts of the symbol stones do not represent Pictish society as a whole, but rather a small aristocratic and military part of the Pictish nation – the equivalent in their own time and place of the medieval knights of England. Finally in this comparison, the frequency distribution of Christian names among the knights shows a remarkable similarity to that of the symbols on the Pictish stones. No longer is there any logical reason to doubt 'the simplest and most obvious possible explanation'[7] that the symbols represent the names of the deceased.

The system of symbols employed on medieval coats of arms has never been forgotten; indeed it has never gone out of use. Almost from the beginning, their interpretation was recorded in 'rolls of arms', illustrated by painted shields. No such records were ever made of the meanings of the Pictish symbols. They went out of use several centuries too early. The medieval writers tell us little enough about the Picts themselves, and absolutely nothing about their symbols.

Having established, on the evidence of the stones themselves, that most of the Pictish symbols (those that generally occur in pairs) represent names, the task that remains is to attach names to as many of the symbols as possible and reconstruct the Pictish equivalent of a medieval roll of arms.

CHAPTER 6

The Ogham Code

The ogham script was an Irish invention. Its alphabet was not really an alphabet at all but rather a code based on an existing alphabet. It bore the same sort of relationship to its parent alphabet as Morse code bears to the modern English alphabet. The ogham characters are formed by short or longer lines either crossing or branching from an axial stem. The stem is generally the more or less vertical edge of a standing stone and the text is read from the bottom upwards. The letters B, L, V, S and N are formed by one to five short lines respectively branching off the stem to the right, and the letters H, D, T, C and Q, by similar lines branching off to the left. The letters M, G, Ng, Z and R are formed by one to five longer lines crossing the stem diagonally, and the vowels A, O, U, E and I by short lines crossing the stem at right angles. Characters like these are quite unlike normal alphabetic characters, such as Roman, Greek or Arabic, whose evolution can be traced back through the centuries from Phoenician or other ancestral forms. The coded nature of the ogham script gives some credence to the story of its origin as recorded in the *Book of Ballymote*, that it was invented for the purpose of secret communication among the learned.

The use of the ogham code for monumental inscriptions became popular throughout Ireland but particularly in the south-west. As Irish influence or colonization affected mainland Britain, the ogham code went with it. We find ogham inscriptions in Wales and Cornwall, in mainland Scotland, and as far north as Orkney and Shetland. The puzzling and frustrating thing is that while in general the Irish, Welsh and Cornish oghams are perfectly intelligible, the Scottish (Pictish) ones remain stubbornly indecipherable. Why should this be so? Are they unintelligible because they were written in a non-Indo-European language or is it because the Picts were illiterate and incapable of mastering the ogham code? Or is it perhaps, as Jackson postulated, that the Picts adapted the code for their own numerical use in predicting local festivals?

Before considering the Pictish ogham inscriptions it is worth looking for clues in the much better understood Irish and Welsh inscriptions. The Irish inscriptions were investigated many years ago by Professor R.A.S. Macalister and he gives some interesting examples in his book on the archaeology of Ireland.[1] A stone at Rathduff (Kerry) has an ogham inscription which reads LLONNOCC. The name should have been LONOC and by doubling three of the letters, the mason has cut twenty-six strokes instead of the required fifteen. He would not have been in full-time paid employment, as his modern equivalent might be, and it is suggested that he was paid a piecework wage so that the more strokes he cut, the more he would have earned. Such doubling of letters is common in Irish ogham inscriptions and is also found in Wales. Double letters are also very common in the Pictish ogham inscriptions.

Whatever the reason for using the ogham code in the first place, the arrival of Christianity put these inscriptions at risk. The reason seems to have been the frequent occurrence in the inscriptions of the formula MAQI MUCOI, meaning 'son of the descendant [of]'. The distant ancestor, whose name appears after the word MUCOI may sometimes have been a god and such visible paganism was not to be tolerated. In many inscriptions the name of the ancestor has been hacked away, leaving the rest of the inscription intact. Other inscriptions were destroyed more or less wholesale.

This did not stop the production of ogham inscriptions. Instead, their meaning was obscured by altering the code. Thus on a stone in County Cork MAQI MUCOI was rendered as GAQIMU, and on another County Waterford, MUCOI was written as GUCOI (G has just one more diagonal stroke than M). A more complex example of additional coding is shown by a stone from Monataggart, County Cork. The inscription reads TENREN MONOI GDUQDEGGEV, but Macalister proposed that the real name was VEQREQ MOQOI GLUNLEGGET. The transformation to the double-coded form was achieved by reversing the direction of all strokes branching off from the stem. Thus V (three strokes to the right) became T (three strokes to the left) and so on. Another device was to cut the inscription on so minute a scale that it was hardly visible.

It might perhaps be argued that this extra coding never really happened at all and that it was all in the mind of a twentieth-century professor whose knowledge of early Irish epigraphy was arguably less good than that of a contemporary monumental mason or his employer. With the Welsh inscriptions the situation is quite different. Ogham and Latin stand side by side on the same stone. The ogham can be compared directly with an actual Latin text rather than with a theoretical idea of what it ought to say.

Among the twenty or so good bilingual inscriptions in Wales,[2] over a third give almost identical ogham and Latin readings. A fine example is the tall stone inside the west end of the church at St Dogmaels, Pembrokeshire. The ogham inscriptions reads SAGRAGNI MAQI CUNATAMI, and the Latin SAGRANI FILI CVNOTAMI. Both inscriptions tell us that this is (the stone of) Sagranus son of Cunotamus, and it is stones such as this that provide confirmation of the key to the ogham script, as given in the *Book of Ballymote*. About the same number of stones have an ogham inscription which gives only part of the equivalent text in Latin. On a stone at Rhuddlan, Cardiganshire, the ogham inscription reads TRENACCATLO, and the Latin TRENECATVS [H]IC IACIT FILIVS MAGLAGNI. There is no doubt that both ogham and Latin refer to the same person, but only the Latin tells us that he is son of Maglagnus (or that he lies here).

A few of the Welsh stones have bilingual inscriptions of roughly equal length but showing only partial agreement. On a stone inside the church at Trallwng, Brecknockshire, the ogham inscription reads CVNACENNIVI ILVVETO, while the Latin says CVNOCENNI FILIV[S] CVNOGENI HIC IACIT. There is no inconsistency here. This is (the stone of) Cunocennius who was sometimes called by the double name Cunocennius Ilveto(s) and sometimes known as Cunocennius son of Cunogenus.

There are also a few Welsh stones with ogham and Latin inscriptions which bear no relationship to one another. The stone in Llandawke Church, for example, has an ogham inscription which reads DUMELEDONAS MAQI M. . ., while the associated Latin inscription reads BARRIVEND FILIVS VENDVBARI HIC IACIT. These two inscriptions presumably refer to different people.

Armed with this knowledge of Irish and Welsh ogham stones, we are now in a position to tackle the problem of the Pictish inscriptions. There are eight bilingual ogham-symbol stones with ten bilingual texts. These are summarized below.[3]

Ackergill, Caithness
Fish above rectangle: NEHTETRI
Latheron, Caithness
Eagle above fish: DUV NODNNATMAQQNAHHTO . . .
Inchyra, Perthshire (A)
Double disc above fish: INEHHETESTIEQ . . . INNE
Inchyra, Perthshire (B)
Fish above serpent: . . . UHTUOAGED
Inchyra, Perthshire (C)
Tuning fork: ETTLIETRENOIDDORS

Brandsbutt, Aberdeenshire
Crescent+V-rod above
    serpent+Z-rod: IRATADDOARENS
Logie Elphinstone, Aberdeenshire
Crescent+V-rod above double
    disc+Z-rod: CALTCHU
Brodie, Moray
Pictish elephant above crescent
    +V-rod: VON . . . ECCO
                       RGINNGCHQODTOSOMBS
                       EDDARRNONN . . . TTI . . . GNG

Scoonie, Fife
Pictish elephant: EDDARRNONN
Golspie, Sutherland
Rectangle above Pictish
    elephant: ALLHALLORREDMAQQNUUVVHRRE.RR

Latheron 1: symbols and associated ogham inscription. (Photo: National Museums of Scotland)

Four of the symbol texts given above include the fish. If the symbol and ogham texts are transmitting the same message, the ogham inscriptions associated with these fish symbols ought to have something in common, quite regardless of the actual meaning of the texts. The common element between the Ackergill and Latheron stones is NEHT on Ackergill and NAHHT on Latheron. Unfortunately the end of the Latheron inscription is missing. The fact that NAHHT on the Latheron stone follows MAQQ, evidently the Pictish equivalent of MAQI on the Irish and Welsh stones, meaning 'son [of]', clearly indicates that the NEHT or NAHT element is a name or part of a name. In the Pictish king lists and Irish annals Nechtan, variously spelt, is one of the commoner names and could well be the name represented by the fish symbol. The next thing to note is the correlation between the position of the fish symbol (top or bottom) and the position of the name in the ogham inscription. The Latheron ogham inscription (standardizing the spelling) gives the full text 'Dunodnat son of Nechtan' as equivalent to 'Eagle above fish'. The Ackergill ogham inscription, in the shorter form 'Nechtan' without the patronymic, is just equivalent to 'Fish', and ignores the rectangle symbol.

The Inchyra stone[4] is more difficult to interpret because it was re-used twice and displays three sets of symbols and three separate ogham inscriptions. This remarkable stone, in its final use as the cover stone of a grave, was found during ploughing in 1945. The stone is rather wedge-shaped, so that it has a narrow end and a wide end. On one face (Inchyra A) the double disc and fish were cut at the narrow end, which must have been uppermost at the time. The associated deeply cut ogham inscription reads from the middle of the left edge upwards and across the top. On the other face (Inchyra B) the fish and serpent were cut at the broad end which must have been uppermost at that time. The associated lightly scratched ogham inscription reads from the middle of the opposite edge towards the top. The third set of symbols (Inchyra C), a 'tuning fork' and a mirror, occupy the wide end of the stone on the 'A' face. These symbols, however, were never finished and some attempt was made to erase them. The associated ogham inscription, lightly scratched like the 'B' inscription, was cut on the same edge as the 'A' inscription, reading from near the middle in the opposite direction.

The Inchyra A inscription begins INEHHET, which seems close to the Ackergill inscription, which begins NEHTET. The problem here is that the associated symbols have the double disc above the fish. Perhaps the stone was set up by another man called Nechtan, possibly the son of the man represented by the double disc and grandson of the Nechtan represented by the fish. The brief

Inchyra: front (left) and back. Symbols with associated ogham inscriptions on both edges (not visible on these views). (Photos: Royal Commission on Ancient and Historical Monuments of Scotland)

Inchyra B inscription seems to say UHTUOAGED but it was damaged when the stone was being moved, and the beginning is defective. The U might be missing a stroke, in which case it would become an E. It is also possible that another complete letter was missing, making it perfectly possible that the inscription really began NEHTU. This may look like wishful thinking but in Wales, where the ogham inscriptions are compared with Latin equivalents, letters from the Latin are used to supplement the ogham and letters from the ogham are used to supplement the Latin. Here in Scotland, using the fish symbol to supplement a defective ogham inscription is shown to produce an internally consistent result.

The Pictish elephant symbol appears in three of the bilingual texts listed above. Two out of these three contain the word EDDARRNONN, the longest recognizable word to appear in any of the Pictish ogham inscriptions (bilingual or not). This is generally believed to represent the Celtic name Edern, which is therefore likely to be the 'translation' of the Pictish elephant symbol. The Golspie ogham inscription contains the element MAQQ and so ought to contain the names of a man and his father, but has nothing in common with the EDDARRNONN inscriptions on the Brodie and Scoonie stones, and yet this stone clearly shows the Pictish elephant in the lower (father) position of the main pair of symbols.

The identical spelling of the name Edern – EDDARRNONN – on stones as far apart as Brodie in Moray and Soonie in Fife is quite remarkable, particularly when compared with the several forms of the name Nechtan – NEHT . . ., NAHHTO . . ., etc. The spelling of names has never been standardized and is certainly not uniform today. My own name, for example, can be spelt in over twenty different ways. If I were to spell it out – C, U, double-M, I, N, S – anywhere in Scotland, the chances are that it would be written down as CUMMING. In most parts of England it would generally be written as CUMMINGS, but in southern Ireland it would be recorded as CUMMINS. Regardless of spelling it out, people tend to write down a name as they hear it and they interpret what they hear in terms of past experience and this often shows a regional variation. In view of the variability in the spelling of our names today, we can hardly expect consistency in the rendering of Pictish names more than a thousand years ago, and yet the spelling of EDDARRNONN *is* consistent. It is perhaps significant that both the stones on which this name appears are Class II stones, whereas only one of the 'Nechtan' stones (Latheron) is a Class II stone. It could be that the Age of Migrating Ideas brought with it some increase in literacy.

It is perhaps surprising that the Pictish elephant, one of the commoner symbols, represents a name that does not appear in any version of the Pictish king lists. It does, however, appear in the genealogy of the kings of Gwynedd in North Wales who traced their ancestry back to Cunedda (Pictish Cinaed=Kenneth), who came from Manau Gododdin to Wales some time in the late fourth or early fifth century. Manau Gododdin was a British kingdom just south of the Firth of Forth, immediately adjacent to the southern Picts. Cunedda came south with eight of his nine sons to drive out the Irish settlers; having successfully completed his mission, he and his sons themselves settled in Wales and founded a number of dynasties. The pedigrees state that Cunedda was son of Oetern (Latin Eternus) and that his youngest son was called Edern and is supposed to have given his name to the district of Edeyrnion in North Wales.[5]

The Pictish elephant is not only the commonest animal symbol, it is also one of the few to show a meaningful distribution pattern. This is best seen on a map showing how its relative frequency, given as a percentage of all the symbols in a given area, varies from place to place. The Pictish elephant shows a clear maximum in the south and a gradual decrease towards the north. Was the name Edern, which is represented by this symbol, introduced from the south not long

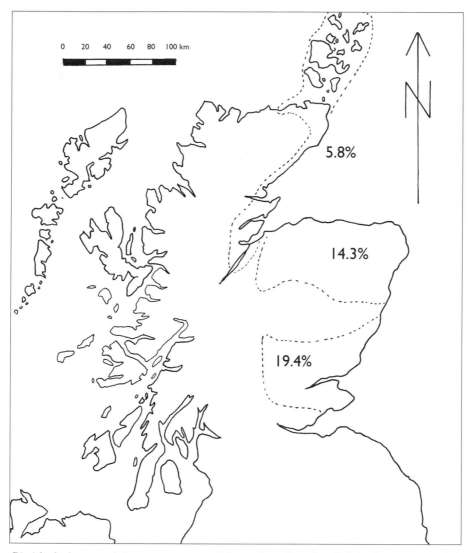

Pictish elephant symbols as a percentage of the total number of symbols in three main symbol stone areas: south of the Mounth (19.4 per cent), Aberdeen to Nairn (14.3 per cent), and Inverness to Orkney (5.8 per cent).

before the Picts developed their system of symbols? Some support for this possibility comes from the names of Cunedda's ancestors in Manau Gododdin. The relevant part of the pedigree states that Cunedda was son of Oetern, son of Patern Pesrud, son of Tacit. These three names, of the father, grandfather and great-grandfather of Cunedda, are considered to be of Latin origin: Eternus,

Paternus of the red tunic, and Tacitus. Cunedda's family seems to have been proud of its Roman connections, however flimsy these may have been thus far north. Paternus of the red tunic might even have held some official position.[6] If this Roman connection is accepted, it would be a good reason for a late adoption of the name Edern by the Picts and a southerly distribution of the Pictish elephant symbol.

The name Edern, whether of Roman origin or not, was in use among the Britons from Manau Gododdin in the north to Wales in the south, but was it really the Pictish name represented by the swimming elephant symbol? If that were so, why was it so carefully recorded in the ogham script as EDDARRNONN? Was the -ONN ending perhaps indicative of the genitive case, so that, as in many of the Welsh inscriptions (both Latin and ogham), the text would have been understood as '(the stone of) Edern'? Or was the man who cut the ogham inscription, presumably an Irishman, simply recording the name as he thought it should be? A brief entry in Latin in the Annals of Ulster under the year 669 supports the second interpretation. *Itarnan et Corindu apud Pictores defuncti sunt*: Itarnan and Corindu, whoever they were, died among the Picts. They were presumably Irish, and Itarnan, not far removed from Edarnon, was probably the Irish equivalent of Edern. There was also a St Ethernan, whose shrine on the Isle of May, off the coast of Fife, became a place of pilgrimage.[7]

The crescent and V-rod, the most abundant of all the Pictish symbols, also appears in three of the bilingual texts, but this time the ogham inscriptions are giving nothing away. There is absolutely nothing in common between them. This is disappointing, but it does not necessarily invalidate the test. What it tells us is that the direct 'translation' of the crescent and V-rod into the ogham script cannot be present in more than one of the associated inscriptions and may not be there in any of them. There are several reasons why it might not be there. It might be so heavily coded as to be unrecognizable. The ogham inscription might be incomplete, either through subsequent damage or because it never did say all that was implied by the symbols. Finally, the ogham inscription and the symbol texts might have been quite unrelated and possibly not even contemporary.

The Brandsbutt stone symbols are a crescent and V-rod above a serpent and Z-rod. The associated ogham inscription is beautifully executed in relation to an incised stem on the same flat surface as the symbols. There can be no doubt at all about the reading of the ogham inscription, but unfortunately it is one of those which continue to resist interpretation.

Brandsbutt: symbols and associated ogham inscription. (Photo: Royal Commission on Ancient and Historical Monuments of Scotland)

The Logie Elphinstone ogham inscription is unusual in being cut along a circular incised stem. The symbols are unusual too and indicate re-use of the stone. The symbols are recorded in Jackson's list as a crescent and V-rod above a double disc and Z-rod but this pair of symbols quite clearly overlies an earlier symbol, of which the most prominent component is a pair of discs. The symbols were deeply incised on both occasions, though the top of the crescent and V-rod seems less well cut. What seems to have happened is that the top of the stone was smoothed down before the circular ogham inscription was cut and this smoothing operation affected the upper part of the crescent and V-rod. If this is so, the ogham inscription is later than both sets of symbols and has no bearing on the 'translation' of any of them.

Finally, the crescent and V-rod appears on the Golspie stone but not as part of a symbol pair (see pp. 42–4). The Golspie inscription is therefore unable to provide any clues to the interpretation of the crescent and V-rod.

The only other symbol to appear more than once in our collection of bilingual texts is the rectangle. On the Golspie stone it occupies the upper position, above the Pictish elephant, but it was concluded earlier that the ogham inscription and the symbol text on this stone are unrelated. On the Ackergill stone it is in the lower position, below what remains of the underparts of a fish. On this stone the ogham inscription is shorter than the symbol text and gives no indication that it ever mentioned the patronymic.

CONCLUSIONS

A few conclusions can be drawn from this examination of bilingual ogham and Pictish symbol texts.

1. As suggested in an earlier chapter, the Pictish symbols *do* seem to represent names.
2. The symbol texts should be read from the top downwards in the form 'A son of B'.
3. The fish symbol represents the name Nechtan, appearing in the ogham inscriptions as NAHHTO, NEHTET, NEHTU, etc.
4. The Pictish elephant symbol represents the name Edern, appearing in the ogham inscriptions (possibly in the genitive case) as EDDARRNONN.
5. The eagle symbol represents the name Dunodnat, appearing in the ogham inscription as DUV NODNNAT, which might mean Black Nodnat.

CHAPTER 7
The Drosten Stone and Trusty's Hill

There are eight bilingual ogham–symbol stones but only one Drosten stone. This unique cross slab stands today in the little museum at St Vigeans near Arbroath. The symbols are a double disc and Z-rod above a simple crescent (without the usual V-rod), accompanied by a mirror and comb. What makes this stone unique is an inscription in Hiberno-Saxon script, set in a panel just above ground level on one side. The inscription, which is unfortunately incomplete, reads as follows:

D R O S T E N

I P E U O R E T

E T T F O R . .

C U S . . . . .

The third and fourth lines of the inscription are incomplete and there should have been three more lines to fill the panel. There are illegible traces of lettering in the blank part of the panel, and it looks as though the lower part of the inscription has been deliberately erased by rubbing the stone down. What can we make of the part that has survived?

Drust, sometimes spelt Drest, is the commonest name in the *Pictish Chronicle* and the form of the name is remarkably consistent, both in this and in the *Annals of Ulster*. The same sources give an equally consistent genitive case of the name. Talorgan son of Drust, King of Athol, who had the misfortune to suffer execution by drowning in 739, is called Talorggan mac Drostain in his obituary notice in the *Annals of Ulster*. With minor variations in spelling, this seems to have been the standard form of the genitive case for Drust. This implies that the reading of the inscription on the Drosten stone should begin '(The stone of) Drust'. The double disc and Z-rod might perhaps be an attempt to render the

St Vigeans 1 (Drosten stone): hunt scene and symbols. Note the archer at bottom left. (Photo: Historic Scotland)

name Drust in pictorial form. Drust is probably the Pictish form of the modern name Tristan or Tristram, which is close to the Welsh word *trystau*, meaning thunder. The symbol could perhaps be interpreted as the clashing of symbols (the two discs) to represent the noise of thunder, combined with a flash of lightning, represented by the Z-rod. This would be close to the heraldic concept of canting arms discussed in Chapter 3, where the symbol or heraldic device is a pun on the name.

In the old Irish language (as in modern Gaelic) a son is *mac*. The genitive case of *mac* was *meic* and this was sometimes shortened to *ic*. The P-Celtic (British Welsh – possibly Pictish) equivalent of the Q-Celtic (Irish Gaelic) *ic* would have been *ip*, and it is therefore quite reasonable to suppose that the IPE in the second line means son of. Taking the first two lines together, we now have 'The stone of Drust son of Uoret'.

Uoret is a name that appears in the Group A versions of the *Pictish Chronicle* as Wrad, Urad or Uurad and in the Group B versions as Ferat, Ferach, Ferech and even Feradhach. These are the Pictish and Irish forms of the name respectively.

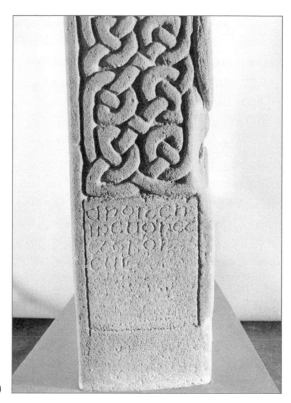

St Vigeans 1: Hiberno-Saxon
inscription. (Photo: Historic Scotland)

Following the pattern of the last chapter, the double disc and Z-rod can be identified as the symbol for Drust and the simple crescent for Ferat. It is reassuring to find Drust, the commonest name in the king lists, represented by one of the most abundant symbols.

A recent reading of the Drosten inscription suggested that the second letter of the word IPE might be an 'R'. *Ire* can hardly be translated in any language as son of, so some other interpretation of the inscription was required. A Gaelic interpretation of the relevant part of the inscription, taking IRE as two words might be *Drosten i re Uoret*, meaning 'Drosten, in the time of (or in the reign of) Uoret'.[1] Drosten, it is suggested, might have been the name of a nobleman or cleric who died in the reign of Ferat son of Bargoit (d. 842); or he might have been a saint connected with the church at St Vigeans; or possibly even the sculptor who carved the stone. There was, however, little certainty about the 'R' in question and it seems that 'on balance it does appear more likely to be a P'.[2] The Drosten stone is still most likely to be the stone of Drust son of Ferat.

As far as the meaning of the symbols is concerned, we have made full use of the damaged inscription. But we can hardly leave the matter there. What does the rest of the inscription say? And why were the bottom three lines erased?

ETT at the beginning of the third line has generally been identified as the Latin *et*, meaning and. It could also be the end of the name on the line above, which would then read UORETETT. It was noted above that the name Ferat could sometimes be written as Feradhach. It is thus possible that if Ferat or Ferech could become Uoret, Feradhach might become Uoretet.

The next word on the third line is the old Irish *for*, meaning great, equivalent of the Welsh *fawr*. If there ever were any other letters on this line after FOR, they have completely disappeared.

The fourth line begins CUS and with that the surviving part of the inscription ends. It has been supposed that this follows directly on the last surviving letters of the third line, making a word FORCUS which might be interpreted as the name Fergus. If this had been the intended word, there was enough room for the final CUS on the third line. It is perhaps more likely that the CUS is the beginning of a new word or name, and the most likely name is Cusantin or Custantin, two common variants of Constantine, the name of one of the greatest Pictish (and Scottish) kings, and the first to have been recognized as king by both Picts and Scots.

When Constantine died in 820, he had ruled at least part of the Pictish kingdom for some forty years. He had defeated his chief opponent, Conall (Canaul in the *Pictish Chronicle*) son of Taedg, in 789 and become King of all the Picts. Conall escaped with his life and retreated to Dalriada, where he may have tried to become King of the Scots on the death of Domnall (Donncorci in the Irish annals) in 792. Exactly when, or how, Constantine became King of the Scots is not recorded. Conall son of Taedg was finally defeated and killed in Kintyre by Conall son of Aedan. Constantine was succeeded in both kingdoms by his brother Oengus, who reigned for a further twelve years. By the time Oengus died in 834, the two brothers had reigned over the combined Picto-Scottish kingdom for a generation, long enough for this to be looked on as the norm. For a short time, however, there was disagreement. Aed son of Boanta became King of the Scots and Drust son of Constantine, King of the Picts. But in the face of the external danger of Viking invasion, unity was soon restored under Eogan son of Oengus. Then in 839 the Viking invaders defeated a combined Picto-Scottish army. Eogan son of Oengus, King of the Picts and Scots, was killed, as was his former rival, Aed son of Boanta. The battle was lost and the Picto-Scottish union shattered.

After the battle Kenneth mac Alpin rallied what was left of the Scottish army and became King of the Scots in Dalriada. Ferat son of Bargoit became King of the Picts. Ferat reigned for three short years before being succeeded by his son Brude, who reigned for one year only. He was followed by Kenneth mac Alpin, though whether by military conquest or peaceful succession is not recorded. Kenneth, however, did not immediately become king of all the Picts. Opposition to his rule continued for a further six years under the leadership of three successive kings, Kenneth (Kinat) son of Ferat, Brude son of Fochel and finally Drust son of Ferat. Drust was defeated and killed, either at Forteviot or Scone. It was generally thought during the Middle Ages, and is widely believed today, that this was a Scottish victory over the Picts. The sons of Ferat and Fochel may even have thought of themselves as leaders of a Pictish national resistance against a Scottish enemy, and this may well have been a good way of drumming up support for their cause. The truth was almost certainly very different from this. This was not a war between the Picts and the Scots, but a civil war within the Picto-Scottish kingdom founded by Constantine half a century earlier.

Kenneth mac Alpin and his opponents – the sons of Ferat and Fochel – may all have been descended from Constantine and each probably had an equally good hereditary claim to the throne. No democratic system had been devised for coping with the succession to a joint Picto-Scottish kingdom and the final solution was achieved by military force. Inevitably some people were unhappy with the outcome.

The Drosten stone is almost certainly a memorial to Drust son of Ferat, the last leader of the resistance against Kenneth mac Alpin. The inscription on the stone was probably too blatant a declaration of his connection with Constantine, of his claim to the throne, or of the manner of his death. Any regime that owes its position to military strength must guard against rebellion, and the public display of rival claims cannot be tolerated. That may explain why half the inscription on the Drosten stone was erased.

There is just one other Class II symbol stone with a partial inscription in Hiberno-Saxon characters. This stone, much less well known than the Drosten stone, was found underneath the pulpit of Fordoun parish church when it was being rebuilt towards the end of the eighteenth century. It is supposed that it might have been hidden there at the time of the Reformation, a suggestion that makes one wonder how many other such stones might have been destroyed at that time. It was then transferred to the nearby remains of an early church known as St Palladius' Chapel, where it stood exposed to the elements for many years until it was moved to its present position inside the west end of the modern church. At some stage in its history it has been shortened for use in some part of the building. The top of the stone, about half the upper arm of the cross and adjacent panels, is missing. Below the cross is a single symbol, the double disc and Z-rod. Below this symbol, the surface of the stone is rough and at a slightly higher level. There never was another symbol, and this lower part of the stone is the part that was set in the ground.

The inscription, in the top left panel, consists of a single line of letters reading PIDARNOIN. The initial P is probably the end of *ip*, meaning son of, as discussed above. It is extremely frustrating that on this bilingual stone, the top line of the inscription is missing and there was only ever one symbol. If we accept the conclusions of this and the last chapter, the inscription should read something like:

D R U S T E N I

P I D A R N O I N

Drusten ip Idarnoin, meaning (the stone of) Drust son of Edern. The symbols equivalent to this inscription would be a double disc and Z-rod above a Pictish elephant, but the elephant was never added. The unfortunate truth is that the damage to this stone prevents it adding any independent evidence to the interpretation of the symbols. Instead, it does something quite different and equally important. The information contained in the inscription was more than that given by the symbol. It tells us that the symbols are not the first clumsy attempts at writing in a pre-literate society. Like medieval heraldry, while giving some of the same information as the written word, they were generally used in different contexts. The ogham inscriptions, most of which do not have associated symbols, lead to much the same conclusion. Little remains of Pictish writing except for the *Pictish Chronicle*, which was probably kept in written form from some time in the sixth century.

These stones are the last bilingual symbol stones to be considered but, far from being the end of the investigation, they point the way forward. The Drosten stone is not just a symbol stone. It is a record on stone of a recognizable incident in Pictish history. What we have to do now is to look for other symbol stones or symbol-bearing artefacts which can be related to their historical context. The symbols carved on a rock face on Trusty's Hill, far away to the south on the other side of the country, provide an ideal starting point.

Trusty's Hill is a small hill-fort near Gatehouse of Fleet, overlooking Wigtown Bay on the northern shores of the Solway Firth. Just across Wigtown Bay, about 4 miles north-west of Wigtown, is a farm called Bartrostan. There are several other place-names in the area beginning with Bar-, a Gaelic word meaning top or summit. Below Bartrostan flows a small stream called Bartrostan Burn, telling us that the hill on which the farm stands received its Gaelic name before the Northumbrian English arrived and named the burn after it. Tristram and Tristan are the English forms of the name Drust and it is likely that Trusty's Hill was originally Drust's Hill and Bartrostan was 'the summit of Drust' (not a very impressive summit, it has to be admitted). The place-name evidence seems to indicate that someone called Drust made an impression in this part of south-west Scotland sufficient for his name to be preserved in the local topography. The first symbol of the Trusty's Hill group (upper left) is the double disc and Z-rod. The fact that the Drosten stone and Trusty's Hill have this symbol in common reinforces the identification of the symbol with the name.

The symbols on Trusty's Hill are unusual in two respects: their geographical location and their physical situation on a solid rock outcrop. Trusty's Hill is a long way south of what is usually regarded as Pictish territory. The Antonine

Trusty's Hill: the double-disc and Z-rod on the rock face by the entrance.

Wall, the more northerly of the two great Roman frontiers, has been a convenient line to take as the southern boundary of the Pictish kingdom. But political boundaries seldom remain fixed for hundreds of years and the symbols on Trusty's Hill are a clear indication of a Pictish presence more than 70 miles south of the Antonine Wall. Their situation at the entrance to a hillfort suggests that they represent a statement by the living rather than a memorial to the dead.

Direct archaeological dating is no help. The symbols were presumably carved during the occupation of the hill-fort, but that is giving very little away. The historical evidence for changes in the position of the Pictish frontier is extremely limited. Indeed the siting of the southern boundary of the Pictish kingdom along the Antonine Wall is not based on historical evidence at all. The main criteria for establishing the boundary are distribution maps of such typically Pictish artefacts as symbol stones and such distinctively Pictish place-names as those beginning with Pit-. Symbol stones and Pit- place-names are rare south of the Antonine Wall but abundant north of it. It has to be admitted, however, that these distributions are not very convincing as evidence of a southern Pictish boundary along the Antonine Wall or along the alternative 'Forth–Clyde line'. The real boundary in the east is the Firth of Forth. West of Alloa, however, a few miles upstream from the head of the firth, there are very few Pit- place-names and no symbol stones at all. West of Alloa, the Forth–Clyde line and, a little to the south, the Antonine Wall, lie within the kingdom of the Strathclyde Britons and do not represent a territorial boundary at all.

The historical indications in late Pictish times are in agreement with the distribution patterns considered above. Bede, writing in 731, relates how Trumwine, who had been appointed English Bishop of the Picts, had to withdraw to the monastery at Abercorn after the decisive Pictish victory at the Battle of Nechtansmere in 685. Abercorn, on the southern shore of the Firth of Forth, a few miles east of Queensferry and the Forth Bridge, was described as being 'situated in English territory but . . . close to the firth that divides the lands of the English from those of the Picts'.[3] Some time after about 850, an unknown writer decided to fill out the Brechin copy of the *Pictish Chronicle* with a summary of historical events.[4] Thus from the reign of Kenneth mac Alpin this work becomes a genuine chronicle. We learn from this *Brechin Chronicle* that in the seventh year of his reign (849), Kenneth mac Alpin invaded Saxonia six times, burnt Dunbar and captured Melrose. This account makes it quite clear that up to the middle of the ninth century, the country south of the Firth of Forth was held by the English. The historical details supplied by Bede and the *Brechin Chronicle* are consistent with the complete absence of Class II symbol stones or Pictish cross slabs south of the Firth of Forth.

Before Bede, we have to go back two hundred years to find another contemporary writer, a British priest called Gildas who wrote a book entitled *The Ruin of Britain*.[5] Unlike Bede, Gildas does not give us a single date and there is considerable doubt about exactly when he was writing. Opinion ranges from about 540 at the latest, through 515–520, to 479–484 as the earliest possible date.[6] Every scrap of evidence is hedged around with uncertainties and there is no possibility of anything approaching absolute proof. Perhaps we should say he was writing in 510 ± 30 years.

Gildas begins his section on 'Independent Britain'[7] with the departure of 'her whole army, her military resources, her governors, brutal as they were, and her sturdy youth, who had followed the tyrant's footsteps, never to return home'. This tyrant was Magnus Maximus, who left Britain for Gaul in 383 in search of imperial power. The departure of the army was the signal for renewed raids by the Scots from the north-west and the Picts from the north. After this the events recorded by Gildas are a confusion of history, legend and speculation, which may be summarized as follows.

1.   The Britons sent a letter to Rome asking for help. A legion was dispatched and quickly defeated the enemy. They instructed the Britons to build a wall and left them to it. Deprived of effficient leadership, they built the wall of turf instead of stone (the Antonine Wall, actually built about AD 142) and it turned out to be a very ineffective barrier. The old enemy soon returned and the situation was as bad as ever.

2.   The Britons once again sent to Rome for assistance and once more their request was granted. This time, however, the Britons were given due warning that in future they would have to look to their own defences. Before they left, the Romans organized the construction of a proper stone wall (Hadrian's Wall, actually built about AD 122–130). Then the Romans departed for the last time. Soon the Picts and the Scots were on the attack again. They 'seized the whole of the extreme north of the island from its inhabitants, right up to the wall'. Then they attacked the wall itself. So ineffectual were the leaderless Britons that they had to abandon the wall and flee to the south.

3.   The Britons wrote yet another letter addressed this time not just to Rome but to 'the Roman commander Aetius'. The letter began 'To Aetius, thrice consul: the groans of the British'. Gildas does not often provide such precise and indeed

helpful detail. Aetius was consul for the third time in 446 and for the fourth time in 454, so the letter must have been written between these dates, most probably in 448, when Aetius was in northern Gaul. Gildas had no need to give such detail and there is no reason to doubt its veracity. This letter was written in living memory of people that Gildas could have known and talked with.

From the point of view of Pictish history, the date of this letter to Aetius is of far greater importance than the date when Gildas wrote his book. If the letter was sent in 448, it means that the Picts, together with the Scots, had already carried out a successful invasion of southern Scotland, right up to Hadrian's Wall, and had taken the wall itself. But this time there was no Roman army to come to the rescue of the Britons. From the middle of the fifth century, for a time at least, southern Scotland was occupied by the Picts (and also, in part, by the Scots). How long this Pictish occupation of southern Scotland lasted we do not know, though it is unlikely to have survived the advance of King Ethelred of Northumbria, who defeated Aidan King of the Scots in a decisive battle 'at a famous place known as Degsastan'[8] in 603. Unfortunately, this formerly famous place can no longer be located. The Picts themselves left very few records of their own history but, for this great period of Pictish military success, there is one small clue contained in the *Pictish Chronicle*.

The Group A version of the *Pictish Chronicle* provides a good chronology back to the reign of Brude son of Maelchon, who reigned for thirty years and died in 584. Brude was baptised by St Columba, was mentioned more than once by the Irish annalists, and was even mentioned by Bede. He is a thoroughly historical character. A recent analysis of the kings listed immediately before Brude[9] has revealed that for most of his long reign, he only ruled over the northern Picts. Contemporary kings of the southern Picts included Drust son of Munait (577–578) and Drust son of Girom (553–558). Slightly earlier than these was Drust Gurthinmoch (506–536), who was King of all the Picts. There is no indication that any of these three might have ruled as far south as Trusty's Hill. But then there are only three kings, before Kenneth mac Alpin, about whom the *Pictish Chronicle* has anything to say at all. One of these is Brude son of Maelchon, and the other two are earlier. Nechtan son of Erip (482–506) is recorded as having given land at Abernethy, near Perth, for the foundation of a church. The king immediately before Nechtan was Talore son of Aniel (478–482), and before him we enter the realm of legend with Drust son of Erp, who is said to have reigned for a hundred years and fought a hundred battles! It is also added that in the nineteenth year of his reign St Patrick came to Ireland. Is this just a legend, or does Drust son of Erp have a real place in history? And what did he have to do with the arrival of St Patrick in Ireland?

The second question is easier to answer than the first, so we will start with St Patrick. The simple answer is that they had nothing whatever to do with each other. St Patrick was in Ireland, Drust was in Scotland, and they almost certainly never met. So why should St Patrick be mentioned at all in this very brief account of the reign of Drust son of Erp? The answer is that the arrival of St Patrick in Ireland was one of the most memorable events in early Irish history and therefore became a reference date in Irish chronology. It is no different in principle from our familiar system of dates AD and BC, with their reference date to the birth of Jesus Christ. So far so good, but why should an Irish reference date be attached to a Pictish king list? For the answer to this we must go to Nechtan son of Erip and the foundation of the church at Abernethy.

Nechtan, before he came to the throne, had spent some time as an exile in Ireland and, while there, had met St Brigid (Bride), Abbess of Kildare. He became interested in the new Christian religion and asked her to plead with God on his behalf. Then, when in due course he returned home and became King of the Picts, he remembered St Brigid and her prayers and sent a message back to Kildare offering land for a Christian mission in his kingdom. St Brigid sent Darlugdach, her favourite pupil, later to succeed her as second Abbess of Kildare, to receive the gift on her behalf. The land he granted was at Abernethy, where the parish church still carries its dedication to St Bride. St Brigid was born about fifteen years after St Patrick's arrival in Ireland, and she founded the first Irish nunnery at Kildare. St Brigid and Darlugdach must both have been familiar with the Irish Christian chronology, in which the years were counted from the arrival of St Patrick, and Darlugdach would have brought this knowledge with her to Abernethy and fixed it in relation to the local chronology. The statement that St Patrick arrived in Ireland in the nineteenth year of the reign of Drust son of Erp does just that and means that the Pictish and Irish chronologies can be synchronized.

The date of St Patrick's arrival in Ireland, as given in several Irish sources, was AD 434. If that was the nineteenth year of the reign of Drust son of Erp, he must have come to the throne about AD 416. That effectively disposes of his 'hundred-year reign'. Had he reigned for a hundred years from that date, St Brigid and Darlugdach would both have been dead before Nechtan could possibly have come to the throne. If the *Pictish Chronicle* is as good a guide as it appears to be, Drust must have died about AD 478, by which time he would have reigned for sixty-two years, just a little short of Queen Victoria's record. What of the legend then? If he did indeed reign for sixty-two years, he had an incredibly long reign by any standards and, in oral tradition, this could easily have been rounded up to a hundred years. As with the reign, so with the battles. He was a great war leader and fought a large number of battles, presumably with a better than average success rate, to account for the legend.

Now we can return to Gildas and the letter to Aetius. In 448, when that letter was sent, Drust son of Erp would have been in his prime, fighting his best battles, pushing the Pictish frontier southwards, attacking and taking Hadrian's Wall, organizing military activity on a wide front and carrying out raids far into enemy territory south of the wall. The correlation could hardly be bettered. Drust son of Erp, who reigned for so many years and was such a famous leader in battle, must surely be the Drust whose double disc and Z-rod symbol is carved on the rock face at the entrance to the hill-fort which to this day bears his name – Trusty's Hill.

The other symbols, to the right of the double disc and Z-rod, are a fish monster, with a deeply incised dagger or sword pointing upwards at its belly.

Trusty's Hill: the fish monster on the rock face by the entrance.

Beneath these is an extraordinary round (insect?) head with two long antennae curled round at the ends. At the point of contact between the dagger and the fish monster, a small spiral is issuing from the underside of the beast. Similar spirals are coming out of its mouth. The dagger and fish monster are clearly connected, but not in the normal manner of a pair of symbols. Is the fish monster mortally wounded? Does it perhaps represent Britain south of the Roman walls? King Edward I of England was known to his countrymen as the Hammer of the Scots. Perhaps the dagger and fish monster are saying something similar about Drust son of Erp. The insect's head remains a mystery.

CHAPTER 8
Symbols on Silver

A heavy silver chain consisting of twenty-two pairs of circular links and a penannular 'napkin ring' terminal, found at Whitecleugh in Lanarkshire, has two things in common with the rock face at the entrance to the Trusty's Hill fort. Both display Pictish symbols, including the double disc and Z-rod, and both sites are well south of the Antonine Wall. The symbols on the chain, the double disc and Z-rod and the notched rectangle, are situated one on each side of the gap in the terminal ring. Like the symbols on Trusty's Hill, these symbols cannot be

Whitecleugh silver chain. (Photo: National Museums of Scotland)

Whitecleugh silver chain: the symbols on the terminal ring. (Photo: National Museums of Scotland)

memorials to the dead and must therefore represent some sort of statement by the living. Perhaps they are statements of ownership, like a name-tape sewn into a school uniform. Or maybe they are statements of authority, perhaps of some high office or military command granted by the king. The Whitecleugh silver chain

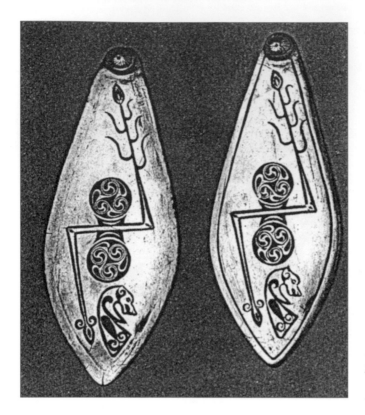

Norrie's Law: silver plaques with symbols. (Photo: National Museums of Scotland)

does not stand alone. Ten such chains are known and all but three were found in the country south of the Antonine Wall. Only five of them were recovered complete with terminal rings and of these only one other, from Parkhill, a few miles north-west of Aberdeen, has symbols engraved on it.

Symbols engraved on silver objects are also known from the Norrie's Law hoard in Fife. The symbols, a double disc and Z-rod above a dog's head, are engraved on a pair of leaf-shaped plaques. The double disc and Z-rod symbols are so like those on the terminal ring of the Whitecleugh chain that they could have been engraved by the same craftsman.

Another symbol from Norrie's Law is a unique Z-rod engraved on the head of a silver hand pin. This Z-rod is similar to those on the Whitecleugh chain and the Norries Law plaques but differs from them in the absence of the double disc. Apart from this single example, the Z-rod is always attached to one or other of three symbols: the double disc, the serpent or the notched rectangle. The other odd thing about this symbol is that it was engraved on the back of the pinhead, where it was partly obscured by the pin when this was attached. The heads of such pins, to judge from the mould found on Traprain Law,[1] were cast as complete units consisting of a semicircular 'hand' and the overlying 'fingers'. There can have been no doubt in the silversmith's mind that he was engraving this Z-rod on the back of the pinhead and that it was never going to be seen. Another hand pin from the Norrie's Law hoard is similar in every other detail but has no symbol engraved on it. It is as if these objects belonged to an experimental period, when new uses for symbols were being tried out. The hand pin was an experiment that failed. The double disc, the most likely symbol to complete the engraving, could not be fitted into the small semicircle of the pinhead.

The silver chains are movable objects and their distribution in southern Scotland does not necessarily indicate an area of Pictish settlement. It has been suggested[2] that they may have belonged to Picts living further north and been carried south as loot by raiders, who presumably lost them before they had a chance to melt them down for their own use. It has even been suggested that they were lost by their Pictish owners while carrying out raids in the south. Accidental loss of such massive and valuable silver objects, either by their Pictish owners or by some foreign raiders, seems a little unlikely. The other possibility is that they were deposited intentionally just where they were found, either stored for safe-keeping in an underground box or possibly buried with their owner. Such a possibility cannot be ruled out in view of the circumstances of their discovery. If this was so, then the distribution of the silver chains must reflect the distribution of some sort of Pictish presence.

Isabel Henderson expressed a widely held view when she wrote: 'the first and most glaring difficulty is the geographical distribution of the chains . . . [of which] . . . all but three were found to the south of the Forth–Clyde line, the political boundary of the historical Picts which was certainly in force by 600 AD'.[3] The distribution of these chains has been treated as if the three northern ones were perfectly acceptable and the seven southern ones were out of place. But that is an over-simplification. There is a huge gap between the southern and the northern silver chains. The three northern chains were all found to the north of another great boundary mentioned by Bede, 'a range of steep and desolate mountains' which separate the provinces of the northern Picts from those of the southern Picts. These mountains, sometimes referred to as the Mounth, extend eastwards from the main mass of the Highlands and reach the sea between Stonehaven and Aberdeen. The continuing importance of this boundary is shown by the obituary notice of Dubhtolargg (782), described in the *Annals of Ulster* as King of the Picts this side of the Mounth. Earlier, in the *Pictish Chronicle*, we find Nechtan son of Erip (482–506) described as king of all the provinces of the Picts,

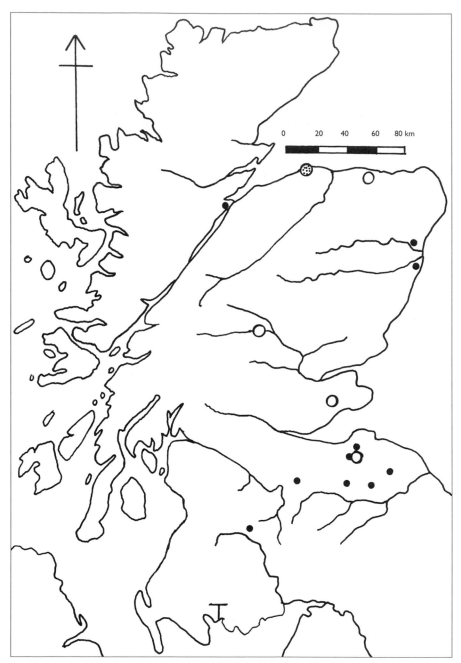

Map showing the distribution of silver chains (dots), hoards of silver (open circles), and Covesea Cave coins (stippled circle).

with the clear implication that some of his predecessors had not enjoyed such wide authority. Classical writers of the fourth century seem to have used the term *Picti* in a generic sense in such phrases as 'Caledonians and other Picts' or 'Picts divided into two peoples, *Dicalydones* and *Verturiones*'. The physical geography of Pictland was the same in the fourth century as it was in the eighth and it is likely that the Mounth was the boundary between the *Dicalydones* and the *Verturiones* just as it was between the northern and southern Picts. It will be convenient to consider the two areas separately.

The distribution of the southern chains may be connected with the Pictish conquest of southern Scotland in the fifth century, as discussed in the previous chapter. One was found in the great hill-fort of Traprain Law, a little over 20 miles east of Edinburgh. A Pictish conqueror of southern Scotland would hardly have left such an important stronghold in enemy hands, and this chain probably belonged to a Pictish leader, perhaps the commander of the garrison. Another chain was found nearby at Haddington, and three more on the southern margin of Lammermuir, north of the Tweed valley. Further west, another chain was found near Walston, about 5 miles north of Biggar. Whitecleugh, where the most westerly of the chains was found, is situated at the head of a pass leading down into Nithsdale and thence to Dumfries and the Solway Firth. Only about 8 miles north-east of Whitecleugh, at Roberton, there stands a Class I stone with just one symbol, a fish, incised on it – perhaps a memorial to someone called Nechtan who died on active service during the campaign. This is the only surviving symbol stone south of Edinburgh. No silver chains have been found south of the Tweed and their distribution seems to reflect an intermediate stage in the Pictish advance, before they reached Hadrian's Wall and perhaps also before they reached the Solway Firth and took over the hill-fort on Trusty's Hill. With such a small sample, however, it would be unwise to push the interpretation too far.

If Traprain Law did indeed fall into Pictish hands during this period, then the great hoard of Roman silver found there would take its natural place as Pictish loot from raids on southern Britain. Two little-worn silver coins of the Emperor Honorius (395–423) included in the hoard are consistent with a Pictish occupation beginning some time before 448, when Hadrian's Wall was over-run and the Britons' letter to Aetius sent. The beautiful silver vessels and other objects in this treasure were crushed and cut into pieces ready to be melted down by Pictish silversmiths to make, among other things, the silver chains which are the subject of the present discussion. A crushed and broken Roman spoon from

Norrie's Law provides a link, if one were needed, between the looted Roman silver and the work of a Pictish silversmith.

Returning to the silver chains, it has already been pointed out that only five of the ten have surviving terminal rings and only two of these have symbols engraved on them. Interest naturally tends to focus on those with symbols, particularly the Whitecleugh chain with the familiar double disc and Z-rod. However we interpret the silver chains themselves, we might reasonably have expected that either all of them or none of them should have symbols engraved on them. A possible explanation for the fact that some have symbols while others do not is that the use of symbols was introduced into this area during the period of use of the silver chains. The historical and geographical evidence discussed above suggests that this period was the middle of the fifth century, though some authorities would consider such a date unacceptably early.[4] This brings us to the thorny problem of dating the symbols themselves, whether engraved on silver or cut on stone.

As with the silver chains, there is a shortage of datable archaeological contexts for the Pictish symbols and, in consequence, much (perhaps too much) reliance has been placed on artistic parallels, particularly with manuscripts such as the *Book of Durrow* or the *Lindisfarne Gospels*. The dog's head symbol on the Norrie's Law silver plaques, for example, has been compared stylistically with 'the standard dog-motif' in the *Lindisfarne Gospels*. For some people, this means that this particular Pictish symbol was modelled on a Lindisfarne-type original and was therefore unlikely to be earlier than about AD 700. This is of course neither more nor less likely than the opposite view: namely, that the *Lindisfarne Gospel* illustrator was following the style of a Pictish original. There is also an equally plausible third possibility, that the Lindisfarne illustrator and the Pictish engraver were independently following a common source. The truth of the matter is that such artistic parallels are a very poor guide to relative chronology, and would carry little weight were it not for the lack of other dating evidence.

In the absence of any evidence to the contrary, it seems reasonable to equate the production of heavy silver chains with the period of material wealth and the abundance of silver resulting from raids into southern Britain during the fifth century, as well as the Picto-Scottish conquest of southern Scotland in the same period. The double disc and Z-rod on the Norrie's Law plaque brings them into line with the Whitecleugh silver chain and into the middle of the fifth century.

Unlike the symbols on the silver chains, those on the Norrie's Law plaques can be interpreted in the same way as the symbol stones. These two plaques both carry the same symbol text – double disc and Z-rod above the dog's head symbol.

Are they a pair of silver plaques or are they, as has been suggested recently, two of a larger series? If so, did all the other members of the series carry the same pair of symbols? And what were they used for? There is no perforation by means of which they might have been attached to clothing and it has therefore been supposed that they may have had 'a ceremonial or votive function'.

Unlike the double disc and Z-rod, the dog's head symbol is extremely rare. It occurs on the two silver plaques from Norrie's Law and also on the unique crescent-shaped bronze plaque found near Monifieth in the eighteenth century and since lost. It was also discovered on the wall of the Doo Cave (since collapsed) at East Wemyss, Fife. In addition to these somewhat exotic occurrences, it is known on just one Class I symbol stone at Rhynie, Aberdeenshire. The remarkable thing is that in every case the dog's head symbol is associated with the double disc and Z-rod, the symbol for Drust. Among all the images carved on the walls of the East Wemyss caves, this symbol pair is the only totally convincing example of Pictish symbols. There must be some exceptional significance in this symbol pair. Interpreted in the manner of symbol stone pairs, these symbols must belong to someone of the greatest importance. With several lines of evidence combining to suggest a date in the middle of the fifth century, that person has to be Drust son of Erp, with the dog's head therefore being identified as the symbol for Erp.

Rhynie 5: compare the symbols with those of the silver and bronze plaques (Norrie's Law and Monifieth). (After ECMS)

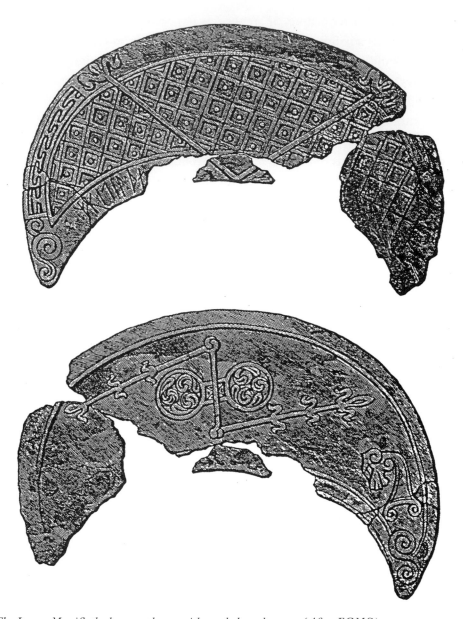

The Laws, Monifieth: bronze plaque with symbols and runes. (After ECMS)

The silver plaques from Norrie's Law might then be symbols of royal authority, carried by the king's messengers and officials as they travelled from place to place through his kingdom. Such a function would compare with the use of the great seals in later medieval times.

The crescentic bronze plaque from Monifieth may also, like the Norrie's Law plaques, be a badge of authority. The particular interest of this object is that not only does it have symbols engraved on it, but it takes the form of a symbol itself, the crescent and V-rod. It was suggested in Chapter 3 that this symbol seems to represent a knowledge of hidden mysteries. The crescent, representing the moon, is shown upside down, an orientation which must exist but is never visible. It is divided by the V-rod into the three phases of the visible moon, waxing crescent, round moon and waning crescent. If, as suggested in Chapter 6, the double disc and Z-rod symbol was an attempt to represent thunder, the crescent and V-rod might be an attempt to represent astrology or perhaps some other form of secret knowledge. Now we happen to know, from Adomnan's account of the meeting between St Columba and the Pictish King Brude son of Maelchon, that the most important member of that king's household was his magician.[5] Broichan, the magician whose contest with St Columba was recorded by Adomnan, had even been foster-father to the king. The Monifieth bronze plaque might perhaps have been the badge of office of the king's magician, and the symbols engraved on it the symbols of the king – Drust son of Erp.

Following this line of thought, if the badge of office of the king's magician took the form of a crescent and V-rod, then the crescent and V-rod symbol might represent a name meaning astrologer or magician. The old Welsh word for magician is *Brudiwr*, close to one of the commoner Pictish names, Brude. Unfortunately the name Brude does not appear on any of the bilingual symbol stones, so there is no direct evidence for this correlation. It is none the less worth keeping it in mind as a provisional interpretation.

The symbols on the Parkhill chain, like those on the Whitecleugh chain, are placed on opposite sides of the gap in the terminal ring. On one side is an ogee, with two triangular arrangements of dots in the concave parts of the figure, and on the other an otherwise unknown symbol consisting of two adjacent isosceles triangles, with a single triangle of three dots. The ogee is known on five Class I symbol stones and is never accompanied by groups of dots as seen on this chain. It seems likely therefore that the groups of dots are a little artistic extravagance and not an integral part of the symbols. The twin triangles, as we may call the second symbol, must be accepted as a genuine Pictish symbol even though it has never (yet) been found on a symbol stone. There are several symbols that have only been found once on a symbol stone. It would be reasonable to expect that more symbols still await discovery.

Parkhill silver chain: the symbols on the terminal ring. (Photo: National Museums of Scotland)

The proper orientation of the twin triangles symbol seems, perhaps a little unexpectedly, to be apex down. On the Whitecleugh chain the notched rectangle has the open end (always at the bottom on symbol stones) facing away from the ring opening. The double disc and Z-rod has the 'point' of the Z-rod also facing away from the opening. On the Norrie's Law leaf-shaped plaques and on the Monifieth bronze plaque the point of the Z-rod is facing downwards, taking the up/down orientation from the dog's head. The symbols on the Whitecleugh chain are thus top to top across the opening in the ring, or base to base along the length of the ring. On the Parkhill chain, we cannot be so definite. The symmetry of the ogee means that it looks the same whichever way we view it, so that it has no top or bottom. However, if we accept the orientation of the symbols on the Whitecleugh chain as applying to both, the symbols cannot be read in the standard symbol stone manner as 'A son of B'.

The double disc and Z-rod on the Whitecleugh chain stands for Drust and probably for the king of that name, Drust son of Erp. The notched rectangle probably stands for someone who owed his position to the king, possibly a military leader. Looking at the Parkhill chain in the same way, one of the symbols probably represents the name of a Pictish king.

Pictish kings tended to use a limited number of favourite names – Brude, Drust, Talorgan, Nechtan, Gartnait – again and again. Thus if either of the symbols on the Parkhill chain represents the name of a king, it is likely to be the commoner of the two, the ogee. The northern silver chains are essentially the same as those in the south and presumably belong to the same general period. If the ogee does represent the name of a Pictish king, he is likely to be fairly close chronologically to Drust son of Erp, though it is not immediately obvious whether he would be earlier or later. The relevant kings, as given in the Group A version of the *Pictish Chronicle*, are listed below with the earliest at the top.

	Gartnait bolc	4 years
	Gartnait ini	9 years
	Breth son of Buthut	7 years
	Vipoig namet	30 years
	Canutulachama	4 years
	Wradech uecla	2 years
	Gartnaich diuberr	60 years
	Talore son of Achivir	75 years
	Drust son of Erp	100 years
	Talore son of Aniel	4 years
	Necton morbet son of Erip	24 years
	Drust Gurthinmoch	30 years
	Galanan erilich	12 years
	Drust son of Gyrom	
and	Drust son of Wdrost together	5 years

The interesting thing about this list is the group of three kings – Gartnaich diuberr, Talore son of Achivir and Drust son of Erp – with extraordinarily long reigns. We might feel quite justified in consigning them to a waste bin for myths and legends, were it not for the fact that the kings immediately before them all have perfectly acceptable reign lengths. It is as if these three towered like giants above the general level of their contemporaries – as if they had, so to speak, become legends in their own time. We have already considered the last of the three, Drust son of Erp, and shown that his reign length was probably increased by nearly 40 per cent, from sixty-two to a hundred years. If we reduce the others in proportion, we come up with the following estimated chronology:

Gartnaich diuberr	333–370
Talore son of Achivir	370–416
Drust son of Erp	416–478

The other interesting feature of the list is that only one of the six kings preceding these three is identified by his father's name, whereas of the six kings following them, only two are not so identified. For some reason, these three kings mark a change in the way Pictish kings were known and remembered. The new way is the way of the symbol stones: A son of B.

We know nothing about Talore son of Achivir, but his predecessor Gartnait (Gartnaich) diuberr was rich. We might reasonably suppose that all Pictish kings were rich as compared with most of their subjects, but for Gartnait to be known as Gartnait the rich, he must have been considerably richer than other kings of his period. How did he come to be so rich? To answer this question, we must summon to our aid the limited archaeological and historical evidence.

The Roman historians make no mention of individual Pictish kings, neither Drust son of Erp nor Gartnait diuberr, but they do tell us about the activities of the Picts.[6] In 360 the Picts and Scots were laying waste to the regions near the Roman frontier, presumably Hadrian's Wall, and the Roman general Lupicinus was sent to restore order. By 365 trouble had broken out again and was all the more serious as by 367 it seemed to be organized by a *barbarica conspiratio*, an alliance between the Picts and Scots and Attacotti. The aim of this alliance was not the conquest of Roman Britain but simply the most efficient exploitation of its potential as a source of wealth, including slaves and cattle. The situation was finally brought under control in 369 by Theodosius, the father of the emperor Theodosius I.

Alliances and combined action against a common enemy imply organization at the highest level; for the Picts and the Scots this meant the kings. If the kings were the organizers and effectively commanders in chief of these concerted raids, we may be sure that they had an administration capable of channelling an appropriately large proportion of the proceeds towards the royal household. For this period there is nothing comparable with the wonderful hoard of late Roman silver from Traprain Law, but there is a well-dated collection of bronze coins from the Sculptor's Cave at Covesea, 5 miles north of Elgin.

Excavations in the Sculptor's Cave (so-called because of the Pictish symbols carved on its walls) were carried out in 1928 and 1929 by Miss Sylvia Benton.[7] The Roman finds consisted of over two hundred bronze coins and miscellaneous small objects such as pins, needles, tweezers, beads and rings. There can be no question about the origin of these objects: they were loot, part of the proceeds of raids on Roman Britain. But they were not in any sense riches. The coins, so far removed from their place of origin, were no longer money – they had absolutely no purchasing power. At best they might be pierced and hung round the neck as lucky charms. Indeed several coins in the cave were so pierced. If that was all the raiders brought back, then a great deal of effort was expended for very little profit. It seems that the Roman finds in the Sculptor's Cave were the scrapings from the bottom of the raiders' barrel, fit perhaps to be handed out to the lowest ranks of the raiding forces. Who else would have been content to live in a damp, dark, cold, north-facing cave? These men did not get rich. The silver, the slaves, the cattle – the real wealth – went to others, higher up the social scale.

The importance of the coins from the Sculptor's Cave is that they provide a date not only for the occupation of the cave, but also for the Roman-derived wealth of which so little trace survives. Of all the coins recovered, only nine were genuine Roman coins struck in the imperial mints. Of the remainder, those that could be identified were barbarous (British) copies of Roman originals. The nine true Roman coins ranged in date from 337 to 354, the earliest being described as very worn and most of the others as in good or excellent condition. The barbarous coins, according to Mr Pierce who studied them, 'do not differ much in date from their prototypes, the last of which is dated 354'. The raid or raids which brought these coins to Covesea Cave took place not long after 354, a date which is consistent both with the Roman historical evidence and with the likely *floruit* of the Pictish king Gartnait the rich.

There is little trace of the riches which must have been brought home with these coins. A hoard of silver, of which only three pieces survive, was found at

Gaulcross, Banffshire, some time before 1840.[8] A hand-pin from this hoard is similar to those from Norrie's Law, but there is no close dating evidence. The Gaulcross hoard was found in a stone circle of which only one stone survives today. The situation is similar to that of the Norrie's Law hoard, which was buried close to a prehistoric burial mound. The Pictish silversmith could not carry all his silver with him, so he had to bury it in a safe place that he could easily remember, and where better than an ancient site. For reasons of security he could not afford to let others into his secret, and as a result when he died his treasure often remained buried where he left it, probably much to the annoyance of his family who must have known it existed, even though they could not find it.

The three northern chains, the Gaulcross hoard and the coins in the Sculptor's Cave have a coastal distribution. If the southern chains were the insignia of generals engaged in the conquest of southern Scotland, the northern ones should have belonged to the admirals in command of the fleets attacking southern Britain by sea. Similarly, if the double disc and Z-rod on the Whitecleugh chain is the symbol of King Drust, the ogee on the Parkhill chain should be the symbol of King Gartnait the rich.

There can be no pretence at certainty in our identification of the ogee symbol with the name Gartnait. As far as the king himself is concerned, most people would consider him to be no more than a proto-historic legend. And yet these legends surely have a basis in half-remembered (half-forgotten) facts. The problem is to recognize the factual needles in the legendary haystack. It seems to me that a king called Gartnait diuberr or Gartnait the rich, like the slightly later King Drust son of Erp, who was said to have reigned for a hundred years and fought a hundred battles, is preserving for us one of those rare gems of historical fact which ought to be treasured and not consigned to the dustbin of meaningless myths and legends.

It is not possible to identify a Class I memorial for Gartnait diuberr. There were four later kings called Gartnait in the sixth and seventh centuries, who should also have had Class I symbol stones, but there are simply not enough to go round. There is only one Class I symbol stone with the ogee definitely in the upper position and one other in which its position is uncertain. Both are from Kintradwell, north of Brora in Sutherland. Perhaps Gartnait, like Drust son of Erp, was a northern Pict. Like Rhynie, Kintradwell and the adjacent Clynemilton Farm show a remarkable concentration of Class I symbol stones.

Clusters of Class I symbol stones are a feature of the country north of the Mounth and, quite apart from such clusters, the general frequency of Class I

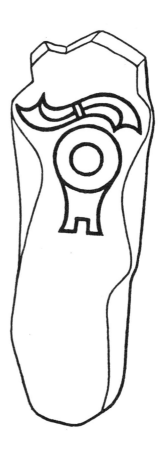

Kintradwell 1: the ogee symbol, as on the
Parkhill silver chain. (After ECMS)

stones in the north is significantly greater than in the south. Did the whole idea originate among the northern Picts in the second half of the fourth century, when the kings and probably their greater subjects began to use patronyms as a form of second name? And did the idea filter through to the south under kings such as Drust son of Erp, who ruled over the united kingdom of the Picts? It seems more likely than the alternative possibility that the north was more densely populated than the south during the period of production of Class I symbol stones.

CHAPTER 9

The Battle and the King

The Aberlemno churchyard cross slab is unique among Pictish symbol stones in its vivid depiction of a battle scene. There are two symbols on this stone: the notched rectangle and Z-rod, separated from the battle raging below by a dividing line; and the triple disc, to the right and a little below, so that it crosses the dividing line between the upper and lower panels. The battle is arranged in three sections, one above the other, each showing the victors on the left and the vanquished on the right. The top section shows the cavalry in action, with an

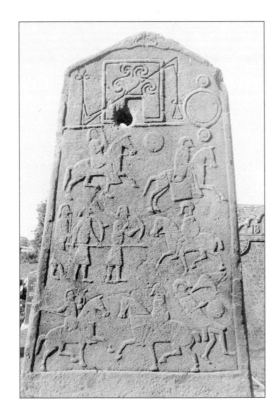

Aberlemno 2: symbols associated with the battle scene.

enemy 'knight', sword and shield thrown to the wind, fleeing for his life. The next section shows the infantry, armed with shields, swords and spears, standing firm against the advancing cavalry. The bottom section shows two mounted knights engaged in mortal combat and, finally, in the bottom right-hand corner, the loser falling to the ground, a prey to the scavenging raven.

This battle scene throws us a challenge across the centuries. There is no accompanying inscription and no obvious means of identifying it with any known historical battle. The most widely accepted interpretation is that it is a monument to the great Pictish victory at Nechtansmere in 685, when the Angles of Northumbria were soundly defeated and their king, Ecgfrith, was killed. In favour of this interpretation is the style of helmet, with long noseguard, worn by the men on the right. Against this interpretation, a Class II stone of this quality is unlikely to have been carved before the middle of the eighth century, about two generations after the battle of Nechtansmere. The evidence of the helmets, similar to one found in the Coppergate excavation in York, seems much more persuasive than it really is. While it certainly suggests that Northumbrian invaders might have worn such helmets, it cannot possibly demonstrate the converse, that such helmets were never worn by the Picts or the Scots.

During the 150 years or so following Nechtansmere, the Picts fought many battles, some against the English, some against the Scots, some among themselves in civil war, and at least one against the Britons. The reporting of these battles, mainly by the Irish annalists,[1] was of variable quality and sometimes even fell short of such basic information as where the battle was fought and who won. However, while the recorded details of some minor battles may be totally inadequate, it is unlikely that any major battle passed unnoticed. In order to consider all the possible interpretations of the Aberlemno battle scene, we must consider the various other battles fought by the Picts in this period and see how they compare with Nechtansmere.

As far as the symbols are concerned, if the battle was fought against a foreign enemy such as the English or the Scots, they must represent the name of the (Pictish) victor. Both symbols belong to the standard range of pair-forming Pictish symbols and therefore neither can represent a foreign enemy. On the other hand, if the battle was between two Pictish armies, the notched rectangle and Z-rod might represent the name of the victor, while the triple disc, slightly below and to the right, above the losing side in the battle scene, might represent the loser.

Brude son of Bile, the victor of Nechtansmere, died in 693. Five years later, in 698, the English attacked again and Bertred 'the royal commander of the

Northumbrians' was killed by the Picts. In 711 there was another battle *in Campo Mannon*, probably somewhere south of the Forth, where the Irish annalists recorded a slaughter of the Picts by the 'Saxons' and also the untimely death of Finguin son of Deileroth. This was the end of hostilities and Bede, who noted both battles, said that at the time he was writing (731), the Picts had a treaty of peace with the English. The next battle on this front would not take place for more than a hundred years. In 848 Kenneth mac Alpin invaded 'Saxonia' six times, burnt Dunbar and took Melrose.[2] It might perhaps be argued that this was a Scottish rather than a Pictish victory, but Kenneth was certainly known to his contemporaries as King of the Picts. In any case, this victory is probably rather late to be the inspiration for the Aberlemno stone.

Peace with the English was followed by a period of civil war among the Picts, in which several rival kings fought for supremacy. The contenders were Nechtan son of Derile, who had reigned from 706 to 724 and then retired to spend the rest of his life in the Church, Drust who succeeded Nechtan, Elpin who displaced Drust in 726, and Oengus son of Fergus. The serious fighting began in 728 with a battle of Moncreiffe (*Monitcroib*), just south of the River Tay near Perth. Here Oengus son of Fergus defeated Elpin and Elpin's son was killed. Later in the same year Elpin was again defeated at Scone (*Castellum Credi*) just north of Perth, this time by Nechtan, who thereby regained the throne. Nechtan's return was short-lived because he was defeated by Oengus in 729 in the battle of Cairn o'Mount (*Monitcarno*) high up in one of the mountain passes between southern and northern Pictland, about 25 miles south-west of Aberdeen. The battle was fought close to *stagnum Loogdae*, possibly the bog of Luchray a little to the north of the summit, and was sufficiently important to be noted by the Welsh annalists as well as the Irish. Three of Nechtan's tax collectors, killed in the fight, were identified by name: Biceot son of Moneit, Finguine son of Drust and Ferot son of Finguine. The decisive battle in this civil war was fought in 729 at Drumdearg (*Dromaderg Blathmig*), about 6 miles north of Blairgowrie, where Oengus defeated Drust and Drust himself was slain. This battle established Oengus son of Fergus as undisputed King of the Picts.

The civil war was over, there was a treaty of peace with the English, and Oengus had a battle-hardened army under his command. Over to the west, beyond the mountainous 'spine of Britain', lay the smaller kingdom of the Scots of Dalriada. Like the Picts, the Scots had been engaged in civil war, but without reaching any decisive outcome. Oengus saw his opportunity and attacked in 731 (possibly not in person). The Picts were defeated in their first encounter, at Murbulg, but won the next battle at an unstated location, between the sons of Oengus (Picts) and the sons of Congus (Scots). Brude son of Oengus was the victor and Talorcan son of Congus was put to flight. In 734 Dunleithfin was destroyed and Dungal son of Selbac (a former King of the Scots 723–726) fled to Ireland to escape from the power of Oengus. In 736 Oengus laid waste to the land of Dalriada, captured Dunadd, north of Lochgilphead, the chief fortress of the Scots, and burnt Creich in Mull. Also in 736 there was a battle at Knock Cariber, in which many nobles fell and Muredach son of Ainfceallach, King of the Scots, was put to flight and hotly pursued by Talorgan son of Fergus. This brought Scottish rule in Dalriada to an end for more than a decade, though Oengus had to use force to maintain his position in 741.

Just how long the Pictish domination of Dalriada lasted in not clear. The next recorded battle was in 768 in Fortrenn, between Aed (King of the Scots) and Cinaed (King of the Picts). The annalists did not say who won, but the fact that it was fought in Fortrenn, which was Pictish territory, suggests that Aed had staged a successful Scottish comeback. Oengus son of Fergus died in 761 and was succeeded by his brother Brude, who died two years later and was followed by Cinaed son of Feradech. The Scots never recognized the rule of Oengus and in their king lists, Muredac son of Ainfcellach, who was defeated by Oengus in 736, was followed immediately by Aed son of Echdach, who died in 778. Pictish rule over Dalriada probably lasted for over thirty years. Any battle between 736 and 768 that was sufficiently important to have brought Pictish rule in Dalriada to an end would hardly have passed unnoticed by the Irish annalists.

The remaining battles in the period under consideration seem rather a miscellaneous collection, unlike the Pictish civil war or the subsequent invasion and conquest of Dalriada. In 750 there was a battle against the Strathclyde Britons at Mugdock, between Milngavie and Strathblane, a few miles north of Glasgow. This may have been part of a plan to incorporate the British kingdom of Strathclyde into the combined Picto-Scottish kingdom. If so, it was a failure. There was a slaughter of the Picts, and Talorgan son of Fergus, the king's brother, was killed. In 789 there was a battle between two Pictish armies in which Connal son of Taidg was defeated by Constantine son of Fergus. Then, just before the end of the century, a new enemy appeared on the horizon. In 794 all the islands of Britain were laid waste by the Vikings. In 839 there was a battle between the Vikings and a combined force of Picts and Scots in which Eogan son of Oengus, Bran son of Oengus, Aed son of Boanta and many others fell.

In order to compare the various battles discussed above in relation to the battle scene displayed on the Aberlemno stone, a system of points has been devised for battles in which the Picts were victorious.

Great victory	4 points
Victory	2 points
English enemy	2 points
Less than 10 miles from Aberlemno	2 points
Fought between 730 and 830	2 points
Death of named enemy	1 point

Points for a battle against the English are given to allow for the evidence of the helmets with noseguards worn by the enemy in the Aberlemno battle scene. Points for battles fought between 730 and 830 are to give credit for battles fought during the likely period for carving the stone. Close dating of the stone itself is not possible. The death of members of the enemy forces sufficiently important to attract the notice of the annalists is used to add to the importance of the battle.

The battles in which the Picts were victorious are summarized in the table below, giving the date, the location of the battle (if known), the nationality of the enemy, the score of points according to the above system, and the name of the victor; Nechtansmere still stands out above all the others as the most likely individual battle to be commemorated in this way. It was the only one fought within 10 miles of Aberlemno, the nearest rival being Cairn o'Mount about 17 miles away. If the Aberlemno battle scene does refer to Nechtansmere, even if it were set up some time later, the symbols should still refer to Brude son of Bile. This would make the rare notched rectangle and Z-rod represent the common (in the king lists) Pictish name, Brude.

Date	Battle	Enemy	Score	Victor
685	Nechtansmere	English	9	Brude son of Bile
698		English	3	
728	Moncreiffe	Picts	3	Oengus son of Fergus
728	Scone	Picts	2	Nechtan son of Derile
729	Cairn o'Mount	Picts	5	Oengus son of Fergus
729	Drumderg	Picts	3	Oengus son of Fergus
731		Scots	2	Brude son of Oengus

734	Dunleithfin	Scots	2	Oengus son of Fergus
736	Dunadd	Scots	6	Oengus son of Fergus
736	Knock Cariber	Scots	5	Oengus son of Fergus
741		Scots	4	Oengus son of Fergus
789		Picts	4	Constantine son of Fergus
848	Melrose	English	6	Kenneth mac Alpin

It has generally been supposed that the battle scene on the Aberlemno churchyard stone represents an individual battle, and Nechtansmere, the most famous Pictish victory, has seemed a natural choice. Most of the other Pictish symbol stones seem likely to be memorials to individuals, sometimes to several individuals. Why should the Aberlemno stone be any different? Could it not be a memorial to a king who was a great and victorious general, rather than a monument to a particular battle? Looked at in this way, the answer seems so obvious that it is surprising that it has not been known for years. Of the thirteen battles shown in the table above, more than half were won by one king, Oengus son of Fergus. On the points system, his score was 25 out of a total of 54. He must have been one of the most successful generals of his age. This stone is likely therefore to be a memorial to Oengus son of Fergus rather than to any individual battle that he or any other Pictish king may have son. If this is accepted, then the notched rectangle and Z-rod becomes the symbol of Oengus, and the triple disc for Fergus.

CHAPTER 10
Pictish Family Trees

Two quite different aspects of Pictish art are displayed on the Class II symbol stones. On the one hand there are the tremendously intricate but still quite formal and geometrical interlace patterns which decorate the crosses, and on the other the much less formal pictorial art such as hunting scenes or the Aberlemno battle scene which often fill the back of such stones. Once an interlace design had been chosen, the sculptor had to stick rigidly to the rules or disaster would be unavoidable. On the back of a cross slab, however, the sculptor could indulge himself and produce a much more personal work of art. Indeed it seems possible that some sculptors may have left such distinctive little marks on their work that they might almost as well have signed it. The carving of these stones was highly skilled and often original work, probably carried out by very few people at any one time, and these few in the employ of some of the greatest families of the land. It may be possible then, in tracing the work of individual sculptors, to trace the family trees of some of the great Pictish families.

A good example of one of these artists' signatures is the rather diminutive figure of an archer, down on one knee, taking aim at a wild animal with his crossbow.[1] The hunt is a popular theme on Pictish stones and hunting scenes appear in all shapes and sizes, with huntsmen singly or in groups, on horseback or on foot, generally with hounds, and pursuing a wide variety of game, but the little archer appears on four stones only, one of which (Meigle 10) is not a symbol stone and so does not come into the present discussion. The archer is in effect a symbol but, unlike the standard pair-forming symbols, he represents an individual artist rather than his name. He can thus be properly considered an artist's signature.

On the Princess stone, in the grounds of Glenferness House about 10 miles north-west of Grantown on Spey, the archer, the remains of a small hunting scene and two pairs of symbols are displayed in the lower of two panels. The upper pair of symbols, sharing the upper third of the panel with the archer and the hunt, are a Pictish elephant above a crescent and V-rod. Beneath these is a much larger pair of

Glenferness: back, showing panel with
symbols. Note the archer in top centre.
(After ECMS)

symbols occupying the lower two-thirds of the panel. These lower symbols are a
double disc and Z-rod above a Pictish elephant. Two names are thus recorded on
this stone, Edern son of Brude and Drust son of Edern, and there can be little
doubt that they are father and son. As both pairs of symbols are clearly part of a
single design, we must presume that they were carved at the same time and it is
therefore probable that Drust erected the stone as a memorial to his father, Edern.
We have here a three-generation family tree: Drust son of Edern son of Brude.

   On the back of the Shandwick stone on the shore of the Moray Firth, about
6 miles south-east of Tain, the archer is aiming at a stag in the bottom right-hand
corner of the third panel from the top. The rest of the panel is filled with an
extraordinary array of wild animals and birds, several huntsmen on horseback, a
man on foot holding a horn, and two men, seemingly unaware of the hunt,
fighting a duel with swords and shields. Above this lively scene are two panels,
each containing one symbol, a double disc in the upper and a Pictish elephant
below. This is a memorial to a son of Edern, whose name was represented by the

Shandwick: back. (Photo: Tom Gray)

Shandwick: detail of hunt scene. Note the archer at bottom right and duelling swordsmen at bottom left. (After ECMS)

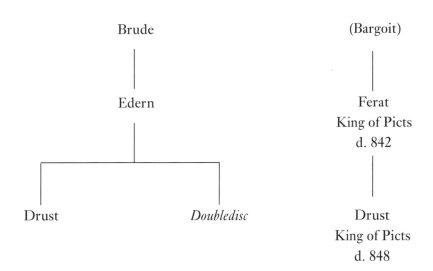

Pedigree 1: based on stones with archer 'signature': Glenferness, Shandwick and St Vigeans 1. Note: in this and subsequent pedigrees, 'names' in italics represent symbols which have not at this stage been interpreted, and names in brackets are known from the Pictish Chronicle, *but have not yet been identified on symbol stones.*

double disc symbol. In the absence (so far) of an interpretation of the double disc symbol, we will have to call him *Doubledisc* son of Edern. He is likely to have been a son of the Edern son of Brude who was commemorated on the Princess stone.

The third stone in this series is the Drosten stone, discussed in Chapter 7. Here the archer, in the bottom left-hand corner of a frame occupying the full height of the stone, is taking aim at a wild boar. Above them is a medley of wild animals with the symbols among them towards the top. This stone is a memorial to Drust son of Ferat, the last Pictish king to resist the rise to power of Kenneth mac Alpin. His relationship to the family commemorated on the Princess stone and the Shandwick stone is not apparent, but may well have been through the female line, so important in Pictish royal inheritance but so totally obscured on memorials which generally only name the father of the deceased. What it does tell us, however, is that this particular sculptor was working in the middle of the ninth century, when Drust's opposition to Kenneth mac Alpin was finally crushed and he himself was killed.

The second artist's signature to be considered also appears in a hunting scene and consists of a pair of long-robed trumpeters, standing together in the top right-hand corner of the picture. Mounted hunters, with their hounds, are riding away to the left in a scene full of action. The trumpeters, standing side by side

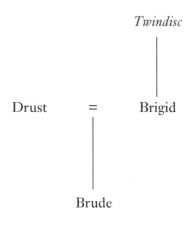

Twindisc

Drust   =   Brigid

Brude

Pedigree 2: based on stones with trumpeters 'signature': Hilton of Cadboll and Aberlemno 3. See Pedigree 10 for alternative interpretation.

and sounding their trumpets, look quite incongruous and most unsuitably dressed for the hunt. This signature appears on two stones. One is the Aberlemno roadside cross (Aberlemno 3) mentioned in the first chapter and the other, now in the National Museum in Edinburgh, formerly stood at Hilton of Cadboll, a little to the north of Shandwick.

There are three symbols on the Hilton of Cadboll stone, two together in a panel above the hunting scene and one in the border above the panel. On Aberlemno 3 the two symbols are together in a panel above the hunting scene. It is clear that the symbols inside the panel on the Hilton of Cadboll stone are a standard symbol pair. These are a crescent and V-rod above the very rare symbol of twin discs. The symbol in the border is a double disc and Z-rod. On Aberlemno 3 the symbols are a crescent and V-rod above a double disc and Z-rod. The main figure on horseback on the Hilton stone is widely recognized as a woman. The crescent and V-rod might perhaps represent the female equivalent of Brude. The name Brude is sometimes spelt Bridei, close to the female name Bride or Brigid, as in the name of the well-known Irish saint. This explanation works quite satisfactorily for Brude but runs into difficulties with a name like Kenneth, for example, which has no obvious female equivalent. (For an alternative explanation, see Chapter 12.) The symbol in the border, for Drust, probably represents the person who had the cross made and set up. The Aberlemno stone is a memorial to Brude son of Drust. An individual sculptor is unlikely to have served more than two generations of a family, so the most likely interpretation of these two stones is that

Drust, the father of Brude on the Aberlemno stone, was the husband of Brigid and son-in-law of someone we can only call *Twindisc*.

The third signature to be considered is not contained in a hunting scene but is inserted in the shaft of the cross. If Pictish cross slabs are any guide, the possession of a fine horse was as much a status symbol in Dark Age Scotland as the possession of a quality car is today. Many cross slabs show men on horseback, sometimes hunting or in battle, but sometimes just standing there looking good. These pictures of mounted Pictish aristocrats must sometimes be portraits of the person commemorated on the stone. One artist hit on the idea of inserting his equestrian portrait into a panel in the shaft of the cross. There are three stones bearing this particular signature, one at Balluderon, just north of Dundee, one at Rossie, about 6 miles west of Dundee, and the third at Fordoun (Auchenblae), already discussed in Chapter 7.

The Balluderon stone is carved on one face only. The top is missing and, reading from the top downwards, the first thing we see is what was the lowest panel of the cross shaft, containing the figure of a man on horseback. Below this and slightly to the right is another man on horseback, with a pair of symbols to his left and below him. The symbols are a Pictish elephant above a serpent and Z-rod.

Balluderon: the symbols associated with man on horseback. Note the equestrian portrait in the panel in the shaft of the cross. (Photo: Tom Gray)

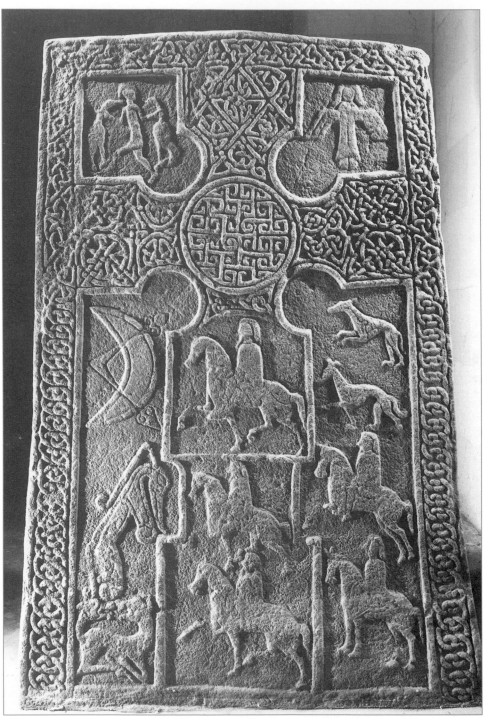

Rossie: back. Symbols associated with equestrian figures in panels in the shaft of the cross. (Photo: Royal Commission on Ancient and Historical Monuments of Scotland)

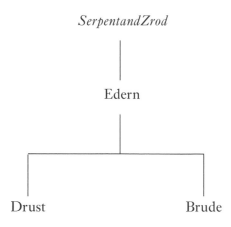

SerpentandZrod

Edern

Drust   Brude

Pedigree 3: based on stones with equestrian portrait contained in a panel of the cross shaft: Balluderon, Fordoun and Rossie.

The Rossie stone is carved on both faces. The front has a cross with a selection of more or less extraordinary animals and monsters filling the spaces either side of the cross shaft and above the arms of the cross. On the back there is another cross, the shaft of which is divided into two unequal panels, the upper one containing one horseman and the lower one two horsemen, one above the other. The symbols, to the left of the cross shaft, are a crescent and V-rod above a Pictish elephant.

The Fordoun stone, like that at Balluderon, is carved on one side only. The shaft of the more or less equal-armed cross consists of a panel containing a man on horseback. On either side of the shaft are two more riders, each armed with a spear, and a hound. Below the cross is a double disc and Z-rod. The top of the stone is missing, but in the top left-hand corner is what seems to be the lower line of a two-line inscription, PIDARNIOIN. The stone can most easily be interpreted as a memorial to Drust son of Edern.

Together, these three stones provide us with a three-generation pedigree in which the central name is Edern. This Edern was the son of a man we will have to call *SerpentandZrod* (Balluderon), and himself had two sons Brude (Rossie) and Drust (Fordoun).

The fourth possible signature to be looked at is that of enclosing the panels on the back of the cross slab in a border of interlace or other design. This is seen on three stones, one at St Madoes, about 5 miles east of Perth, one at Nigg, about 3 miles south-west of Shandwick, and also the Hilton of Cadboll stone already considered above.

PidaRNOIN

*Fordoun: symbol
associated with riders and
equestrian portrait in the
panel in the shaft of the
cross. The inscription at
top left is very worn.
(After ECMS)*

On the St Madoes stone there are six panels enclosed by the border. Each of the top three, one above the other, contains an equestrian figure. Below these are two panels side by side, each impinging on the adjacent border and containing a crescent and V-rod to the left and a double disc and Z-rod to the right. Below these two is a single panel containing a Pictish elephant. The horsemen in the upper panels are presumably the two brothers Brude and Drust and their father Edern. On the Nigg stone the border itself is divided into panels, leaving the central pictures undivided. A pair of symbols, an eagle above a Pictish elephant (most of which has broken away), can be seen at the top of this central area.[2]

The St Madoes and Nigg stones tell us about the family of a man called Edern. He had three sons: Brude and Drust are commemorated together on the St Madoes stone, and Dunodnat (eagle) is commemorated on the Nigg

St Madoes: back, showing unusual association of three symbols with three equestrian portraits. (Photo: Perth Museum)

Nigg: symbols as drawn before the Pictish elephant and the feet of the eagle were lost during 'restoration'. (After ECMS)

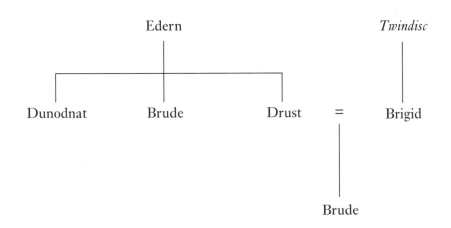

Pedigree 4: based on stones on which the symbols and figures are enclosed in an ornamental border: St Madoes, Nigg and Hilton of Cadboll (incorporating Aberlemno 3: see Pedigree 2).

Flower

Fergus

Deershead

Pedigree 5: based on Class II faces of Glamis 1 and Glamis 2.

stone. The connection with the Hilton of Cadboll stone suggests that the Drust who had that stone set up may have been the Drust son of Edern of the St Madoes stone.

The next two stones to be considered are not linked by any artist's signature, but by the fact that they are both re-used Class I stones; for this reason they are carved on one face only in the Class II phase of their use. Both stones are at Glamis, one in the manse garden (Glamis 2) and the other in a wood about half a mile southeast of the village (Glamis 1). Both Glamis stones have a pair of symbols to the right of the cross shaft: Glamis 2 has a deer's head above a triple disc, and Glamis 1 a triple disc above a flower symbol. Between them, these two very similar stones give us a three-generation pedigree in which only one of the symbols can so far be translated into a name. We have *Deershead*, son of Fergus, son of *Flower*.

The two Class I stones may well have been chosen for re-use as Class II stones because they were themselves the memorials of earlier members of the same family. With this in mind, the interesting thing is that the Class I symbols can also be arranged in a three-generation pedigree. Glamis 2 has a serpent above a fish, and Glamis 1 a beast above a serpent. As with the Class II symbols on these stones, only one of the symbols can so far be translated. The pedigree is *Beast*, son of *Serpent*, son of Nechtan. The connection between the Class I and Class II pedigrees is not apparent. There may be a missing generation, or the connection may be through the female line.

Nechtan

Serpent

Beast

Pedigree 6: based on Class 1 faces of Glamis 1 and Glamis 2: later re-used as Class II stones (see Pedigree 5).

The twelve Class II symbol stones considered above have been grouped into five sets on the basis of what seem to be artists' signatures. Analysis of the symbols on these stones has yielded five pedigrees, four of three generations and one of four generations. Only one of the fifteen stones failed to link up with other members of its set to form an internally consistent pedigree. The weakness of this analysis is that each sculptor had a limited working life and was unlikely to have served more than two generations of the same family. It is therefore difficult to extend the pedigrees to earlier or later generations.

In each three-generation pedigree there is a link-man in the middle generation holding the loose ends of the pedigree together. In the first pedigree this link-man is Edern son of Drust. His father's name is contained in his own as a patronymic, and his own name is preserved in the names of his sons in exactly the same way. It stands to reason that Edern's father Drust must himself be the link-man for an earlier generation of the pedigree. Unfortunately, even if his father's memorial has survived, it would be difficult to identify it, as we would have no direct means of connecting it with his family. It is perfectly possible that he is staring us in the face from one of the other pedigrees. He could, for example, be the Drust who set up the Hilton of Cadboll Stone, the father of Brude on the Aberlemno roadside cross slab. Alternatively, he might be the Drust of the Fordoun stone, whose father's name was inscribed in Hiberno-Saxon characters above the left arm of the cross. Both these Drusts were sons of Edern and both had brothers called

Meigle 6: back, showing equestrian portrait, symbols and part of hunt scene. (After ECMS)

Brude. It is immediately apparent that better progress is likely to be made with the less common symbols, where there is less chance of confusing different individuals bearing the same name.

The Drosten stone provides a good starting point for an attempt to extend a pedigree. It has two symbols, the very common double disc and Z-rod for Drust, and the much rarer crescent (without the V-rod) for his father Ferat. The most likely stone to show a family connection with the Drosten stone is at Meigle (Meigle 6). This stone is broken, with the top and bottom both missing. The back of the surviving part has, at the top, a man on horseback with a circular shield. Below him are two symbols, a double disc (without Z-rod) and a crescent (without V-rod), and below them a hound. It is perfectly possible that this stone was the work of the same sculptor who produced the Drosten stone. His signature of a little archer with a crossbow, hiding away in the corner of the picture, could easily have been lost. Drust son of Ferat, commemorated on the Drosten stone, was a king and had two brothers who were kings before him.

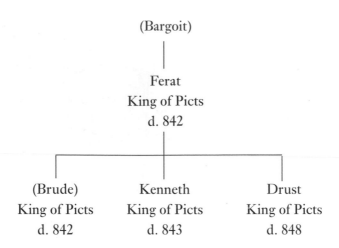

Pedigree 7: based on Drosten stone (see Pedigree 1), extended by reference to Meigle 6.

According to the Group B version of the *Pictish Chronicle*, the succession was as follows (spelling standardized):

Ferat son of Bargoit	3 years
Brude son of Ferat	1 year
Kenneth son of Ferat	1 year
Brude son of Fochel	2 years
Drust son of Ferat	3 years
Kenneth mac Alpin	16 years

The Group A version of the Pictish king list begins the reign of Kenneth mac Alpin immediately after that of Brude son of Ferat, omitting all mention of the next three kings who kept a resistance movement alive for the next six years. The importance of linking Meigle 6 with the Drosten stone is that we are also linking it with a historical pedigree. We can therefore identify the double disc symbol with the name Kenneth. Brude, the name of the other son of Ferat, is already identified with the crescent and V-rod.

The next loose end to be looked at is the serpent and Z-rod on the Balluderon stone. This is the symbol of the father of Edern, the link-man in the third pedigree. Among several other occurrences of the serpent and Z-rod on Class II

Meigle 1: back, showing large symbols and smaller symbols (below the fish), above a hunt scene with strange animals. (Photo: Royal Commission on Ancient and Historical Monuments of Scotland)

symbol stones, one at Meigle (Meigle 1) is of particular interest. The main symbols on the back of this stone are a fish above a serpent and Z-rod. Beneath these are a mirror and comb and then a group of riders and a selection of more or less strange animals. The curious feature of the symbols at the top of this stone is that between the fish and the serpent and Z-rod are two much smaller symbols, a horse's head and a Pictish elephant. The stone is clearly a memorial to Nechtan (fish) son of *SerpentandZrod*. Perhaps the little symbols represented his brothers, one of whom could then be identified with Edern, the link-man on the Balluderon stone.

There are only three other fish symbols on Class II stones and two of these, the Golspie stone and the Ulbster stone, are outside the normal range of symbol stones. The third, at Latheron, has already been discussed in Chapter 6 on account of its ogham inscription. This stone, carved on one face only, is a memorial to Dunodnat (eagle) son of Nechtan. Meigle 1 is the only Class II stone commemorating anyone called Nechtan. It is quite possible that it is a memorial to the only King Nechtan who could possibly have been commemorated on a Class II stone, namely Nechtan son of Derile, who died in 732. If this is so, the serpent and Z-rod is the symbol for Derile. This is not by any means a certain identification but, in view of the shortage of bilingual inscriptions, we can only proceed by making such provisional identifications and testing them as we go.

The identification of Meigle 1 as a memorial to Nechtan son of Derile opens up an interesting possibility. Nechtan was the king who sent messengers to Ceolfrid, Abbot of Wearmouth and Jarrow in Northumbria, asking for guidance about the proper date of Easter and the tonsure that his clergy should wear. He also asked 'that architects be sent him in order to build a stone church for his people in the Roman style, promising that he would dedicate it in honour of the blessed Prince of the Apostles'.[3] Meigle has one of the finest collections of Class II symbol stones in the country, all of which were found in the immediate vicinity of the parish church, and it is one of a small group of Angus churches dedicated to St Peter. It was clearly an important place during the eighth and ninth centuries and it could well be that this is the site of Nechtan's stone church built under the direction of Northumbrian architects.

Much of the follow-up to Nechtan's initiative seems to have been undertaken by St Boniface (Curitan), who arrived by boat and landed at Invergowrie, a few miles west of Dundee. He founded churches at Invergowrie, Tealing and Restenneth before crossing the Mounth and continuing his work among the northern Picts. He eventually settled at Rosemarkie, north of Inverness, where he died. The priory at Restenneth has been proposed as the site of Nechtan's stone church on the basis of primitive architectural features in the lower part of the existing tower.[4] This argument fails on three counts:

1. The tower is not generally considered to be as early as the eighth century.

2. Even if it were that early, it could not necessarily be identified by that fact alone. The example of Nechtan's Northumbrian architects was there to be followed and his first stone church would not have stood alone for long.

3. The lack of symbol stones at Restenneth suggests that, apart from the church, it was a place of very little importance, certainly not the Pictish equivalent of a royal borough.

The church at Meigle, also dedicated to St Peter, is not mentioned among the churches founded by St Boniface, though the abundance of Class II symbol stones indicates that it could not have been founded much later. The most likely interpretation is that Meigle was indeed Nechtan's original stone church and that it was already in existence when St Boniface arrived in Angus.

Nechtan son of Derile had an older brother Brude, who was king before him and died in 706. There is no surviving Class II stone commemorating Brude son of Derile (crescent and V-rod above serpent and Z-rod). There is, however, a Class I stone with the appropriate symbols – the Brandsbutt stone with its incomprehensible ogham inscription, IRATADDOARENS. This would be consistent with the interpretation of Meigle 1 as a memorial to Nechtan son of Derile. Brude died before the contact with Monkwearmouth and Jarrow and the subsequent development of Pictish cross slabs.

We must, however, beware of being too quick to identify symbol pairs including the crescent and V-rod with particular individuals. The crescent and V-rod is the most abundant of all the pair-forming symbols and accounts for one in five in all such symbols. The same remarks apply to the double disc and Z-rod and to the dolphin, each of which accounts for one in eight of all pair-forming symbols. Thus, out of every five occurrences of the serpent and Z-rod as the lower member of a pair, it is likely that one will have a crescent and V-rod above it. There are in fact eight symbol pairs with the serpent and Z-rod as the lower member. One of these has a crescent and V-rod above it, two have double discs and Z-rods above them, and one a dolphin – all very close to what one might expect by chance. We must conclude that there is no good reason for connecting the Brandsbutt stone with Brude son of Derile, the King of the Picts who died in 706.

*St Vigeans 2: shaft of cross and symbols.
(After ECMS)*

Linking Meigle 1 to this set of stones has extended the pedigree laterally but not vertically. In order to reach back to an earlier generation, we need to find the memorial to Derile. The search takes us no further than St Vigeans, where there is a broken cross slab (St Vigeans 2) carved on one face only. The top of the cross is missing but the symbols, to the right of the cross shaft, are unaffected. The serpent and Z-rod above an eagle indicate that this is a memorial to Derile son of Dunodnat. The only other Class II symbol stone with the serpent and Z-rod in the upper position is the Gask stone, now in the grounds of Moncreiffe House a few miles south of Perth. The symbols, a serpent and Z-rod above a flower symbol, are displayed to the right of the cross shaft between some strange-looking animals above and a pair of equestrian figures below. This would be an interesting connection for

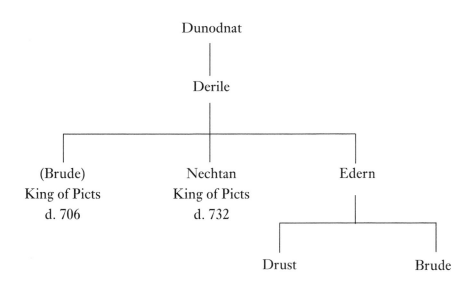

Dunodnat

Derile

(Brude)
King of Picts
d. 706

Nechtan
King of Picts
d. 732

Edern

Drust

Brude

Pedigree 8: extension of Pedigree 3 by reference to Meigle 1 and St Vigeans 2.

the pedigree of Nechtan son of Derile because, as has been shown above, the flower symbol also occurs in the pedigree of Oengus son of Fergus. However, the style of this ringed cross, with the spaces between the angles of the cross and the encircling ring cut right through, argues against the possibility of such an early date.

The third and final pedigree to be considered for extension is that given by the Glamis stones, in which the link-man is Fergus, represented by the triple disc; his father and son are represented by the flower and deer's head symbols respectively. All three symbols are relatively uncommon. The triple disc occurs on three other Class II stones, including the Aberlemno churchyard stone discussed in the previous chapter, the memorial to the great warrior king, Oengus son of Fergus. The other two are both rather irregular-shaped pillars of granite, with cross and symbols on one face only. One of these, at Monymusk, about 17 miles west of Aberdeen, has a pair of symbols beneath the foot of the cross. These are a step symbol above a triple disc. The other, at Dyce, a couple of miles north of Aberdeen airport, has two pairs of symbols. To the left of the cross shaft are a crescent and V-rod above a triple disc and, to the right of the cross shaft, a mirror case symbol above a double disc and Z-rod, which extends beneath the foot of the cross. The triple discs on the Monymusk and Dyce stones have internal

Monymusk: cross and symbols. Compare the ornamented triple disc with the plain ones on Aberlemno 2 and Glamis 2. (After ECMS)

decoration and are quite unlike the plain symbols on the Glamis and Aberlemno stones. There is no good reason to attribute them to members of the same family.

Oengus son of Fergus, King of the Picts, commemorated on the Aberlemno churchyard stone, is known to have had two brothers – Brude, who succeeded him as king and died in 763, and Talorgan, who was killed in a battle against the Strathclyde Britons in 750. For the reasons given above in connection with Brude son of Derile, we cannot be sure of identifying the Dyce stone, with its crescent and V-rod above a triple disc, as a memorial to Brude son of Fergus, King of the Picts. What is much more likely is that the deer's head above a triple disc on the Glamis manse stone belongs to his brother, Talorgan. We can therefore identify the deer's head as the symbol for the name Talorgan.

In order to extend this pedigree vertically downwards, we need to find Class II stones with pairs of symbols representing the sons of the youngest generation in the pedigree, that is to say symbol pairs with either the notched rectangle and Z-rod or the deer's head in the lower position. Such symbol pairs have not been found on Class II stones. The alternative is to extend the pedigree upwards, which means finding a symbol pair with the flower symbol in the upper position. No such Class II stone has survived. The most likely possibility is the Class I stone at Dunichen, which has a flower above a double disc and Z-rod. This stone could represent an earlier generation of the pedigree. Oengus, Brude and Talorgan, sons of Fergus, were all adult in the 720s. Their father Fergus is

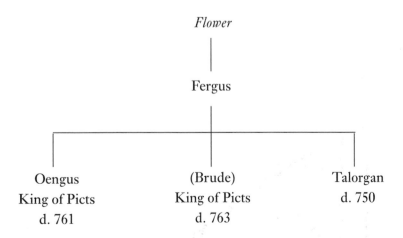

Pedigree 9: extension of Pedigree 5 by reference to Aberlemno 2.

Dunichen: Class I stone extending the
Class II stone pedigree of King
Oengus son of Fergus (d. 761).

commemorated on Glamis 1. His father, represented by the flower symbol, would
have died too early to have a Class II memorial. The pedigree, based on the
available symbol stone evidence, is consistent with the historical information for
the family of Oengus son of Fergus, King of the Picts.

Of the pedigrees discussed in this chapter, two belong to the first half of the
eighth century, the dating being established by reference to kings whose dates are
known. Most Class II symbol stones are carved on both faces, the cross on the
front and the hunt, symbols and other scenes on the back. A few Class II symbol
stones are carved on one face only and five such stones belong to pedigrees
discussed in this chapter. Three of these appear in the pedigree of Nechtan son of
Derile who died in 732, probably at a fairly advanced age, as he had succeeded his
elder brother Brude twenty-six years earlier in 706. The Balluderon stone
commemorates Edern, an otherwise unknown brother of Nechtan; the Fordoun
stone commemorates Drust, son of this Edern; and St Vigeans 2 is a memorial to

Nechtan's father. The other two stones, Glamis 1 and 2, have carving on both faces, incised symbols of Class I on one face and a cross and relief carvings of Class II on the other. As far as their Class II carvings are concerned, they were carved on one face only. These two stones belong to the pedigree of Oengus son of Fergus who died in 761, also at a fairly advanced age, his recorded fighting career having started thirty-three years earlier. Glamis 1 is a memorial to Fergus son of *Flower*, the father of Oengus, and Glamis 2 commemorates Talorgan son of Fergus, the brother of Oengus who was killed in battle in 750.

These stones, all datable to the first half of the eighth century, are close in principle to their Northumbrian models. The Herebericht stone (Monkwearmouth 5), for example, has a cross carved in strong relief and an inscription in Latin occupying all the available space above and below the arms of the cross: HIC IN SEPULCRO REQVIESCIT CORPORE HEREBERICHT PRB (Here in the tomb rests Herebricht the priest in the body). Such were the Northumbrian models for the Pictish cross slabs – a plain cross and a statement about the deceased. The Picts, with their long-established artistic tradition, soon realized the potential of this model and elaborated on it. St Vigeans 2, possibly the earliest, has a decorated cross, two symbols to the right of the cross shaft, and a possible mirror to the left (the top of the stone is missing). A little later equestrian portraits were added (Balluderon and Fordoun) and centaurs, angels and a variety of animals (Glamis 1 and 2). Then the narrow spaces on either side of the cross shaft could no longer contain the artistic drive of the Pictish sculptor and he turned his attention to the back of the cross slab. The sequence is not strictly chronological. Glamis 2, carved on one face only for Talorgan son of Fergus, is twenty years later than Meigle 1, carved on both faces for Nechtan son of Derile.

CHAPTER 11

Unusual Stones – Unusual Symbols

The Dunfallandy stone, situated about a mile south of Pitlochry on the west side of the River Tummel, is unique in showing the 'portraits' of three people, each with his or her own symbols. At the top are two figures seated in chairs, facing each other across a small plain cross. Beneath them is a figure on horseback, riding towards the left. Finally, beneath the horseman, are three more symbols – a hammer, an anvil and pincers – which, like the mirror and comb, do not belong to the main series of pair-forming symbols. The seated figure at top left has one symbol, a Pictish elephant. The other seated figure has two symbols, a double disc above a crescent and V-rod. The equestrian figure also has two symbols, a crescent and V-rod above a Pictish elephant. Interpreting the symbols as before, the man on the horse was Brude son of Edern, so the seated figure on the left, whose name was Edern, was presumably his father. It seems likely that the seated figure on the right was his (Brude's) mother, whose name might have been the female equivalent of Kenneth (if there was one), daughter of Brude. (For an alternative explanation, see Chapter 12.) If this interpretation is correct, Brude son of Edern was named after his maternal grandfather.[1]

Now we come to the three symbols at the bottom: the hammer, the anvil (a crucible according to Dr Katherine Forsyth) and the pincers. These are all tools connected with metal-working. Perhaps the simplest explanation would be to take them at their face value and say that Brude son of Edern was a metal-worker. The alternative is that these pictures of objects associated with metal-working may be symbolic of manufacture in a more general sense. The clue on this particular stone lies in the small cross situated on a little mound between the two seated figures. Generally, when crosses are shown on the back of Class II symbol stones they are large and decorated with interlace patterns. This cross is very small and quite plain. It is really not a cross as such, but a symbol of a cross,

Abernethy: mutilated Class I symbol stone with hammer, anvil and pincers. Compare with the Dunfallandy Class II stone.

and the metal-working tools below are telling us that Brude son of Edern had this cross made and set up as a memorial to his parents.

The only other stone showing the hammer and anvil (but not the pincers) is a badly mutilated Class I stone at Abernethy. This stone, which has been reduced and trimmed to shape for re-use as a building stone, is now built into the foot of the eleventh-century round tower of Abernethy. The symbols on this stone are a tuning fork, shown vertically, flanked by a hammer to the left and an anvil to the right. Beneath these symbols is a crescent and V-rod, cut off on the right and the base. On the evidence of the Dunfallandy stone, this ought to refer to the making of something, perhaps for somebody. This is one of the all-too-rare stones for which we have a possible historical context. In or about AD 484, Nechtan son of Erip (or Wirp), King of all the provinces of the Picts, gave land at Abernethy 'to St Brigid in perpetuity to the day of judgement'. St Brigid sent Darlugdach, later to succeed her as Abbess of Kildare, to Abernethy to meet Nechtan and found a church. There has been a church at Abernethy ever since, a continuous history of over

1,500 years. St Darlugdach's church was probably a wooden structure and the great round tower may have been the first stone building on the site. The modern parish church is still dedicated to St Bride, perhaps the more familiar form of St Brigid.

It is possible that the hammer and anvil on the Abernethy symbol stone may refer to the building of the first church for St Brigid. St Brigid is often called St Bride. The Pictish name Brude is often spelt Bridei. The use of the crescent and V-rod interchangeably for Brude and Brigid therefore seems perfectly reasonable. We might then suppose that the tuning fork was the symbol for Nechtan,[2] though it is perhaps more likely that Nechtan would have used his full name, Nechtan son of Erip. It is a pity that the stone has been cut down and we will never know whether or not there was a fish above the tuning fork. In view of the identification of the fish as the symbol for Nechtan, it is likely that the tuning fork was the symbol for Erip (or Wirp), Nechtan's father.

If this is the correct interpretation of the Abernethy stone, there is just one Class I symbol stone which we can attribute to Nechtan son of Erip and it is in almost mint condition. It was found at Dunrobin, a few miles south-west of

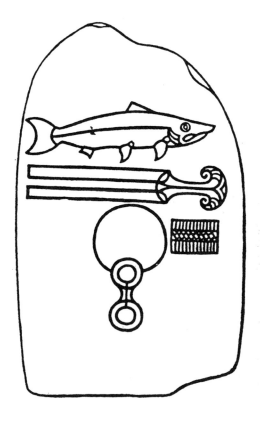

Dunrobin 1: this Class I stone was found in (probably primary) position as a capstone at the head end of a long cist burial. (After ECMS)

Brora, in 1854 in position as one of three capstones covering a long cist burial containing two adult male skeletons.[3] The symbol stone was covering the head end of the cist. Part of an iron spearhead was recovered with the skeletons. The symbols – a fish above a tuning fork, both arranged horizontally, and a mirror and comb – are beautifully carved with minute attention to detail, especially in the ornament on the middle bar of the double-sided comb. The stone had clearly not been exposed to the weather for any length of time and it is quite possible that this was its primary use. Long cist graves were generally fairly shallow and it is possible that this capstone was intended to be visible at the surface. Some (later) continental sarcophagi 'with the decoration on the lid rather than on the sides, may have been intended to be buried level with the ground'.[4] If this was the situation, the capstone would soon have become overgrown and the freshness of its carving preserved under a protective layer of turf.

The vast majority of Pictish symbol stones, whether of Class I or Class II, commemorate one person with one pair of symbols. A few have been reused and have four symbols. A few also record the name of the person who set the stone up, and a few commemorate more than one person. The Dunfallandy stone, which does both, has five symbols, excluding the hammer, anvil and pincers. The Golspie stone, with its seven symbols, is a special case, to be considered later in this chapter, but the record is held by the Ulbster stone with ten symbols. The front of the Ulbster stone is badly weathered, but two symbols can be recognized: a serpent to the left of the cross shaft and a flower symbol to the right. There are also a few wild animals and two people squatting either side of a cauldron.

   On the back of the stone there is an equal-armed cross with a pair of symbols in each of the inter-arm spaces: a Pictish elephant above a fish in the top left; a crescent and V-rod above a beast, variously identified as a lion, a dog or a black cat,[5] in the top right; a double disc above a double crescent in the bottom right; and a step symbol above a fish monster in the bottom left. Ten symbols in all, and not one of them duplicated. This lack of duplicates serves to emphasize the significance of the common symbols linking stones with the same artists' signatures. On the Ulbster stone we have a memorial to at least four individuals (the four symbol pairs on the back of the stone) who seem to have been quite unrelated.

Ulbster: front and back, with record number of ten symbols. (After ECMS)

Apart from having the record number of symbols, the Ulbster stone also has one of the rarest and most controversial symbols, the fish monster, with its tail tightly coiled backwards. Two similar sea-beasts face each other (above a Pictish elephant and a double disc and Z-rod) on the Brodie stone. This symbol also resembles the fish monster on a rock face at the entrance to Trusty's Hill, though it differs in some details of the head and mouth. Jackson accepts all of these as symbols. Katherine Forsyth, in a recent paper, reaches exactly the opposite conclusion on the basis that they only occur on late (Class II) stones and do not combine in pairs to form statements. This conclusion is difficult to sustain in the face of the evidence. Trusty's Hill must surely be assigned to Class I and the Ulbster fish monster is equally surely one of a perfectly normal symbol pair. Alastair Mack, in his *Field Guide to the Pictish Symbol Stones*, follows the middle road and says 'this rare symbol should not be confused with decorative sea-horses or fish monsters, like the pair on the Brodie cross slab'.

A possible interpretation of the Trusty's Hill symbols was discussed in Chapter 8. There the fish monster is shown to the right of a double disc and Z-rod, with a sharp-pointed dagger piercing its heart. The interpretation was that Drust son of Erp, the great warrior king of the Picts, was being portrayed as a thorn in the flesh of the Britons, with the fish monster representing the Britons. If we now transfer this interpretation to the Ulbster stone, the symbol pair in the bottom left can be read as *Step* the Briton. This is an interesting possibility, as it is the first suggestion we have had of a second symbol that might not represent a patronymic. This is comparable with a Latin inscription on a stone at Penbryn in south-central Wales[6] – CORBALENGI IACIT ORDOVS – which is translated as '(The stone) of Corbalengus. (Here) he lies, an Ordovician.' The Ordovices were a tribe in north-central Wales. *Step* the Briton was probably a Briton of Strathclyde who, for whatever reason, had left home and gone to live in the far north.

We can read the names of some of the other people commemorated on the Ulbster stone. They are Edern son of Nechtan in the top left, Brude in the top right, and Kenneth in the bottom right, but that is all we know about them. The art-work on this stone gives every impression of being a uniform design, with no suggestion that the symbols were added at different times. This suggests that the four people commemorated on the back of the stone died together, while involved in some joint venture. What this venture was we shall probably never know but, with Ulbster overlooking the North Sea, it may well have ended in shipwreck. The two symbols on the front of the stone are quite clearly dissociated from those on the back. Were they survivors of the wreck? Were they also perhaps the same two people who are depicted to the left of the cross shaft, squatting either side of a cauldron?

Is the cauldron a symbol of a ritual meal being eaten in memory of those who have died in the service of their country, possibly in the hope that the survivors may take on some of their characteristics of courage and endurance? The only other stone with a comparable cauldron 'symbol' is Glamis 2. If the interpretation of this stone suggested in the last chapter is correct, this is a memorial to Talorgan son of Fergus who was killed in action in a battle against the Strathclyde Britons in 750. On this stone we can see the meal being prepared. The cauldron is hanging from a rod suspended between two forked sticks firmly dug into the ground. Rising out of the top of the cauldron are several human legs! 'Is this an execution by drowning or a scene from Pictish folklore?' asks Anna Ritchie in a well-known book on the Picts.[7] All we can do is ask questions. Execution by drowning was certainly practised by the Picts, but to carry it out in a cauldron suspended on two sticks would have been rather difficult. A scene from Pictish folklore or a symbol for a ritual meal could have a common origin. There can be no certainty on such a question, but the Ulbster stone and the Glamis manse stone on which the cauldrons appear may both commemorate people who died 'on active service'.

Some symbols, like the fish monster discussed above, are still in dispute. Others, like the centaur seen on several Class II stones, are universally rejected. One of these rejected symbols deserves further consideration. It looks just like a walking stick, but there has never been any doubt that it is in fact a crosier. It occurs only once, on a small fragment of a cross slab at St Vigeans (St Vigeans 4). Exactly similar crosiers can be seen in the hands of priests on two stones from Shetland, one from the Isle of Bressay and the other from Papil on West Burra, both now in the National Museum in Edinburgh. The St Vigeans crosier differs from the Shetland examples in being 'disembodied'. In company with a double disc symbol (unusually shown in a vertical orientation), it is shown behind the cleric to whom it refers. The double disc represents the name Kenneth, and the crosier is clearly telling us that he was a priest. We might interpret the symbol pair as 'Brother Kenneth', 'Father Kenneth', or even perhaps 'Bishop Kenneth'. This compares

St Vigeans 4: fragment of back showing an isolated crosier between a man and his symbol. Compare with the Bressay crosiers. (After ECMS)

with a Latin inscription from Aberdaron in North Wales[8] – VERACIUS PBR [presbyter] HIC IACIT – which is translated as 'Veracius the Priest lies here'.

The normal quota of symbols, excluding the mirror and comb, is two per person, one for his or her own name and another for his or her father's. The Golspie stone is unique among Pictish symbol stones because, though it commemorates one man only, his portrait on the back of the stone is almost surrounded by seven symbols. At the top are two large symbols occupying the full width of the stone: a rectangle above a Pictish elephant. These are evidently the symbols giving the man's name. Below them, the man, on the left side of the stone, is marching – almost goose-stepping – towards the symbols on the right. In his right hand he is wielding an axe at the head of a beast (lion, dog or cat). A fish, approaching him beneath this animal, is in danger of being stabbed by a dagger held in the man's left hand. Beneath the fish are two symbols side by side: a flower on the left being spurned by the man's left foot, and a crescent, with just a hint of a V-rod, on the right. Below these two symbols is a double disc about to be trampled under foot by the advancing man. At the very bottom are a pair of intertwined serpents, each biting the other just above its fish-like tail. The man himself, quite unlike the rather formal representations of men on horseback or sitting in chairs, is full of character and vigour as he goes about his business. But who was he and what was his business?

Bressay: note the priests holding their crosiers. (After ECMS)

Until the rectangle symbol has been deciphered we can only call him *Rectangle* son of Edern. We do, however, know that his family had strong Irish connections. There is a long ogham inscription on a round moulding along one edge of the stone. His father was probably the Edern son of Drust (Pictish elephant above a double disc and Z-rod) commemorated on the Brodie stone, which has a similar ogham inscription on a round moulding. This raises the possibility that the bilingual ogham–symbol stones, already discussed in Chapter 6, might be used, regardless of whether or not the oghams can be interpreted, as indicators of Hiberno–Pictish family connections.

The Golspie and Brodie Class II stones yield a simple three-generation pedigree. Turning now to Class I stones, another three-generation pedigree is given by the Inchyra stone, which has symbol pairs on both faces: a fish above a serpent on one and a double disc above a fish on the other. This gives another three-generation pedigree: Kenneth son of Nechtan son of *Serpent*. The Latheron stone, which seems to be transitional between Class I and Class II, has an eagle above a fish giving Nechtan another son, Dunodnat. We now have two three-generation pedigrees of our Hiberno-Pictish family, one on Class I stones and the other on Class II stones, with a gap between them.

There is one particularly interesting stone which seems to belong in that gap. The top of the Ackergill stone is missing but enough remains to identify the symbol pair. The belly and ventral fins of a fish are recognizable above a rectangle. This stone does not make a direct connection with either of the three-generation pedigrees mentioned above. The fish is, however, consistent with a family connection with the Class I pedigree, and the rectangle with the Class II pedigree. The other interesting feature of this stone is that the ogham inscription is arranged along a stem line on the flat surface to the left of the symbols, instead of the more usual situation along the edge of the stone. There are two other stones with this arrangement of the ogham inscription. These are the Latheron stone mentioned above and the Class I Brandsbutt stone, whose crescent and V-rod above a serpent and Z-rod represent Brude son of Derile, possibly the King of the Picts (elder brother of Nechtan) who died in 706. The Ackergill and Brandsbutt stones are so similar that we may treat them like the Class II stones displaying artists' signatures. The simplest (but certainly not the only) interpretation of these two stones is to consider them as memorials to first cousins. The resultant pedigree suggests that we have one Hiberno-Pictish family which encompasses almost all the surviving bilingual ogham–symbol stones and has the unique Golspie man as the last of the line.

In the previous chapter the identification of Brude son of Derile on the Brandsbutt stone was treated with justifiable caution. Three points in the above discussion of the symbol stones with ogham inscriptions seem to support this identification. One is the transitional nature of the Latheron stone, which has a curious 'double rectangle' (probably the lower part of rather a crude cross) in relief (primitive Class II style) above two incised (Class I style) symbols. This would make it more or less contemporary with King Nechtan son of Derile, who was largely instrumental in the development of Class II symbol stones. The name Dunodnat (eagle) appears in the Hiberno-Pictish pedigree and was also the name

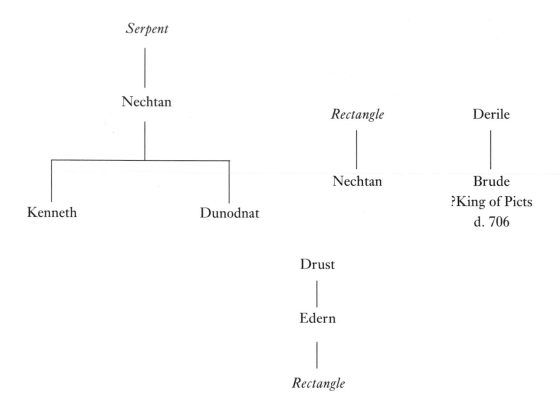

Pedigree 10: fragments of a Hiberno–Pictish pedigree based on symbol stones with ogham inscriptions: Inchyra, Latheron, Ackergill, Brandsbutt, Golspie (Craigton 2) and Brodie.

of Nechtan's grandfather (Meigle 6). The Hiberno–Pictish pedigree also has two Nechtans. Nechtan son of Derile, with his strong attachment to Rome, would probably not have wished for an ogham text on his memorial. Such inscriptions had already become unpopular with the Church in Ireland (see Chapter 6). This digression into Hiberno-Pictish genealogy shows that though the pedigree of the Golspie man is not complete in every detail, he seems to have belonged to one of the greatest families in the land, a family with royal connections in the first quarter of the eighth century.

Taking the scene on the back of the Golspie stone at its face value, the man is clearly attacking a lion (dog or cat) and a fish. In view of this, it is not surprising that these symbols have received special attention. A popular view, initially championed by Joanna Close-Brooks,[9] is that the lion is the lion of St Mark and the fish is the symbol of Christ. On this view, the Golspie man is a pagan fighting against his Christian enemies, but there are two reasons why this interpretation is difficult to maintain. On the front of the stone is a large cross, typical of Class II symbol stones and clearly stating that this is a Christian monument. The fish is a moderately common Pictish pair-forming symbol and it is difficult to see why this particular fish should be treated as a special case. The lion (referred to as a beast in the symbol list) is much less common but does appear on a few symbol stones in the usual way. It seems much more likely that all the symbols on the Golspie stone represent the names of Pictish people, just as they do on other symbol stones. It also seems likely that his activity, displayed on such a large and public monument, was not only acceptable to his fellow Christians but also perhaps admirable.

The Pictish army in the eighth century was one of the most effective fighting forces in Britain. Such success could not be achieved without adequate training and, then as now, training involved mock combat on all scales. In later centuries this took the form of tournaments, and successful warriors, like William Marshall (1147–1219), could build up a considerable reputation and also make a fair living from the misfortunes of their defeated adversaries.[10] The tournament provided training for battle and at the same time provided the medieval equivalent of sport. On the evidence of the Class II symbol stones the chief sport among the Picts was hunting, but it was not the only sport. On the Shandwick stone there is a lively hunting scene, with men on horseback, hounds, deer, and a variety of other animals. In one corner of the panel, beneath a horseman armed with a spear, two men are engaged in single combat, armed with swords and square shields. They have nothing to do with the hunt and seem quite oblivious of all that is going on around them. They are certainly fighting one another but, like the huntsmen above them, they are probably also engaged in a sporting activity. The same may be true of the two men fighting each other with axes on the Glamis manse stone. The Golspie man may have been a great warrior famed for his success in the Pictish equivalent of the tournament. His memorial stone shows him striding forward to victory, with the symbols recording the names of his defeated adversaries.

There are eight Pictish symbol stones in the west of Scotland: three on Skye, one on Raasay, one each on Benbecula and Pabbay in the outer Hebrides and two on the mainland at Gairloch and Poolewe. All are Class I stones and show the usual paired arrangement of symbols (except for Poolewe, which is broken). An unusual feature is that two of them display incised crosses above the symbols and only one of them has a mirror and comb. The Pictish presence indicated by these symbol stones is supported by historical evidence and by a sprinkling of Pictish place-names.

Some 70 miles south of Skye is a Pictish symbol that seems totally out of place. Carved on a rock face at the entrance to a fort, its situation is immediately reminiscent of Trusty's Hill. But this fort, Dunadd, is not only far outside Pictish territory, but is in the very heart of Scottish Dalriada. Dunadd is situated on a rocky eminence rising above an extensive area of mud-flats a few miles north of Lochgilphead. At the foot of the crag the River Add meanders across the flats to Loch Crinan, which opens out into the Sound of Jura and the open sea. The symbol, still recognizable as a boar, was discovered during excavations in 1904.[11] The back, which had been exposed to the weather ever since it was carved, had virtually disappeared. The lower part, which had been protected by a cover of turf, is much better preserved and shows considerable attention to detail and also some traces of the internal scroll features so characteristic of Pictish animal symbols.

Dunadd, unlike Trusty's Hill, has a place in the contemporary historical records maintained by the Irish annalists. It was besieged in 683 and in 736 was captured by the Picts under Oengus son of Fergus, who thereby became effectively King of the Scots as well as the Picts. His rule did not go undisputed and in 747 he was once again hammering the Scots of Dalriada. It has been suggested that the boar symbol was carved at the entrance to Dunadd at the time of its capture by Oengus. This date seems rather late for what must be considered a Class I symbol. Furthermore, if the symbol really had been cut by the Picts in 736, it would surely have been erased when the Scots returned a few decades later. They managed to eliminate Oengus son of Fergus from their king lists, with consequent confusion in the chronology. Surely they would not have tolerated such a blatant display of the Pictish conquest to remain at the principal gate leading into their fort. It seems likely therefore that the boar was carved at a time when the Picts and Scots were allies rather than enemies.

Whatever Gildas said about the Picts, he also said about the Scots. After the departure of the Roman army, he said, Britain was over-run 'by two exceedingly savage overseas nations, the Scots from the north-west and the Picts from the north'. Later on, the letter to Aetius in 448 was written because of the 'foul hordes of Scots and Picts' who, though 'they were to some extent different in their customs . . . were in perfect accord in their greed for bloodshed. So they seized the whole of the extreme north of the island from its inhabitants, right up to the wall.'[12] And the Roman writers back this up by speaking of a barbarous alliance between the Picts, the Scots and the Attacotti.[13] This is a much more likely period for the carving of a Pictish symbol at Dunadd, a fort which was serving exactly the same purpose as Trusty's Hill. We may perhaps imagine a returning Scottish raiding party taking shelter from a storm in Wigtown Bay and seeing the rock-cut symbols at the entrance to Trusty's Hill. A Pictish artist might have been commissioned on such an occasion to carve an appropriate symbol at the entrance to their own fort. Unfortunately there is nothing in the records of the Scots of Dalriada to indicate the name of any individual king who might have had such a symbol carved. But whoever he was, his (Pictish) symbol carved under such circumstances would have been well established before war broke out between the old allies some 250 years later, and the need to erase it never arose.

CHAPTER 12

Mirror and Comb: Pictish Sex Symbols?

The mirror and the comb are among the most abundant of Pictish symbols. The mirror, with 65 occurrences on symbol stones, is second only to the crescent and V-rod (86). The comb, with 41 occurrences, comes fifth in order of abundance, following the double disc and Z-rod (57) and the Pictish elephant (54). Unlike almost all the other non-animal symbols, the mirror and comb are not mere abstract designs. Instead they are carefully drawn representations of familiar objects and their identity has never been in doubt. It is a different matter when it comes to their interpretation as symbols.

The mirror and the comb do not belong to the main series of pair-forming symbols with which we have been largely concerned up to now, and it is therefore highly unlikely that they represent names. They are generally shown together, below a 'normal' symbol pair, but side by side rather than one above the other. The mirror and comb position on a symbol stone may be occupied by the mirror alone. Indeed about one-third of all the mirrors are not accompanied by a comb. The very rare occurrences of combs without mirrors can all be attributed to the fragmentary nature of the stones on which they occur.

The pairing of mirror and comb seems perfectly natural. After all, you look in the mirror and comb your hair. But who among the Picts looked into the mirror and combed their hair? Why, the women of course. This highly sexist interpretation of these symbols has been accepted almost without question. For Thomas, the mirror and comb indicated that the stone had been set up by a woman. For Samson, it meant that the stone was a memorial to a woman. Jackson, who believed that the stones recorded dynastic marriages, thought that the mirror and comb recorded the giving and receiving of bride-wealth. Did men not comb their hair, or did they do it without looking in the mirror?

Alastair Mack, in his *Field Guide to the Pictish Symbol Stones*, looked at the thirteen mirror-bearing Class II symbol stones in his search for evidence to interpret the mirror and comb symbols. He noted that seven of these stones show human figures, among which the principal figure may well represent the person for whom the stone was erected. On five of these, the principal figure appears to be female. Furthermore, a Class I stone with mirror and comb, found in 1977 during ploughing near Dunrobin Castle, was situated above a low cairn covering a long cist containing a female skeleton. The connection between the burial and the symbol stone was confirmed by radiocarbon dating of the skeleton to some time between the mid-sixth and mid-eighth centuries. 'The find provides compelling evidence that stones carved with a mirror-and-comb were carved for females.'[1] This argument loses some of its force in connection with the other stone, also with mirror and comb, found at Dunrobin (see Chapter 11) in use as a capstone at the head end of a long cist containing two adult male skeletons. Even if this was a secondary use of the stone, the meaning of the symbols must have been perfectly clear at the time.

The best-known portrait of a female Pict must surely be the lady riding side-saddle on the Hilton of Cadboll stone. She is looking 'straight out of the picture', in marked contrast to the two men below her, who are looking where they are going – to the left. The men are further distinguished from her by being armed with spears and round shields. A curious feature of this stone is that the lady is riding alongside a man whose horse, identical with hers both in size and stance, is shown a fraction ahead of her own. His nose is just visible, protruding to the left from behind her hair. The lady and her companions, together with their hounds and two long-robed trumpeters, are contained in a square panel. The mirror and comb are fitted into the picture just in front of the lady's horse. The upper panel is occupied with two symbols, a crescent and V-rod above a pair of discs. A third symbol, a double disc and Z-rod, is displayed in the border at the top. Who was the lady; who was riding beside her; and why was it deemed necessary to provide a mirror and comb to symbolize the perfectly obvious fact that the lady in the picture was indeed female?

A seated (enthroned?) female figure, facing to the front, occupies a central position in the lower of two panels on the back of a cross slab from Kirriemuir. To the left is a mirror above a comb occupying the full height of the panel. The space to the right of the seated lady is occupied by an unidentified object. The remarkable thing about this stone is the complete lack of other (pair-forming) symbols. A third female portrait is on the back of a cross slab turned up recently

Hilton of Cadboll: back, showing hunt scene with a lady riding side-saddle. Note the detail showing another rider beside her. (Photo: National Museums of Scotland)

during ploughing at Wester Denoon near Glamis. Like the Kirriemuir lady, she is facing to the front and the space to her left is occupied by a mirror above a comb. The area to her right is occupied by a vertical column of interlace. There are no other symbols. As with the Hilton of Cadboll lady, we are bound to ask why it was necessary to provide a mirror and comb to indicate that the perfectly clear portrait of a lady was female. Far from being evidence that the mirror and comb symbols represent the female sex, these stones might well be taken as evidence that the mirror and comb have nothing whatever to do with the sex of the deceased. Apart from the mirror and comb, why are there no other symbols on these two stones?

The sex of the remaining two figures cited as female by Mack is less easy to determine. The seated figure on the back of the Kingoldrum stone is incomplete, as the top of the stone has been damaged, but is dressed in a long garment, and facing to the left. In the absence of the head, there are no distinctive features on which a sexual identification can be based. There are five equestrian figures on the back of Meigle 1 but, unlike the Hilton of Cadboll stone, there is nothing to identify the leading rider as female or to suggest that it is in any other way different from the others.

The evidence of the female portraits, while a considerable advance on earlier work, is not as strong as it seemed at first sight. As a further test of the hypothesis that the mirror and comb have some female connotation, let us see what the neighbouring and related people of Ireland and Wales have to say on the matter.

The Irish ogham inscriptions, of which more than three hundred survive,[2] are much more amenable to interpretation than their Pictish equivalents. The message of the inscriptions is simple and clear: 'This is the stone of ——'. The name, in the genitive, is given with varying amounts of supplementary information to ensure accurate identification. In order of decreasing abundance, the inscriptions follow the patterns indicated below.

A *maqi* B	(The stone of) A son of B
A	(The stone of) A
A *maqi mucoi* X	(The stone of) A son of a descendant of X
A *avi* C	(The stone of) A grandson of C
A *maqi* B *mucoi* X	(The stone of) A son of B descendant of X
A *mucoi* X	(The stone of) A descendant of X

There are a few other variations on the same genealogical theme, but the record is consistently male. There is no trace of daughters or wives or sisters. The fifty of so ogham inscriptions in south-west England, Wales and the Isle of Man are generally similar to those in Ireland. There is, however, one female ogham inscription on a stone in the churchyard at Eglwys Cymin in Dyfed. The ogham inscription reads: INIGENA CUNIGNI AUITTORIGES – (The stone of) the daughter of Cunignus, Avittoriga. The Latin inscription on the same stone reads: AVITORIA FILIA CVNIGNI – Avitoria daughter of Cunignus (lies here).

The Britons of Wales, and other parts of the highland zone of southern Britain, looked on themselves as the survivors of a once-thriving Romano–British culture. Most of their memorial inscriptions are in Latin[3] and a small number of these relate to women. Among them are Velvoria, daughter of Brohomaglus; Bona, wife of Nobilis; Culidor, son of Secundus, and his wife, Orvvita; and Rosteece, daughter of Paterninus, who died aged thirteen years. The Latin language of the inscriptions and the inclusion of memorials to women both have their origin in Roman Britain, an influence whose effect on Pictish culture was minimal. Furthermore, in the Welsh inscriptions, as in their Roman prototypes, there is nothing anonymous about these women. Their names and family relationships are just as real and detailed as those of their menfolk. The suggestion that the mirror and comb symbols indicate that the stones on which they occur were either memorials to, or set up by, unnamed women has little to recommend it.

Pictish symbols are not restricted to symbol stones. They were engraved on objects of silver and bronze, scratched on pebbles and bones, carved on cave walls and natural rock outcrops, and cut on slabs of stone. The mirror and comb, in spite of their general abundance on symbol stones, have not a single representative among the sixty or so symbols found in these various other situations. One positive conclusion to be drawn from this is that the mirror and comb, whatever their exact meaning, have their place on memorial stones in the Pictish equivalent of monumental inscriptions. It is therefore necessary to look once again at such inscriptions from Roman Britain, Wales and Ireland, in the hope of shedding some light on the interpretation of the mirror and comb.

On pre-Christian Roman tombstones[4] the standard phrase is *Dis Manibus*, generally abbreviated to DM and translated as 'To the spirits of the departed'. 'This was a conventional phrase and continued in use among Christians. It remains doubtful whether in any particular instance it has a specific meaning.'[5] On the early Christian memorials of Wales,[6] its place is taken by *Hic iacit* (Here lies) or, occasionally, *Hic in tumulo iacit* (Here in the tomb lies) – a simple statement about the body of the deceased, with no religious overtones. Much less common than this is *In pace* (In peace), sometimes abbreviated to IP, like the familiar RIP of more modern tombstones.

The Irish ogham inscriptions carry no such set piece phrases, just the name of the deceased and that of his father or other ancestors. With the arrival of Christianity, the ogham inscriptions gradually went out of fashion. The new inscriptions in Hiberno-Saxon characters often carried supplementary phrases appropriate to the new religion. The most common of these was *Oroit do*, commonly abbreviated to *Or do*, meaning 'A prayer for ——'. Another phrase which appeared on these monuments was *Bendacht for*, meaning 'A blessing on ——'.

These set phrases do not all mean exactly the same thing, nor is it likely that any one of them gives an accurate rendering of what was meant by the mirror and comb. They do, however, all perform a similar function. They fulfil a need to say something. Go round any churchyard or cemetery today and you will find memorials to single individuals or to whole families, with all their relationships, ages and dates recorded for the eager genealogist. And at the top, above all the names, some such phrase as 'In loving memory'. To the spirits of the departed, here lies, a prayer for, a blessing on, rest in peace, in loving memory of – all of these, in their different ways and different times, represent the meaning of the mirror and comb.

If I had to choose one of these phrases to represent the meaning of the mirror and comb, it would be *Dis manibus* (to the spirits of the departed). There is widespread belief that the reflection seen in the mirror represents in some way a person's soul, and the shamans of eastern Asia all carry a metal mirror in which they can 'see' the souls of the dead. The many superstitions connected with mirrors, such as the bad luck supposed to follow the breaking of a mirror, have their origins in such beliefs.

Returning to the two female figures with mirror and comb but without any other symbols, we must consider the possibility that women were not normally entitled to use symbols. The phrase 'not normally' is used advisedly, because the Hilton of Cadboll lady is clearly female and is equally clearly using symbols. How exceptional is she? In order to answer this question, we need to look at Class II symbol stones with human figures, with or without mirror and comb, in an attempt to determine the sex ratio of these 'portraits'.

There are about a hundred human figures on Class II stones. Of these, nearly two-thirds are on horseback and one-third on foot, with just a few seated in chairs or (on one stone) in a boat. Nearly half of them are out hunting and a much smaller number fighting. Only a dozen or so can be identified as principal characters in the scenes portrayed on the stones. Most are merely anonymous members of the hunt or soldiers in the army – just walk-on parts in the crowd scenes. The principal characters include the equestrian portraits set into a cross in a special panel (Baluderon, Fordoun and Rossie); lone figures with associated symbols (Logierait horseman, Kingoldrum seated figure); or figures that stand out from the rest, like the Hilton of Cadboll lady or the Kirriemuir horseman (the upper of two) with his double disc and Z-rod. Finally, there is the Dunfallandy stone with three figures, one on horseback and two seated in chairs, each with his or her own symbols.

Two of these principal figures are definitely female: the Hilton of Cadboll side-saddle lady and the upper right seated figure on the Dunfallandy stone. The two Dunfallandy seated figures are both dressed in long robes and their heads are very weathered, so they cannot be recognized as male or female by their clothing. The evidence of the symbols suggests that the one on the left is the father of the equestrian man, and it is therefore likely that the other is his mother. The seated Dunfallandy lady has two symbols, a double disc above a crescent and V-rod. If she were a man, we would call her Kenneth son of Brude, but she is not a man. Was there a Pictish female equivalent of the name Kenneth? Or were the symbols not really hers at all? On the Hilton of Cadboll stone the lady's symbols are probably the crescent and V-rod above twin discs in the panel immediately above her. If she were a man we would call her Brude son of *Twindisc*. But she is not a man. Should we call her Brigid, a reasonable female equivalent for Brude? Or were the symbols not really hers at all? If the symbols did not belong to the woman, who did they belong to? The stones cannot provide an answer to this question directly but the circumstantial evidence, that we are looking at the symbols of a military aristocracy, is helpful and points us once again to the analogy with medieval heraldry.

A medieval knight, completely encased in armour, could be recognized by the symbols (heraldic devices) on his shield. Warfare was a male activity, knights were men, and heraldry was a correspondingly male attribute. If you look at any of the early rolls of arms, such as Glover's Roll, dating from the middle of the thirteenth century, you will see row upon row of carefully painted shields, each one labelled with the name of its owner. Each shield was the symbol of an individual knight. These armorial bearings soon became hereditary and, along with the land which gave the knights their status and power, they passed from father to son. If there were no sons, the land would be inherited by the daughters, who thus became desirable properties in the marriage market. The fortunate sons of such heiresses could then record the source of their advancement by quartering the arms of their maternal grandfathers with their own. This is not unlike biological sex-linked

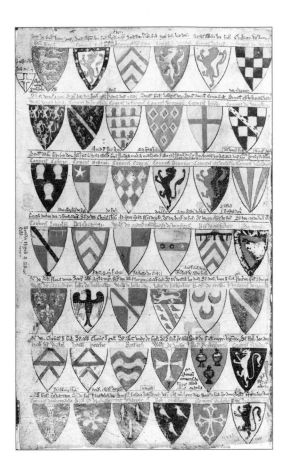

Medieval symbols: a roll of arms illustrating the shields and naming the individual knights who were entitled to use them. (British Library, Nero. D.I. f171ᵛ)

inheritance, of which colour blindness is a good example. The daughters of a colour-blind father all carry the gene for colour-blindness and pass it on to about half of their children. Their sons have a 50 per cent chance of being colour-blind, but none of the female members of the family will be affected.

Pictish symbols were not inherited like medieval coats of arms, but it seems quite probable that they were sex-linked and held only by male members of a family. Whether or not the Kings of the Picts were chosen from the female royal line, it is likely that the descent of property among the aristocracy went from father to son. Thus, if a man decided to erect a memorial to his mother, through whom he had inherited considerable property and status, he might decide to embellish the monument with the appropriate symbols: *those of her father*. The double disc above a crescent and V-rod, shown with the old lady (top right) on the Dunfallandy stone, give the name of her father, the maternal grandfather of the man (equestrian figure

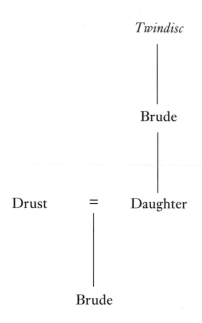

Twindisc

|

Brude

|

Drust   =   Daughter

|

Brude

Pedigree 11: possible alternative interpretation of pedigree based on stones with trumpeters (see Pedigree 2).

below) who set the stone up. Instead of having to imagine a female version of Kenneth (double disc) for her, we can say that her father was Kenneth son of Brude (crescent and V-rod). The same applies to the Hilton of Cadboll lady, whose father would have been Brude son of *Twindiscs*.

Quite apart from Pictish symbol stones, this might be an explanation for those ogham inscriptions in Ireland which, instead of naming the father of the man commemorated, name his grandfather. His *maternal* grandfather might be the ancestor from whom he inherited the greater part of his land and status in society.

The two Pictish stones with female portraits accompanied only by the mirror and comb probably have no other symbols because they did not, in their own right, have any symbols at all. The mirror and comb indicate not their female sex, but a prayer for their souls – a prayer equally appropriate for man or woman.

Finally the mirror and comb symbols, like all the other Pictish symbols, while they certainly had their origin in pre-Christian times, continued into the Christian period with full vigour. There is no indication of an anti-symbol movement associated with the arrival of Christianity. Indeed some of the most elaborate and beautifully designed symbols are associated with Class II cross slabs. Why did they survive, when *dis manibus* and the ogham inscriptions aroused the intense opposition of the Church. The answer probably lies in the special feature of symbols. They are not written out in words that can be read and interpreted or perhaps misinterpreted by strangers. They remain symbolic, with the possibility that their interpretation may be modified to suit changing circumstances.

CHAPTER 13

Who Used the Symbols?

Who used the symbols? This question can be answered in two quite different ways. Now that so many of the symbols can be deciphered, it is relatively easy to look at a symbol stone and put a name to it. The Aberlemno roadside cross, for example, has a crescent and V-rod above a double disc and Z-rod. These symbols identify it as the stone of Brude son of Drust. This in itself is interesting and useful information. It tells us that though the symbols themselves are unique to the Picts, the message of the symbol stones is not. This is just the sort of thing the ogham inscriptions of Ireland and the Latin inscriptions of Wales are telling us. Almost all these stones, Irish, Welsh and Pictish, are memorials to named individuals.

But who was Brude son of Drust? Perhaps the question should be rephrased. What was Brude son of Drust? What sort of man used these symbols and had such a splendid stone set up in his memory? To answer this question we must return to the fifty Class II symbol stones, which are sufficiently complete for meaningful analysis, and to the pedigrees discussed in Chapter 10. The first thing to notice is that four of these stones (8 per cent) have been identified as memorials to kings.

Aberlemno 2	Divided rectangle and Z-rod above triple disc
	Oengus son of Fergus (728–761)
Meigle 1	Fish above serpent and Z-rod
	Nechtan son of Derile (706–724, 726, d. 732)
Meigle 6	Double disc above crescent
	Kenneth son of Ferat (842–843)
St Vigeans 1	Double disc and Z-rod above crescent
	Drust son of Ferat (845–848)

Another six have been identified as the memorial stones of close relatives of the above-named kings.

Balluderon	Pictish elephant above serpent and Z-rod
	Edern son of Derile (brother of King Nechtan)
	Unknown to history
Fordoun	Double disc and Z-rod and inscription PIDARNOIN
	Drust son of Edern (nephew of King Nechtan)
	Unknown to history
Glamis 1	Triple disc above flower
	Fergus son of *Flower* (father of King Oengus)
	Unknown to history
Glamis 2	Deer's head above triple disc
	Talorgan son of Fergus (brother of King Oengus)
	Killed in battle (750)
Rossie	Crescent and V-rod above Pictish elephant
	Brude son of Edern (nephew of King Nechtan)
	Unknown to history
St Vigeans 2	Serpent and Z-rod above eagle
	Derile son of Dunodnat (father of King Nechtan)
	Unknown to history

Two factors frustrate any further development of these pedigrees. The first is that the succession to the Pictish throne was, as Bede records, through the female royal line. Kings of the Picts were never succeeded by their sons until after the union of the Pictish and Scottish kingdoms under Constantine son of Fergus, early in the ninth century. The second problem is that the symbol stones, like the *Pictish Chronicle* and the *Annals of Ulster*, are almost wholly male-dominated. Eithni daughter of Cinadon, whose death in 778 was recorded in the *Annals of Ulster*, is a rare exception. Her father was Ciniod son of Wradech, King of the Picts, who died in 775. Had she lived longer and produced a son and heir, her own death would have passed unnoticed. Her son might have become king and would have been known as the son of his (otherwise unknown) father, with nothing to indicate any connection with his maternal grandfather from whom, through his mother, he would have succeeded to the throne.

Among the stones mentioned so far in this chapter, we have memorials to four kings, two fathers of kings, two brothers of kings and two nephews (sons of brothers) of kings – that is, a total of ten members of the Pictish royal family (20 per cent of the sample studied). Eight other stones – Aberlemno 3, Dunfallandy, Glenferness, Hilton of Cadboll, Meigle 4, Nigg, St Madoes and

Shandwick – provided three more pedigrees. Any one of these might have been connected to the royal family by what we may now term a 'missing link' and the links that are most notably missing are the female ones. All that would be required is that the mother, sister, daughter or wife of someone in one of the pedigrees might be the mother, sister, daughter or wife of someone in another pedigree. The most likely pedigrees to be linked in this way are those given by the Drosten stone (St Vigeans 1) on the one hand, and the Glenferness and Shandwick stones on the other. All three share the little kneeling figure of an archer as an artist's signature. It is impossible to say which of the many possible connecting links might have been present – and sadly it will remain impossible because of the complete lack of information about Pictish ladies.

If one-fifth of the Class II symbol stones are memorials to members of the Pictish royal family, and over one-third of them can be linked together in the pedigrees of a restricted number of other families, it seems that these symbol stones belonged to a very exclusive elite of Pictish society. We can form an idea of the general character of this Pictish aristocracy in the eighth and ninth centuries by looking at the figures portrayed on the stones. Of the fifty Class II stones we have been considering, over thirty show human figures and the great majority of these are equestrian, with a few seated in chairs and a few on foot. Some of the equestrian figures are clearly individual portraits, while others are participants in more general scenes involving a number of people. Taking them all together, we can begin to form a picture of a typical Pictish aristocrat. His favourite sport was deer hunting, riding out with a group of his friends and their hounds. He may also have enjoyed hawking for smaller game.[1] His possessions would have included his horse and hounds, his saddle and bridle, a spear and sword, and a circular shield. As well as being a keen hunter he was also, perhaps most importantly, a warrior – a member of a highly trained, high-speed cavalry unit. He is beginning to sound just like a medieval knight.

According to St Anselm, Archbishop of Canterbury from 1093 to 1109, the horse, with its bridle and saddle, was the knight's most important possession; for his own protection he had a hauberk, helmet and shield and, for attack, a lance and sword. Without any one of these he could not properly be called a knight.[2] Our Pictish aristocrat, some three hundred years earlier, fell short of these essentials only in the matter of hauberk and helmet. The resemblance between the Pictish aristocrat and a medieval knight is reinforced by the pictorial evidence, for example in the Bayeux Tapestry, where we see King Harold and his knights out riding with their hawk and hounds on their way to his manor at Bosham.

Bayeux tapestry: a scene showing King Harold and his knights hunting with hawk and hounds, while on their way to his manor of Bosham in Sussex. (The Bayeux Tapestry, 11th century. By special permission of the City of Bayeux)

The above conclusions, based on an examination of Class II symbol stones, can be tested for the earlier Class I symbol stones by a consideration of Pictish cemeteries.

There have been several demonstrations in recent years of a close association of Class I symbol stones with Pictish burials.[3] In 1974 fragments of a Class I symbol stone, with a crescent and V-rod, were unearthed on top of a low circular cairn at Garbeg, near Drumnadrochit. Subsequent excavation showed that the cairn covered an unlined pit.[4] Three other cairns in the immediate vicinity were also excavated. One contained a few badly decayed human bones in the underlying pit, but there were no further finds of symbol stones or fragments. Another Class I symbol stone, with a double crescent above a serpent and Z-rod and a mirror and comb, was found in 1977 while ploughing not far from Dunrobin Castle, Sutherland. Excavation showed that the stone had been lying on a low rectangular cairn covering a long cist grave.[5] The cist, walled and roofed with sandstone slabs, contained an extended female skeleton, radiocarbon-dated to 550–750. Two pieces of another Class I symbol stone, with a crescent and V-rod, were discovered on a low cairn at Watenan, Caithness, in 1977,[6] when a heather fire burnt through the overlying layer of peat. This cairn was not excavated.

From the above examples and others like them, we may conclude that some symbol stones are associated with burials and are, in effect, gravestones. Looked

Map showing the distribution of long cist cemeteries. Note the geological controls: the Highland Boundary Fault (HBF) in the south and outcrops of Old Red Sandstone (stippled) providing suitable raw material in the north.

at the other way round, we may similarly conclude that some Pictish burials have associated symbol stones. To what extent can we generalize from these few examples? Are all symbol stones likely to have been gravestones, and are all Pictish graves likely to have been marked by symbol stones? The answer to the first question must remain a matter of opinion and conjecture. Many symbol stones are known to have been moved from the place where they were found, some several times. Many were found in situations which were obviously not primary, as in the walls of buildings. For most of them there is no possibility of testing their connection with Pictish burials. The second question is more easily answered. Several Pictish cemeteries have been excavated in recent years, quite independently of the discovery of symbol stones, and it is these we must now consider.

The long cist cemetery at Hallow Hill near St Andrews, first noticed in the nineteenth century, was rediscovered during building operations in 1975. A total of 145 graves were excavated[7] and an unknown number had been destroyed before the archaeological investigation began. It has been estimated that the cemetery originally contained somewhere between two hundred and five hundred graves. Most were lined with slabs of sandstone set on edge, and were floored and roofed with the same material. These contained well-preserved extended skeletons. A few of the graves were simple unlined pits. In these the skeletons could be seen at the bottom of the pit, but the bones became a fine sandy powder when any attempt was made to remove them. Nothing could be recovered apart from a few teeth.

Bone samples from twenty individuals were radiocarbon-dated and the bulk of these yielded seventh-century dates. It is thus clear, both chronologically and geographically, that Hallow Hill was a Pictish cemetery – a cemetery with two hundred or more graves and not a single symbol stone. It should perhaps be pointed out that there are very few symbol stones anywhere in Fife.

At the other end of the Pictish kingdom, in Orkney, a small long cist cemetery has recently been excavated at Westness on the island of Rousay.[8] As at Hallow Hill, some of the graves were lined and roofed with sandstone slabs, while others were simple unlined pits. The graves were identified as Pictish by radiocarbon-dating. Most of the graves were marked by a headstone, but these stones had no symbols; indeed no symbol stones have yet been found on Rousay.

We now come to a difficult question. Why do these two cemeteries, at opposite ends of the Pictish kingdom, have no symbol stones associated with them? There are several possibilities. They may contain only the burials of the lower classes,

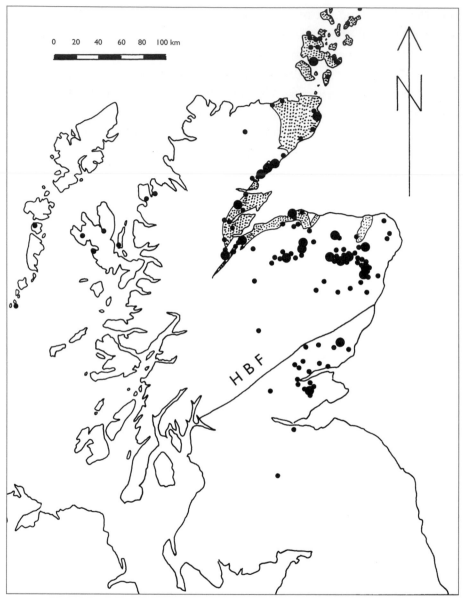

Map showing the distribution of Class I symbol stones. Compare with the distribution of long cist cemeteries (p. 156).

people who did not have symbol-bearing status. On the other hand, it may be a matter of cultural affiliations. The developed Pictish kingdom was a multicultural entity resulting from the military and political alliance of a number of smaller kingdoms. Perhaps these two marginal cemeteries were used by people who did not use symbols because, though politically part of the Pictish kingdom, neither they nor their ancestors had ever used them. Or maybe it was all a matter of time. The fashion for using symbols may have died out in these two areas before the period of the cemeteries, or perhaps the cemeteries had gone out of use before the idea of using symbols caught on.

Long cist cemeteries are difficult to miss when they are encountered during building or other engineering activities, and sooner or later they come to the notice of museums and other archaeological organizations. Symbol stones, more often found while ploughing, are also of obvious interest and tend to get reported. It is therefore possible to make a meaningful comparison of the distribution of long cist cemeteries and symbol stones. Two things stand out on these distribution maps. First, long cist cemeteries reach their greatest concentration south of the Firth of Forth, well beyond the generally accepted southern boundary of the Pictish kingdom. Secondly, long cist cemeteries are completely absent over a large area north of the Mounth, precisely the area of greatest abundance of Class I symbol stones. Class I symbol stones may sometimes be associated with long cist burials, but the correlation between them leaves a lot to be desired.

Three long cist cemeteries south of the Firth of Forth have been partly excavated in recent years: one at Longniddry in East Lothian,[9] one at the Catstane near Kirkliston in Midlothian,[10] and one at Linlithgow in West Lothian.[11] Between them, these provided radiocarbon dates from ten bone samples, ranging from the fifth to the seventh centuries, with one sample possibly as late as the eighth. We have already seen evidence from Gildas that this area was conquered by the Picts in the fifth century, and Bede gives a couple of hints that it may still have been culturally Pictish in the late seventh and early eighth century. He tells us that Peanfahel was the Pictish name for a place at the eastern end of the Antonine Wall (not far from Linlithgow).[12] This would seem to imply that the local inhabitants were Pictish even though the place was, at the time of writing, in English territory. He also tells us that when Trumwine was appointed 'bishop of those Picts who were then subject to English rule' in 678, he established the administrative centre of his see in the monastery of Abercorn[13] on the southern shore of the Firth of Forth, east of Linlithgow and north-west of Kirkliston. The

Map showing the distribution of Class II symbol stones. Compare with the distribution of long cist cemeteries (p. 156).

implication, once again, is that the people of this area were Picts under English rule. This conclusion is reinforced by the fact that after the resounding defeat of the English army at the battle of Nechtansmere in 685, Trumwine felt obliged to withdraw from Abercorn and retire to Whitby.

There are no symbol stones associated with these southern long cist cemeteries, though the area is not entirely without such memorials. A Class I symbol stone with a crescent and V-rod above part of a double disc and Z-rod was discovered, face down, in use as a footbridge in the Princes Street gardens, immediately below Edinburgh Castle. While this was clearly not its original location, there is no reason to suppose that it had been brought from any great distance.

The Catstane, within the confines of the Kirkliston long cist cemetery, is a rough glacial boulder with a Latin inscription on one face.

```
I  N   O  C  T  V
M  V  LO   I  A C
V  E  T T A   F
V   I C T  I
```

In [h]oc tumulo iac[it] Vetta f[ilia] Victi: 'In this tomb (mound) lies Vetta daughter of Victus'. Or it could be that Vetta was the son of Victus. A recent reading of the inscription on the Catstane[14] makes the last word VICTR instead of VICTI, and it has been tentatively suggested that Vetta might have been the daughter of Victricius. Whatever its exact interpretation, the fact is that this inscription, like those at Whithorn, would be more at home in Wales than a few miles to the north, in the kingdom of the Picts. These Picts of Lothian, who came under English domination some time before the middle of the seventh century, had been converted to Christianity much earlier as a result of St Ninian's mission in south-west Scotland. These people, south of the Forth-Clyde line, were the 'southern Picts' who, according to Bede 'are said to have abandoned the errors of idolatry long before this date [565] and accepted the true Faith through the preaching of Bishop Ninian'.[15]

The long cist cemeteries north and south of the Firth of Forth are a reflection of the cultural similarity between the Picts under Pictish rule, north of the Firth, and those under English rule, south of it. If this is so, does the sharp boundary between abundant long cist cemeteries in Fife and Angus and the absence of such cemeteries to the north and west represent an equally sharp cultural divide? The possibility can be tested by looking for a similar boundary in other distribution maps.

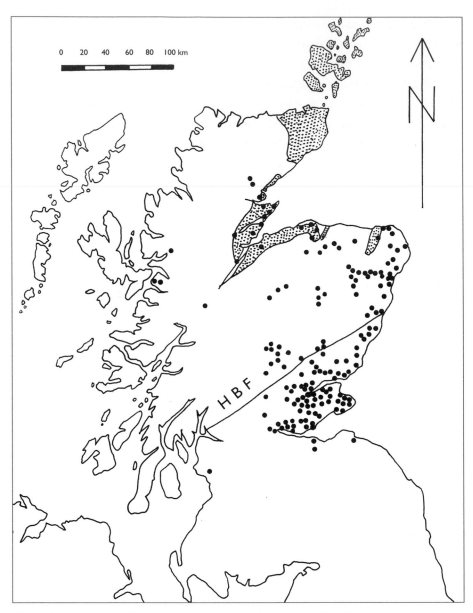

Map showing the distribution of place-names beginning with Pit-. Compare with the distribution of long cist cemeteries (p. 156).

The two things most frequently cited as indicators of the geographical spread of Pictish culture are place-names and symbol stones. We have already seen that the distribution of Class I symbol stones shows no hint of the north-western limit of the long cist cemeteries. Place-names beginning with Pit-, the most popular of Pictish place-name indicators, show not the slightest hint of such a cultural or ethnic boundary. Class II symbol stones, on the other hand, while they do step across the boundary, seem much more abundant within the confines of the long cist cemetery distribution, particularly in Angus. Why should there be a connection between the distribution of Class II symbol stones and that of the generally earlier long cist cemeteries? The question is an archaeological one, but the answer has nothing to do with cultural affinities or ethnic origins. Class II symbol stones and long cist burials require similar raw materials, namely rocks that split readily into slabs. It is a matter of geology.

The north-western limit of long cist cemeteries corresponds very closely to one of the most significant geological boundaries in Scotland: the Highland Boundary Fault. This great fault, running from Stonehaven in the north-east to Campbeltown in the south-west, separates the metamorphic and igneous rocks of the Highlands from the Upper Palaeozoic Old Red Sandstone and Carboniferous rocks to the south and east. These Upper Palaeozoic rocks include many sandstone beds which split readily to form slabs or flagstones. In contrast, the rocks of the Highlands are much more massive and do not split readily, either naturally or mechanically. The absence of long cist cemeteries north-west of the Highland Boundary Fault is entirely due to the lack of suitable raw material. Further confirmation of this conclusion comes from the far north, where long cist cemeteries reappear along the shores of the Moray Firth, northwards as far as John o'Groats, and then across the Pentland Firth to Orkney. The occurrence of these northern cemeteries, their graves lined with sandstone slabs, corresponds exactly with outcrops of Old Red Sandstone overlying the metamorphic and igneous rocks of the Highlands. This answers one question only to raise another. How did the poor Picts in the intervening areas dispose of their dead?

It has been suggested that round and square barrows, which have in some instances been shown to cover Pictish graves, have a distribution complementary to that of the long cist cemeteries. There is, however, a fundamental difference between the two which should be considered. The long cist cemeteries are very economical in their use of space, with graves arranged neatly side by side in long rows. About twenty long cist graves could be fitted into the area occupied by a single six-metre square barrow. Replacement of long cist graves by barrows, round or square, would seem an unlikely response to a shortage of slabs to line the graves. The most natural response would have been to have cemeteries organized as usual, but with the graves being simple unlined pits. Such unlined-grave cemeteries would never be detected during building operations, road works or ploughing. There would be no structural remains and all skeletal material would be completely decayed with the possible exception of a few scattered teeth. There would be nothing to draw attention to such a cemetery. This is not to say that the graves would have disappeared without trace – the unlined graves at Hallow Hill give the lie to that. But a cemetery composed entirely of unlined graves would generally go undetected. Aerial photography is one way in which such a cemetery might be discovered, as recently demonstrated at Forteviot.[16]

The Class II symbol stones, which have similar raw material requirements to the long cist cemeteries, are not quite so constrained by the geological boundaries. Two different solutions to the problem were found. The one most commonly adopted by the Class II sculptors was to make use of the rougher and less workable local stones such as granite. The other was to transport top quality sandstone from its relatively distant source to the place where it was required. The Dunfallandy stone, for example, is a fine slab of Old Red Sandstone which must have been dragged at least 20 kilometres along the valley of the Tay and Tummel, from the nearest outcrop of such rock south of Dunkeld. The wealthy clients of the Class II sculptors were easily able to bear the extra costs involved.

The long cist cemeteries seem to have been broadly contemporary with the Class I symbol stones. If we knew the average number of long cist cemeteries (and their equivalent unlined-grave cemeteries) per unit area and the average number of graves per cemetery, we would know how many graves there were per unit area, provided that all the burials took place in such cemeteries. Then, if we knew the area occupied by the Picts in eastern Scotland, from John o'Groats in the north to the Firth of Forth in the south, we could make a realistic estimate of the number of Pictish burials in that area and compare that figure with the number of Class I symbol stones in the same area. Of course we do not really know any of these things, but it is none the less worth making an attempt.

In the best long cist cemetery areas, there are about eight cemeteries in a 20 kilometre square, that is, about two per 100 square kilometres. This would mean that some people would have to transport their dead up to 3.5 kilometres to the nearest cemetery. There may well be unlined-grave cemeteries within the long cist areas. The construction of long cist graves depends not only on suitable underlying rock formations, but also on accessible sources of slabs at the surface.

It has been pointed out that the distribution of long cist cemeteries in Fife is largely coastal. This is because erosion of the coastal cliffs provides a readily accessible supply of suitable slabs. The inhabitants of inland areas of Fife may have preferred to bury their dead in unlined graves rather than travel to the coast. The average number of cemeteries per 100 square kilometres may therefore be greater than suggested by the distribution map. On the other hand, in less populated areas there may be fewer cemeteries. Perhaps we might allow a range of from one to four per 100 square kilometres. The average number of graves in a cemetery is even harder to guess. At Hallow Hill the original number of graves was estimated as somewhere between two hundred and five hundred. If this was perhaps a rather larger than average cemetery, perhaps we should allow a range from fifty to five hundred. From these figures, we may *guess* that the average number of burials per 100 square kilometres is between fifty and two thousand, which we might perhaps narrow down to between one hundred and one thousand.

The area of eastern Scotland occupied by the Picts during this period, estimated from the distribution of Class I symbol stones, backed up by place names beginning with Pit-, is approximately 15,000 square kilometres. The number of Class I symbol stones in this area is almost 150, that is, close to one per 100 square kilometres.

None of these figures can be considered much better than reasonable guesses but taken together they suggest that Class I symbol stones were erected for one person out of every few hundred members of the population (somewhere between 1 in 100 and 1 in 1000). This conclusion is consistent with the more specific interpretation of the Class II symbol stones, that these memorials were the prerogative of a more or less exclusive elite of Pictish society.

By the close of the tenth century it was fairly generally believed that society was divided into three main categories – one might almost say classes – those who fought, those who worked, and those who prayed.[17] This idea, originally proposed by King Alfred towards the end of the ninth century, had been taken up by continental writers as well as his English successors. The Picts of the Class II symbol stones in the eighth and ninth centuries clearly identified themselves with the fighting class. They, like the Anglo-Norman knights and their continental equivalents, were maintained in their position by the great bulk of the population who worked on the land. Such evidence as we have suggests that the Class I symbol stone users may have enjoyed much the same position in society.

CHAPTER 14
Pictish Graffiti

The use of Pictish symbols on memorial stones and on the silver or bronze insignia of high officials in the king's service might be termed their 'formal' use. It is the sort of use that, in later centuries, might have been acceptable to the Lord Lyon King of Arms. But these are not the only occurrences of Pictish symbols. They were also carved on the walls of caves, scratched on bone gaming pieces, cut on to pebbles, and incised on slabs of stone that are unlikely ever to have been set up as memorial stones. All these miscellaneous occurrences of Pictish symbols have been grouped together under the general heading Pictish graffiti.

The Sculptor's Cave[1] at Covesea near Elgin and a range of caves at East Wemyss[2] on the Fife coast are well known for their Pictish carvings. The casual visitor might be excused for being a little disappointed at the seeming lack of recognizable symbols. As Elizabeth Sutherland has written of the Sculptor's Cave (and her remarks apply equally to the Fife caves), 'every inch is carved with initials ancient and modern, indecipherable doodles and a collection of undoubtedly Pictish symbols'.[3]

During the last few centuries many people have visited the caves and made their own contribution to the decoration of their walls. Some have produced entirely original carvings, some have modified existing ones, and others have simply carved their initials, leaving a lasting and completely anonymous record of their visit. Some relatively recent carvings can be recognized by their subject matter, like the eighteenth-century cannon in Jonathan's Cave, East Wemyss. Others can be identified by comparing drawings made in the 1860s with recent surveys of the cave walls. How many of the carvings are truly Pictish, how many prehistoric, and how many medieval, it is difficult to say. All that we can do is consider those that are certainly or probably Pictish – and that is a very small proportion of the total.

Crescent and V-rod Several examples can be seen in the Sculptor's Cave. The general form is fairly standard but the execution somewhat inferior.

Double disc and Z-rod above a dog's head This symbol pair, in the former Doo Cave, East Wemyss, can be matched on the silver plaques from Norrie's Law, on the lost bronze plaque from Monifieth, and on a Class I symbol stone at Rhynie. These are also the only occurrences of the dog's head symbol. These were discussed in Chapter 8 and considered to be the symbols of Drust son of Erp, a fifth-century King of the Picts.

Mirror case There are two examples in the Sculptor's Cave, both simple outlines with no distinctive features.

Step symbol One example appears in the Sculptor's Cave, an outline of standard shape.

Triple oval There is one example in the Sculptor's Cave showing the 'ovals' with pointed ends, instead of the usual rounded form.

Fish There is one in the Sculptor's Cave and another in Jonathan's Cave, East Wemyss; both were drawn vertically (standing on their tails).

Rectangle The two rectangles, one in the Sculptor's Cave and one in the Sliding Cave, East Wemyss, both have their long sides vertical, whereas those on the symbol stones are generally elongated horizontally. Furthermore, the internal designs on the cave rectangles are quite unlike those on the symbol stones.

Pictish elephant There is one example in the former Doo Cave. The supposed elephant symbols in Jonathan's Cave and the Glass House Cave, East Wemyss, are much less convincing.

Ogee One example appears in the Doo Cave, of fairly standard form.

Double disc With a dozen or so examples in several of the East Wemyss Caves, this is more abundant than any of the other cave symbols. They differ from the symbol stone double discs in the relative proportions of their component parts, in the shape of the connection between the two discs, in their orientation and in their relative abundance. The only cave double disc which compares well with those of the symbol stones is the one with a Z-rod in the former Doo Cave.

Pentagram (Pentacle) There are two examples in the Sculptor's Cave, one with a central spot. This design was certainly known to the Picts (see below) but was probably not a Pictish symbol in the usual sense.

Hexagram (Star of David) One incomplete (probably damaged) example occurs in the Court Cave, East Wemyss. This design, like the pentagram, was known to the Picts but was probably not a symbol in the usual sense.

Various birds in the East Wemyss caves have been referred to as examples of the 'bird symbol',[4] but they bear little resemblance either to one another, or to the eagles and geese of the symbol stones. Some are identifiable, for example the swan in Jonathan's Cave and the peacock in the Doo Cave, but neither of these has yet been found on a symbol stone and there can be no certainty that they are Pictish.

Various animals in the East Wemyss caves, more or less identifiable as lion, horse, deer, etc., may or may not be Pictish symbols. None of them has the characteristic internal scrolls of Pictish symbol animals and they may just be pictures of animals.

There are three important differences between the cave symbols and their equivalents on the symbol stones. With the exception of the double disc and Z-rod and its associated dog's head in the Doo Cave, the cave symbols do not occur in the pairs so characteristic of the symbol stones. The mirror and comb, which are such a common feature of the symbol stones, are completely absent from the cave walls. The cave symbols are, almost without exception, rather poorly executed.

Symbols displayed publicly and openly on symbol stones, and symbols carved in the dark recesses of subterranean caves, while they may have had the same basic meanings, must surely have served very different purposes. The symbol stones were intended to be seen and their symbols to be read. The single symbols on the cave walls, like the initials which are their modern equivalent, conveyed very little meaning except to the person who carved them. They carried a very simple message: 'I was here and, to prove it, this is my symbol.' The symbols – those that can definitely be identified as Pictish – represent single names like Brude (crescent and V-rod), Nechtan (fish), Edern (Pictish elephant) and so on – just like writing Jack, Bob or Bill, without giving the surname. Identification of the person who carved the symbol was never the intention. The people who carved symbols on the walls of the caves were simply writing their own names.

The idea of Picts writing their names on the walls of caves may seem a little far-fetched, but it is worth considering a better-known example of writing on walls, not too far removed from the Pictish caves either chronologically or geographically. Thousands of people visit the great chambered cairn or Maes Howe in Orkney every year and learn about the beautiful Ingeborg, the crusaders and the great treasure. A recent study of some thirty runic inscriptions on the walls of Maes Howe gives a table of their texts with suggested English translations.[5] Six of them make references to the missing treasure, five describe how the tomb was penetrated, and the remainder contain little more than names as, for example:

I	Eyjolfr Kolbeinssonr carved these runes high
IV	Vemundr carved
XIX–XXg	Simun
XXIV	Benedikt made this cross

The absence of the mirror and comb symbols from the cave walls is entirely consistent with their interpretation in Chapter 12 as some formula equivalent to the Latin *Dis manibus* or *Hic iacit*. The cave symbols were not memorial inscriptions and so had no need for such formulae.

The poor draughtsmanship of many of the cave symbols may be attributed to a variety of factors. They may be early attempts at symbol carving and as such have been referred to as proto-symbols. They may be the products of unskilled hands and thus compare unfavourably with the output of professional monumental masons. On the other hand the poor lighting and generally atrocious working conditions may be quite sufficient explanation for substandard carving, without invoking any other cause.

The proto-symbol idea has gained much of its strength from Covesea Cove, where the Pictish occupation has been dated to the second half of the fourth century. The significance of this date has been understandably exaggerated because of the quite exceptional quality of the dating evidence. The Picts were in occupation of the cave when, about the year 360, there was a sudden influx of highly datable Roman coins,[6] part of the loot from a successful raid on southern Britain. How much longer the Pictish occupation of the cave lasted we simply do not know. The Roman coins are silent on the matter and there is no other dating evidence worth looking at. As for the symbols on the walls, they could have been carved as early as the fourth century, but there is nothing remotely approaching proof on the matter. There is no real evidence that any of the cave symbols are earlier than the main sequence of Class I symbol stones, very few of which can be dated with any confidence. There is therefore no reason why they should be classified as proto-symbols. If, on the other hand, the cave symbols represent names carved from time to time by Pictish visitors, then their generally inferior quality can be put down to inexperience on the part of the symbol carver, combined with the difficult working conditions.

Mention has been made of fertility symbols in the East Wemyss caves. In Jonathan's cave there are several symbols which look like the vertical double disc symbols in the same cave, but without the lower disc. These possible phallic symbols could be interpreted as fertility symbols. They might also be symbolic references to real or imaginary encounters, like runic inscription IX in Maes Howe, which has been crudely but confidently translated as 'Thorny fucked; Helgi carved'.[7]

Another group of symbols which resemble those on the cave walls in some respects were carved on slabs of stone but do not seem ever to have been symbol stones as such. These symbols generally occur singly or accompanied by rather indefinite scribbling. Most of them bear sufficient resemblance to known Pictish symbols to provide a basis for discussion.

Rectangle A tall narrow rectangle, containing a smaller one within it, is the left-hand symbol of a group of three on a block of stone found on top of a partition wall outside the Broch of Gurness.[8] This differs from the standard rectangle of the symbol stones, which is almost invariably elongated horizontally rather than vertically. Its closest parallel is the rectangular symbol in Covesea Cave. It is perfectly possible that these are two examples of a genuine Pictish symbol which has yet to be found on a symbol stone.

Mirror case The middle symbol on the Gurness stone has been identified as a mirror case, otherwise known as a disc with divided rectangle. An alternative identification is a tuning fork. Its closest parallel is with the upper symbol on the Strathmiglo Class I symbol stone, which has been given the same alternative identifications.

Divided rectangle The right-hand symbol on the Gurness stone is another tall thin rectangular symbol, rather like a laterally compressed letter H. It differs from the divided rectangle of the Class I symbol stones in having the division at both ends.

Double disc A poorly executed double disc symbol, very like some of the examples in the East Wemyss Caves, was found during the excavation of a habitation site at Pool on the island of Sanday, Orkney.[9] The water-worn slab of sandstone on which the symbol was carved was found face-down in a sixth-century paved area. This datable archaeological context has given this symbol some credibility as a proto-symbol.

Several symbol-bearing stones were found at Dunnicaer, about a mile south of Stonehaven. Dunnicaer 1 has a double disc and Z-rod, the effect of which is marred by a tangle of extra lines and curves. Dunnicaer 3 has a crescent superimposed on the apex of an equilateral triangle. This seems to be a perfectly clear symbol, but one that has not yet been recorded elsewhere. Dunnicaer 5 has two discs, each with a central spot. This may be an example of the rare twin disc symbol.

Some of these symbols may be proto-symbols, some may be trial pieces carved by apprentice craftsmen, others may be idle scribblings with no particular purpose. We will probably never know why they were carved. What does seem to be clear, however, is that most of them are genuine Pictish symbols, some of which are clearly identifiable with symbols known on symbol stones. There is nothing final about our current list of symbols found on symbol stones. Seven of the thirty-five pair-forming symbols (one-fifth of the total) listed by Mack in his recent guide have only been found once each on symbol stones. One fewer find of each and they would not be on the list at all; indeed one of them, the square, was not discovered until 1974. The dog's head, with only one example on a symbol stone, is well known from its occurrence on the Norries Law silver plaques, the Monifieth bronze plaque and the wall of the Doo Cave at East Wemyss. There are four symbols on two of the Pictish silver chains, three of which are also known on symbol stones. The fourth, the twin triangles, has not yet been found on a symbol stone and consequently does not find a place in any list of Pictish symbols.

The pentagram and hexagram are magical symbols that transcend national boundaries. They are mentioned here because, as well as being carved on the cave walls, they have been found carved on either side of a sandstone pebble from the Broch of Burrian on North Ronaldsay, Orkney. They are not Pictish symbols and are never likely to be found on a symbol stone. They are nevertheless international symbols with which the Picts, like many other people, were familiar.[10]

The symbols and other designs carved on gaming pieces from Shetland and Orkney differ from those on the cave walls and slabs of stone, discussed above, in that they are clearly the work of skilled craftsmen. Excavations at Jarlshov, Shetland, in 1932 and 1934 yielded numerous sandstone discs, shaped like the pieces for a game of draughts but rather larger. They were all well made and polished, and one was distinguished from all the others by a double disc and Z-rod incised on one face.[11] Another unusual sandstone disc, ornamented with a complex spiral design, was found at Jarlshof in the 1898 excavation.[12] This design can hardly be called a symbol and just seems to serve the purpose of making this particular disc special and different from the general run of unornamented discs. Two other examples of such special discs were found in the ruins of a broch just across the bay, to the west of Jarlshof.[13] One has a rectangular pattern divided into nine smaller rectangles, each with a diagonal line through it. The other has, on one side, a circular design just inside the rim, and on the other side a pattern that looks just like the wire device for holding plates so that they can be hung on a wall.

Excavations at the Broch of Burrian in 1870–1 produced two ox phalanges inscribed with Pictish symbols.[14] One has a crescent and V-rod on one side and a mirror case on the other. The other has a damaged design on one side which cannot be matched with any known Pictish symbol. The identification of these bones as gaming pieces is supported by excavations at a Cheardach Mhor on South Uist, where the abundance of such bones was contrasted with the relative scarcity of any other ox bones. The absence of such unmarked bones from the Broch of Burrian may simply be due to the selective nature of the collections. Objects made of bone (pins, needles, hair combs, weaving combs, spindle whorls) were recovered in considerable numbers during the excavations of the Broch of Burrian, but bones as such were not kept. Thus we can only guess that the ox phalanges with symbols on them must have been, like the inscribed sandstone discs at Jarlshof, special members of sets of similar but unmarked bones.

Decorated stone discs from Shetland.

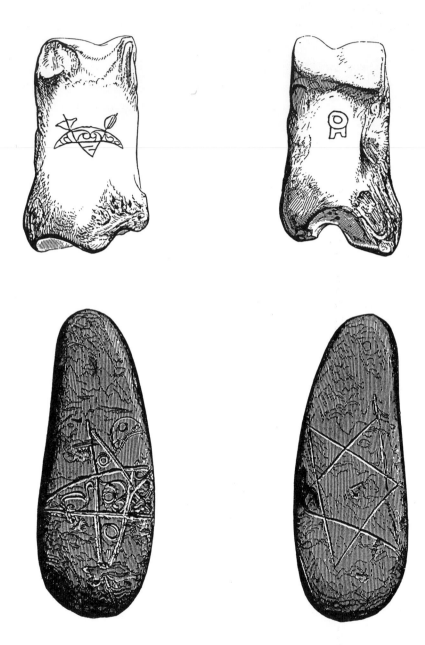

Broch of Burrian, Orkney: ox phalange with symbols and pebble with incised designs.
(After ECMS)

The best example of a gaming set of this sort comes from an Anglo-Saxon cemetery at Caistor-by-Norwich. One urn (N 59) contained a collection of gaming pieces.[15] One set consisted of thirty-six plano-convex counters, of which twenty-two were white (bone) and eleven black (probably shale). Another set consisted of at least thirty-six astragali (number uncertain due to fire damage), mostly of sheep and some of roe deer. Of these, one roe deer astragalus stood out from all the others by its larger size and a runic inscription on one side, the equivalent of the symbols and other designs on the Pictish gaming pieces. A single ox phalange similarly inscribed with runes was found in a Saxon context at Southampton.

In a board game known in Norse literature as *hnefatafl*, the king, a piece different in some way from all the others, starts at the centre of the board surrounded by defenders. The attackers, arrayed round the edge of the board, have to break through the defence and capture the king, while the defenders endeavour to bring him safely to the edge. Another board game in which one piece is different from all the others is fox and geese. In this game, the fox has to take the geese by jumping over them, while the geese try to surround the fox in such a way that he cannot move. The symbols, runes and other designs on the various gaming pieces are probably all the distinguishing features of the kings or foxes in some such games as *hnefatafl* or fox and geese.[16] The problem with *hnefatafl* is that the unornamented pieces have to be divided into recognizable teams and, apart from the plano-convex pieces from Urn N 59 at Caistor-by-Norwich, such a division has not been demonstrated.

The runic inscription on the roe deer astragalus has been read as *raihan*, but there seems to be no certainty about the exact meaning of *raihan* in the context of this astragalus. According to Dr R.L. Page,[17] who reported on the runes, *raiho* might mean painter or runemaster, and from being an occupation might have become a name. Then *Raihan* might mean (the property) of *Raiho*. Or *raiho* might apply to the astragalus itself, rather than its owner, and might mean marker. Then *raihan* might mean a piece (acting as) a marker. Alternatively, *Raihan* might be some sort of distinguishing name for the king in a board game. A more remote possibility is that *raihan* might be a form of the word *raha*, meaning a roebuck. On general grounds the least likely of these possibilities is that the person who owned this particular roe deer astragalus was called Raiho. Whoever he was, he owned the complete set of astragali that were deposited in Urn N 59 along with his cremated bones. Why should just one of them be singled out to have his ownership inscribed upon it?

The runic inscription on the ox phalange from Southampton has been read as *catae*.[18] This could be a personal name *Cat*, which occurs as an element in the place-name Catwick and in the patronymic *Ranulphus cattessone*, or it could simply be the animal, a cat. This inscribed ox phalange was recovered from a rubbish pit and was an isolated find.

The runic inscriptions are not much help when it comes to the interpretation of the Pictish symbols and other designs. If the inscribed gaming pieces all relate to the same sort of game, the only thing that can be said with any certainty is that all the inscriptions are different. Indeed, if there is only one piece to be distinguished from all the others, whether it be a king or a fox, it matters very little precisely how that distinction is made. The name of the owner might be inscribed on the special piece, not so much a mark of ownership as a mark of distinction. Equally effective as distinguishing marks within a set of gaming pieces are the various non-symbol designs on the stone discs from Shetland.

CHAPTER 15

Constantine: the King without a Symbol

Constantine son of Fergus, who died in 820, was one of the greatest Pictish kings. By the time he died, he was not only King of the Picts, but had also been undisputed King of the Scots of Dalriada for nearly a decade. His long and successful reign invites comparison with that of his predecessor, the warrior King Oengus son of Fergus (a different Fergus), who died in 761.

Oengus came to the throne after a period of anarchy following the abdication of Nechtan son of Derile in 724. For four years he fought battle after battle until he had defeated all his rivals. Once he was secure on the Pictish throne, and with a battle-hardened army at his command, he turned his attention to the west. Across the mountains, along the western seaboard, lay the smaller kingdom of the Scots of Dalriada, a tempting target already weakened by years of inconclusive civil strife. After a few years of skirmishing, the attacks began in earnest in 734. Dungal, King of the Scots, was wounded and forced to take refuge in Ireland. Two years later Dungal returned to defend his kingdom but once again was defeated by Oengus. This time the Dalriadan fortress of Dunadd was captured and Dungal and his brother Feradech were taken prisoner. Oengus was unbeatable. He ruled over the kingdom of Dalriada by military strength, crushing rebellions and laying waste the land of those who opposed him. The Scots of Dalriada suffered his rule, but never really accepted it, and his name finds no place in the list of their kings.

Constantine began his career in a weakened and divided Pictish kingdom. He came to the throne sometime between 775 and 780, probably in the northern half of the kingdom, north of the Mounth. South of the Mounth, the Picts were ruled by a king known as Dubhtolargg or Black Talorgan. There were two contemporary Talorgans, both of whom became kings, Talorgan son of Drust and Talorgan son of Oengus. Talorgan son of Drust was probably Black Talorgan. One cannot help wondering if Talorgan son of Oengus was known as Red

Talorgan – like the much later Black Comyn and Red Comyn, and later still the Black Douglas and Red Douglas. When Black Talorgan died in 782, Constantine extended his kingdom southwards, apparently without opposition. However, he was still not king of the whole of the old Pictish kingdom. The south-western part, known as Fortrenn, had been in the hands of the Scots probably since the battle between Aed, King of the Scots, and Kenneth (Ciniod, Kinet), King of the Picts in 768. In 789 Constantine fought the only recorded battle of his career and defeated Connall son of Taidg. This was recorded by the Irish annalists as a battle among the Picts, but Connall was probably a Scottish king of a Pictish province.

From this point onwards any resemblance that may have existed between the careers of Constantine and Oengus came to an end. Oengus would surely have followed the victory over Connall with a punitive expedition into the heart of Dalriada. Constantine did nothing – at least nothing that attracted the attention of the media (the Irish annalists). Unlike Oengus, Constantine had a perfectly valid claim to the Scottish throne. His father Fergus had been King of the Scots before him. Why, we might wonder, did he wait twenty years to claim a throne that was his by right? The answer is a slightly unexpected one. Such a delay was standard practice. In a sample of ten Scottish kings between 673 and 820, the average interval between the death of a king and the accession of his son was twenty-three years. Direct succession from father to son was the rare exception rather than the rule.

In an age when kings often died young, either in battle or from natural causes, their heirs were often young children, quite unready for the demanding role of absolute monarch. The solution to this problem was to have, at any given time, a number of recognized candidates from among whom a new king could be chosen with a minimum of delay. The system was very similar to that operated by the Picts except that, where they selected their kings from the female royal line, the Scots chose theirs from the male royal line. As a result, it is much easier to study the genealogy of the Scottish kings and to follow the order of succession.

Constantine must have been one of the candidates for the Scottish throne from the time of his father's death in 781, twenty-eight years before he eventually became King of the Scots. Four other kings were chosen before him: Eochaid, Domnall, Connall son of Taidg and Connall son of Aed. It is impossible at this distance in time even to guess what qualities these four might have possessed to put them ahead of Constantine. It is less difficult, however, to appreciate that Constantine's CV gave him one great disadvantage as a candidate for the Scottish throne. By the time his father died, he was already a king over at least some of the Picts and as time went on he became king of all the provinces of the Picts. The Scots had no wish to be ruled by another Pictish king, even if his father had been Scottish and had been their own king. Memories were not that short and when Constantine's father died, Oengus, the Pictish king who had conquered Dalriada and subjugated the Scottish people, had been dead for less than twenty years. This was the problem Constantine had to overcome before he could be accepted by the Scots of Dalriada.

One of the more unusual of Constantine's attributes was his name. The parents of possible future Pictish kings were very conservative in their choice of names, determined that their little kings-to-be should be equipped with names to match the role they might one day take on. Drust, Brude and Talorgan, the names of ancient heroes and kings, were popular choices and between them accounted for half the total. A list of forty-seven kings, from Drust son of Erp in the fourth century to Kenneth mac Alpin in the ninth, yields only fifteen names for the kings themselves, including Drust (10), Brude (7), Talorgan (7), Gartnait (4), Kenneth (4) and Nechtan (3). The twenty-nine known fathers of these forty-seven kings (some fathers not known, others fathered several kings) provide us with twenty-six different names, of which only three occur more than once and only four appear in the list of the kings' names. So strong was the tendency to use traditional king-names for sons of the female royal line that the kings provide us with a heavily biased sample of Pictish names. Their fathers, on the other hand, very few of whom had been kings or even potential kings, give us a totally different and presumably more random sample of Pictish names.

An interesting sample of Pictish names from outside the king lists is provided by the thirteen noble Picts who were present when King Oengus son of Fergus (Oengus II, the younger brother of Constantine, see Chapter 16) founded his Church of St Andrews,[1] the predecessor of the great medieval cathedral. The first four of these witnesses, arguably the most important of them, were Talorgan (Thalarg) son of Ythernbuthib, Nechtan (Nactan) son of Chelturan, Gartnait (Garnach) son of Dosnach and Drust (Drusti) son of Wthrosst, all names which would have looked quite at home in the king lists. They were not kings and never became kings, but it is quite possible that they were born of the female royal line and were given king-names, just in case! The rest of the names, like the fathers' names of the first four, are a seemingly random sample of Pictish names.

The choice of Constantine as the name for a possible future King of the Picts was a break with long-standing tradition. Not only was it not one of the relatively small number of traditional king-names, it was not even Pictish. With a son who might one day become either King of the Scots or King of the Picts, his parents decided on a name which could not be seen either as a Pictish threat to the Scots or a Scottish threat to the Picts, but might just perhaps be acceptable to both. The name of a great Roman emperor, who had died some four hundred years earlier, was in a sense an international name – and it was an international destiny that his parents planned for the young Constantine, half Pictish and half Scottish.

Constantine, a name never before given to a Pictish boy, naturally had no symbol associated with it. The Pictish symbols were uniquely Pictish and a measure of their importance is the fact that their use on memorial stones survived the arrival of Christianity from Ireland in the sixth century and the conversion to Rome, via Northumbria, in the eighth. What was to be done about a symbol for Constantine? One simple answer would have been to create a new design – the equivalent of a new grant of arms from the Lord Lyon King of Arms in Edinburgh or the College of Arms in London. The other solution would be to complete the break with tradition and abandon the use of symbols altogether.

The cross that was erected as a memorial to Constantine – the Dupplin Cross – serves to illustrate the extent of his departure from Pictish tradition. It differs from earlier Pictish crosses in two important respects: first, it is a free-standing cross and not a cross slab, and secondly, there are no symbols on it. The ornament on the shaft of the cross is divided up into a number of panels. On the east face,

Dupplin cross. (Photo: Tom Gray)

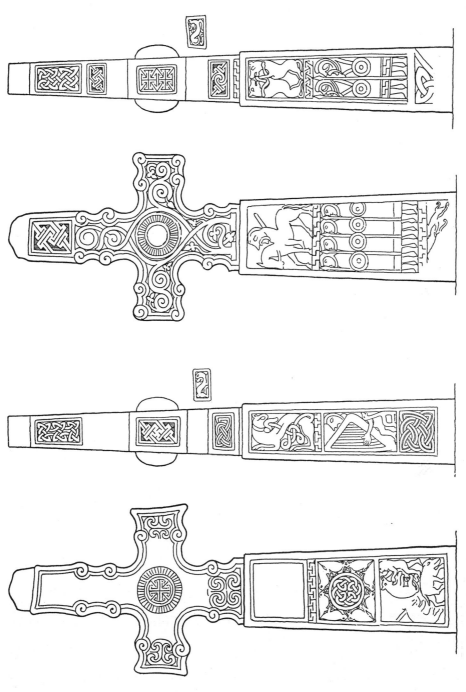

Dupplin cross: detail of sculpture. Note David and the lion (bottom panel on front of shaft). Note also the moustaches and shields on the two soldiers on the right side of the shaft. The recently discovered inscription occupies the 'blank' panel on the front of the cross shaft. (After ECMS)

Dupplin cross inscription. Compare with the inscription on St Vigeans 1 (Drosten stone). (Photo: National Museums of Scotland)

the upper panel contains an equestrian portrait of the king. Below him is a panel containing four foot soldiers with spears and round shields, and below them is a panel with what remains of a hunting scene, with a hound leaping on to a fleeing animal. On the opposite face, the upper panel had for years appeared completely devoid of ornament until in 1991 a fibre-glass replica of the cross was made for an exhibition in Edinburgh. The replica could now be examined in a way that had never been possible with the original. Feeling her way across the blank panel and marking any slight indentations with chalk, Dr Katherine Forsyth was able to read the beginning of what had been a seven-line inscription:[2]

C U [S T A] N T I N
F I L I U S F I R C U
S . . . .

Constantine son of Fergus. It would be interesting to know what the rest of the inscription said but, as with the Drosten stone, we have enough to identify the king for whom the memorial was set up.

By playing down the most blatant attributes of Pictish nationalism, Constantine King of the Picts became King of the Scots of Dalriada – king by right of descent and not king by right of conquest. But in keeping with his international aspirations, he did not style himself King of the Picts or King of the Scots, but King of Fortrenn, one of the original seven provinces of the Picts. Fortrenn, extending from Perth and Abernethy westwards along Strath Earn to Crieff and Auchterarder, then along Strath Allan to Dunblane and into Menteith, between Callander, Stirling and Aberfoyle, reaches almost into Dalriada. Since the death of Oengus son of Fergus in 761, Fortrenn had been disputed territory. Aed, King of the Scots, and Kenneth, King of the Picts, had fought there in 768, and it may well have been the site of the battle in which Constantine defeated Connall son of Taidg in 789. In calling himself King of Fortrenn, Constantine was implying that he was not just king of one old Pictish province, but rather the king of the middle ground between the Picts and the Scots.

Constantine was succeeded by his brother Oengus. Both brothers founded churches which were to become great medieval cathedrals, Constantine at Dunkeld and Oengus at St Andrews. Oengus is said to have marked out the land granted for his new church by erecting twelve stone crosses and to this day, St Andrews Cathedral has one of the largest collections of early Christian sculptured stones in the country. Unlike comparable collections elsewhere in eastern Scotland (Meigle, St Vigeans), St Andrews is notable for the complete absence of symbol stones. In part this may be related to the general scarcity of symbol stones in Fife. It may also, however, be an indication that Oengus was following his brother's policy of discouraging such displays of Pictish nationalism.

Oengus son of Fergus died in 834 and for a few years the union of the two kingdoms fell apart. Aed son of Boanta became king in the west with Scottish support. In the east Drust son of Constantine and Talorgan son of Wthoil ruled (in the word of the *Pictish Chronicle*) 'together'. This is unlikely to mean that they were joint rulers and probably means that they ruled apart, in the geographical sense, but simultaneously – quite possibly one north of the Mounth and the other south of that mountain barrier. This period of divided rule came to an end when Eogan son of Oengus was accepted as king by both sides. All would then have been well but for a disastrous battle in 839 in which the Vikings defeated 'the men of Fortrenn' and killed their king, Eogan son of Oengus, as well as Aed son of Boanta, Bran son of Oengus, and many others.

The period which followed this battle saw Kenneth mac Alpin rise from obscurity to become the undisputed ruler of the whole of Constantine's united kingdom of the Picts and Scots. The sources are generally agreed that Kenneth's reign over the Picts lasted for sixteen years and the *Annals of Ulster* record his death in 858. A chronicle of the lives of Kenneth mac Alpin and his successors contains useful supplementary information. A copy of this chronicle, the source of the only surviving version, was made towards the end of the tenth century for the new church at Brechin, whose round tower adjoining the medieval cathedral still stands today. The original chronicle was written further to the west, possibly at Dunkeld, possibly at Abernethy. Just how close this chronicle was to its subject is revealed by its account of the death of Kenneth mac Alpin: 'He died at last from a swelling of the anus, the Ides of February on the third day of the week [probably Tuesday the 9th of February 858] in the palace of Forteviot.'[3] This reads like an eye-witness account, with the expression of relief that he had died 'at last' after his painful illness. It might have been written or perhaps dictated by the priest who attended him at the end.

This chronicle tells us that Kenneth mac Alpin ruled over the kingdom of Dalriada for two years before coming to Pictavia. The seventh year of his reign was particularly eventful. He transported the relics of Saint Columba to the church he had built (presumably the church where the chronicle was written) and then invaded *Saxonia* (southern Scotland) six times, burning Dunbar and taking Melrose. Later on the Danes wasted Pictavia as far as Cluny and Dunkeld. Notable for its absence is any mention of his dealings with the Picts.

The career of Kenneth mac Alpin is important, not only for the general history of Scotland, but also for the study of Pictish symbol stones. To some extent the converse is also true, that the study of symbol stones can throw some light on the history of the period. Symbol stones at this time may be taken as an indication of a narrow Pictish nationalism, in contrast to the broader Picto-Scottish internationalism of Constantine and indeed of Kenneth mac Alpin himself.

The chronology of the period between the battle of 839 and Kenneth's death in 858 can be set out in a series of columns derived from the various sources. The length of Kenneth's reign, as shown in these columns, ranges from sixteen years in the *Brechin Chronicle* through fourteen in the group A version of the *Pictish Chronicle*, to only eight years in the group B version. The explanation of these differences must be that the beginning of his reign was dated from the moment he first became king of some part of Pictavia.

The administration of a kingdom divided by mountain barriers can never have been easy and whenever the old Pictish monarchy was weakened the kingdom tended to split into two parts, north and south of the Mounth. After the defeat of 839 the situation was more complex and the combined Picto-Scottish kingdom suffered a three-way split. Kenneth mac Alpin acquired the Scottish kingdom of

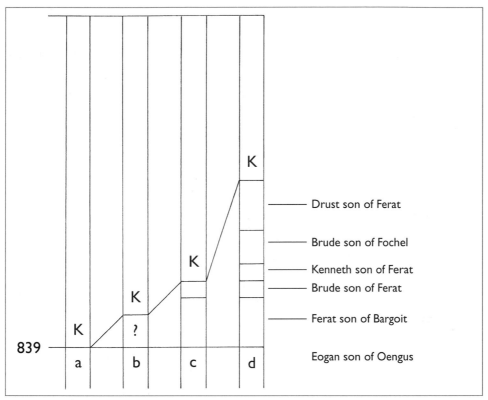

Chronological columns showing the rise to power of Kenneth mac Alpin (from left to right): (a) Scottish kingdom of Dalriada, (b) Northern Picts, (c) Southern Picts (western part, including Abernethy), (d) Southern Picts (eastern part, St Vigeans, Meigle and St Andrews).

Dalriada and Ferat son of Bargoit became king of the southern Picts. What happened north of the Mounth we do not know, because of the unfortunate lack of surviving chronicles or king lists originating in that area.

Ferat son of Bargoit reigned for three years and was succeeded by his son Brude, who was succeeded after only one year by Kenneth mac Alpin. That is the sequence according to the Group A versions of the *Pictish Chronicle*, probably written at Abernethy. According to the group B versions of the king lists, possibly written at St Andrews, Brude son of Ferat was followed by three other kings (Kenneth son of Ferat, Brude son of Fochel and Drust son of Ferat) who reigned for a total of six years. Symbol stones commemorating two of these kings (Kenneth and Drust, sons of Ferat) have been identified at Meigle and St Vigeans (see Chapters 7 and 10). It is possible that Kenneth mac Alpin started his Pictish career north of the Mounth, following some unknown king of that area who had reigned for only two years. Then he moved through Fortrenn as far east as Abernethy and finally, after conquering much of southern Scotland, gained control of the rest of southern Pictavia. As with his great predecessor Constantine, there is little evidence to show how much of his progress was military and how much the result of waiting patiently for the right opening.

The symbol stones for Kenneth son of Ferat at Meigle and Drust son of Ferat at St Vigeans may be an indication that these kings were making a nationalist stand against the advance of the Picto-Scottish union. If this is so, their narrow nationalism may have been partly responsible for the view that Kenneth mac Alpin was, by contrast, a Scottish conqueror. The decline of Pictish nationalism, begun under Constantine son of Fergus, reached its climax under Kenneth mac Alpin. It seems likely that this period also saw the end of the great Pictish tradition of erecting symbol stones as memorials to their dead. We can investigate this possibility by looking at a selection of the so-called Class III stones, originally defined by Allen and Anderson as 'all monuments having Celtic ornament sculptured in relief, which are not included in Class II'. Inevitably this Class III contained a wide variety of sculptured stones whose only common feature was the absence of symbols. Many of the Class III fragments may perfectly well be pieces of Class II symbol stones which by chance do not have any symbols on them. There are, however, some complete Class III cross slabs which differ from Class II symbol stones only in the absence of symbols. There are indications that two of these Class III cross slabs are more or less contemporary with the Dupplin cross.

The first of these, at Benvie, about 5 miles west of Dundee, has two panels on the back, each occupied by a horseman armed with spear, sword and shield. Equestrian portraits are common enough on Class II stones, but these two Class III portraits are different. They have highly distinctive long curved moustaches, and their shields, represented by three concentric circles, are slung over their shoulders on straps. Identical moustaches and shields are seen on two foot soldiers in a panel on the side of the Dupplin cross shaft. Whether the moustaches and shield straps were new fashions at the time, or whether they are the distinctive products of an individual artist, we cannot tell, but there can be little doubt about their contemporaneity.

The second Class III stone, at Aldbar near Brechin, has a representation of David and the lion just above the equestrian portrait of the deceased. David and the lion are drawn in profile, facing each other, with David wrenching the lion's jaws apart. The lion, lifted clean off the ground, has its tail curled between its hind legs and is pushing against David with all four paws. The only difference between this and the equivalent scene in the lowest panel on the front of the Dupplin cross

Benvie: back. Note the moustaches and shields on the two equestrian figures. Compare with the Dupplin Cross. (After ECMS)

shaft is that at Aldbar David is wearing a tunic, whereas at Dupplin he has not been provided with clothing. The close relationship between Aldbar and Dupplin is accentuated by the totally different and far more realistic treatment of the same subject on the front panel of the St Andrews sarcophagus. Once again, it seems reasonable to conclude that the Aldbar cross slab is broadly contemporary with the Dupplin cross. It seems that members of the Pictish aristocracy, with the resources to erect symbol stones, were falling into line with Constantine and dispensing with the symbols of their Pictish heritage.

Perhaps even more interesting than the Aldbar and Benvie stones is the great cross slab that stands in the centre of the little museum at Meigle. Meigle 2 has a remarkable ringed cross on the front, its centre marked by a circular boss surrounded by eight smaller bosses, and with twenty-four smaller bosses arranged symmetrically on the ring and the arms of the cross. The top of this stone is curved to follow the outline of the ring surrounding the cross. This stone was classified as a Class II symbol stone by Allen and Anderson[4] but has been removed

*Aldbar: back. Note
David and the lion (left,
just above middle).
Compare with the
Dupplin Cross and the
St Andrews sarcophagus.
(Photo: Tom Gray)*

Meigle 2: back. Note the three horsemen riding abreast (below and to the left of the top horseman) and compare with Hilton of Cadboll. Note also Daniel in the lion's den (middle) and the centaur carrying a branch (near bottom) – compare with Aberlemno 3. (Photo: Royal Commission on Ancient and Historical Monuments of Scotland)

from that class by subsequent writers. The centaur, its only symbol, is no longer recognized as a Pictish symbol. However, the centaur, brandishing two axes and dragging a branch along, is not without interest. It occurs on one other stone, the Aberlemno roadside cross. The branch being carried by the Aberlemno centaur is treated in a much more stylized manner but the concept is the same. Above the centaur on Meigle 2 is a picture of Daniel in the lions' den, a subject treated in a similar style on a Class III stone at Dunkeld. At the top of the stone, above Daniel and the lions, is a group of horsemen. A single horseman, probably a portrait of the deceased, is riding after two hounds in the uppermost curved part of the stone. Beneath him are four more horsemen, a group of three riding side by side and one following on behind. The group of three is particularly interesting. The nearest of the three is shown in full, while the others are indicated by outlines of the head, neck, breast and legs of the horses, shown slightly ahead and in lower relief. This very effective device for showing riders alongside one another is also used on the Hilton of Cadboll stone. This tends to confirm the link between Meigle 2 and Aberlemno 3, because Hilton of Cadboll and Aberlemno 3 are already linked by the artist's signature of two robed trumpeters (see Chapter 11).

Here we have a correlation between four stones, two of Class II (Aberlemno 3 and Hilton of Cadboll) and two of Class III (Meigle 2 and Dunkeld 2). Perhaps these four stones spanned the period during which the use of Pictish symbols was beginning to be discouraged. A Class III stone without a symbol, or more usually a pair of symbols, is like a tombstone without a name on it. It soon loses its identity and after well over a thousand years there seems little hope of recovering that identity. But Meigle 2 is an exceptional monument and was clearly erected for someone of considerable importance – a king perhaps.

Meigle 2 has links with another stone, now lost for over a century, Meigle 10. The dimensions of this stone, which was illustrated several times before it was lost,[5] suggest that it may have been the front panel of a sarcophagus like that at St Andrews. The left-hand side of this panel is largely occupied by a covered cart drawn by a pair of horses. One man is sitting outside driving the cart and he has two passengers inside, under cover. The two horses pulling the cart are shown side by side, using exactly the same device as on the Hilton of Cadboll stone and on Meigle 2. There is more action elsewhere on the stone, but the important detail, from our point of view, is a little man below the cart, down on one knee, aiming his bow at one of the animals to the right. This is the artist's signature found on the Drosten stone, which should be dated to about 848. Indirectly therefore, the Drosten stone gives an approximate date to Meigle 10 and, rather

Meigle 10: probable sarcophagus panel. Note the two horses pulling the carriage and compare with Hilton of Cadboll and Meigle 2. Note also the archer (below carriage) and compare with St Vigeans 1, Glenferness and Shandwick. (After ECMS)

less exactly to Meigle 2. Do we know enough about any Pictish king of this period to connect him with Meigle and, in the absence of symbols, with this particular stone at Meigle?

There is just one Pictish king who has a documented connection with Meigle. Ferat son of Bargoit commissioned Thana son of Dudabrach at Meigle to write an account of that great day when the relics of St Andrew were brought to Kilrymont and the new church of St Andrew was founded there. This account[6] was preserved in the registry of St Andrews. Added to this, Ferat's son Kenneth is commemorated by a Class II symbol stone at Meigle. Finally, there are the three horsemen riding side by side on Meigle 2. Ferat son of Bargoit, who died in 842, had three sons, Brude, Kenneth and Drust, who all became kings after him. For a stone without symbols and without an inscription, that is about as near as we can ever hope to come to an identification.

From the middle of the ninth century onwards, Pictish symbols ceased to be used. Their meaning was soon forgotten and within a century or two the language of the people who used them followed them into obscurity. The Picts themselves became almost a forgotten people.

CHAPTER 16

Shifting Centres of Power

Katherine Forsyth in her recent discussion of the Pictish symbol problem has warned against treating the symbols 'as a glorified crossword puzzle, the solution of which is an end in itself'. Our concern must be, she says, 'to understand the symbol-stones not for themselves but for what they tell us about Pictish society'.[1] The concern has been there throughout this book and only time will tell whether it has borne fruit. Now that the investigation is drawing to a close, what can be said of these extraordinary Dark Age monuments? The texts are so brief that they tell us nothing whatever about the Pictish language, and the sources for their analysis are so slight that some of the interpretations are much less well-founded that we might wish. Perhaps the chief result of the analysis presented in the previous chapters is that many of the symbol stones have become historical documents in a way that would have been inconceivable before. They have acquired names and dates as well as geographical locations. The importance of dates has recently been stressed by Isabel Henderson. 'From now on', she says, 'no discussion of the date of any Pictish relief sculpture can be without reference to the monument now recognized as having a fixed date, the Dupplin Cross.'[2] In whole-hearted agreement with this sentiment, I venture to suggest that we now have at least ten such directly dated monuments and many more that have acquired slightly less precise dating by association with these ten.

Starting at the early end of the series, we have identified three kings with Class I symbol stones: Drust son of Erp, who died about 478; Nechtan son of Erip, who died about 506; and Brude son of Derile, who died in 706. The historicity of Drust son of Erp and Nechtan son of Erip, has been discussed elsewhere.[3] Assuming that the identification of the symbols associated with the names of these kings and their fathers is correct, the question that needs to be considered is how far we can be sure that these particular symbol stones really belonged to these particular kings. It is a problem familiar to anyone who has tried to build up a family tree. Let us suppose you have found a record of the marriage of your ancestors John Smith and Anastasia Discobolus but the record gives no information as to their ages or their place of birth. In pursuing the matter further, you are fortunate enough to find a baptismal record for Anastasia daughter of Edward Discobolus in a neighbouring parish nineteen years earlier. You know you are on the right track. But what about poor John Smith? It is all a matter of probability.

The relative frequency of the various symbols on symbol stones is given in Chapter 3. The double disc and Z-rod (for Drust) is relatively common at 12.9 per cent, but the dog's head (for Erp) very rare at 0.2 per cent. Based on these figures, the probability of finding another stone with a double disc and Z-rod above a dog's head is about 1 in 7750. On the same basis, the probability of finding another stone with a fish above a tuning fork would be about 1 in 2700. When it comes to a crescent and V-rod (for Brude) above a serpent and Z-rod (for Derile), the chances of finding another are much better, at about 1 in 320. If the sample of Pictish names was better, we could carry out a similar exercise on the probability of duplicating the names of these particular kings. On the basis of these figures, it seems that we can be fairly confident about the identification of Class I memorial stones for Drust son of Erp and Nechtan son of Erip. As far as Brude son of Derile is concerned, supplementary evidence supporting the identification was discussed in Chapter 11.

The interesting thing about these three dated Class I memorials to kings is that they are all north of the Mounth. Drust son of Erp, in spite of the evidence linking him to military activity in southern Scotland, has a memorial stone at Rhynie, north-west of Aberdeen. Nechtan son of Erip, in spite of the evidence linking him with the first Christian mission to Tayside and the founding of the church at Abernethy, has his memorial stone at Dunrobin, north of Inverness. Brude son of Derile, in spite of his younger brother Nechtan's interest in Northumbria, has his memorial stone at Brandsbutt near Inverurie, north-west of Aberdeen. Not only are these three Class I memorials to Pictish kings all north of the Mounth, but all are associated with notable concentrations of such stones. Such concentrations of Class I symbol stones are a feature of the country north of the Mounth and are virtually absent in the south. Indeed it is true to say that Class I stones are generally more abundant, both in absolute terms and per unit area, in the north than in the south.

The greater frequency of Class I symbol stones in northern Pictland may be due to a variety of factors. There may have been a greater population density in the north, or the use of such memorials may have started earlier (or ended later) in the north, or the symbol-using aristocracy may have been predominantly northern. The first of these suggestions is probably the least likely. The evidence of the three kings whose memorials we are considering suggests that the power base of the Pictish union, which became the Pictish kingdom, was situated north of the Mounth during this early period. We may also remember that when St Columba made his great journey to meet the Pictish King Brude son of Maelchon about 565, he travelled up the Great Glen to Brude's headquarters somewhere near Inverness, once again in northern Pictland.

Moving on to Class II symbol stones, we have identified the memorials to four kings and one king's brother: Nechtan son of Derile, who died in 732; Oengus son of Fergus, who died in 761; Talorgan his brother, who was killed in battle in 750; Kenneth son of Ferat, who died about 843; and Drust son of Ferat, who died (was killed) about 848. Unlike the Class I memorials discussed above, all five of these are south of the Mounth. Nechtan son of Derile and Kenneth son of Ferat have memorial stones at Meigle; Oengus son of Fergus at Aberlemno, Talorgan son of Fergus at Glamis, and Drust son of Ferat at St Vigeans. Like the Class I memorials to kings discussed above, these Class II memorials are associated with concentrations of such monuments, generally connected with early churches. Such concentrations are a feature of southern Pictland, particularly the country between the Tay Estuary and the Mounth. Quite apart from such concentrations, Class II symbol stones are generally more abundant in the south than in the north, even though some of the finest individual stones are northern.

The relative scarcity of Class II symbol stones over much of northern Pictland is partly related to the lack of suitable sandstone, as discussed in Chapter 13. But the concentration of memorials to kings south of the Mounth must surely represent a shift of the centre of power from the north to the south. This shift can be dated to the reign of Nechtan son of Derile and his decision to join the mainstream of European Christianity and turn the face of his kingdom to Rome via Northumbria.

There are Class III monuments which can be attributed to two kings: Constantine son of Fergus, who died in 820, and Ferat son of Bargoit, who died about 846. Constantine's well-known memorial is the Dupplin Cross. Constantine, who died earlier than Ferat, and indeed earlier than the two sons of Ferat whose Class II monuments are discussed above, was the innovator of these two. His monument at Dupplin breaks with Pictish tradition in several respects (see Chapter 15) and is situated south-west of Perth, a long way from the Class II stone concentration in Angus. This move is in keeping with Constantine's new role as King of Fortrenn, with the centre of gravity of his combined Picto-Scottish kingdom being in the low ground between Perth in the east and Aberfoyle in the west.

We now come to a break in the monumental record. There are no more symbol stones and no inscribed memorials to take their place. Where, for example, was Kenneth mac Alpin buried and where is his memorial? He died in his palace at Forteviot, not far from Dupplin, and may have had a similar memorial nearby. There are several fragments at Forteviot, of which Forteviot 1 and Forteviot 3 might be the base and one arm of a cross like the Dupplin Cross.

There is one remaining Pictish power centre to be considered and that is St Andrews. Here, there is a fine collection of Class III sculptured stones but not a single Class II stone – not a single Pictish symbol. This is in complete contrast

St Andrews sarcophagus: the surviving panels assembled. (Photo: Historic Scotland)

to such centres as Meigle and St Vigeans, where Class II and Class III stones are found together. By far the most famous monument in the St Andrews collection is the sarcophagus, which was exhibited in London and Edinburgh in 1997, was the subject of a conference in Edinburgh in September 1997 and has since been published in a fine volume edited by Sally Foster and entitled *The St Andrews Sarcophagus: A Pictish Masterpiece and its International Connections*. The front panel of the sarcophagus is carved in high relief, in complete contrast to the usually rather flat relief of the Class II Pictish symbol stones. The principal figure in this dynamic scene is David wrenching open the jaws of the lion. This David is definitely the adult King David and not the boy shepherd of the biblical account. But who was the sarcophagus built for? The general consensus of opinion is that it was either for an eminent cleric or, perhaps more likely, a king. Before looking into the matter of the sarcophagus any further, it is necessary to look at the evidence for the foundation of the Church of St Andrew.

The building of the Church of St Andrew is mentioned in two copies of the group B *Pictish Chronicle*. In one it was attributed to Constantine son of Fergus and in the other to his brother Oengus. One of these two must be a scribal error – a slip of the pen from one line to the next. The matter is settled by the so-called *Legend of St Andrews*,[4] which confirms Oengus son of Fergus as the founder of the church. Unfortunately there were two kings of that name, the conqueror of the Scots of Dalriada, who died in 761, and the younger brother of Constantine, who died in 834.[5] In view of the general unreliability of the Group B *Pictish Chronicle*, some people have felt quite justified in assuming that the attribution was totally misplaced and should have referred to the earlier Oengus son of Fergus.

Tuathalan, Abbot of Cinnrigh Monai (Kinrymont, later Kilrymont and finally St Andrews), died in 747. The fact that his death was noticed by the Irish annalists has been taken to mean that the church of Kinrymont, so far removed from areas of Irish interest, was already a place of national, perhaps even international importance. Such an interpretation would lend some support to its foundation by the earlier Oengus. On the other hand, no other abbots are mentioned by the annalists, from which we might infer that it was Tuathalan himself who was well known to the Irish, rather than his church. Tuathalan's obituary notice tells us that there was a church at Kinrymont in 747, but not that it was the church founded by Oengus son of Fergus.

Confirmation that the later Oengus son of Fergus was indeed the founder of the Church of St Andrew at Kinrymont comes from the *Legend of St Andrews*, which itself is a mixture of legend and contemporary record. The earlier part of this document is said to have been copied from the ancient books of the Picts (*Haec ut praefati sumus, sicut in veteribus Pictorum libris scripta reperimus, transcripsimus*). Immediately before this statement about the copying is another to the effect that Thana son of Dudabrach wrote this record for King Ferat son of Bargoit at Meigle (*Thana filius Dudabrach hoc monumentum scripsit Regi Pherath filio Bergeth in villa Migdele*). The important distinction between these two statements is that Thana wrote (*scripsit*), whereas 'we' copied (*transcripsimus*).[6] What Thana wrote, which seems to have been an eye-witness account of the events at Kinrymont, was only a part of what was later copied, but from the historical point of view it was the most important part. The second Oengus son of Fergus died in 834, only five years before Ferat son of Bargoit came to the throne. Thana, writing for Ferat son of Bargoit, could easily have been at Kinrymont for the foundation ceremony. But why should Ferat have gone to Meigle for an account of his predecessor's foundation of a church at Kinrymont – an account which finished up in the library of the Cathedral at St Andrews? The most probable answer is that Meigle was an established, probably royal, church with a well-equipped scriptorium and a good scholastic tradition, whereas Kinrymont, though equally royal, was still in its infancy, with none of these advantages.

Returning now to the sarcophagus itself, one notable feature of the recent studies has been a marked reluctance to give it a date. Thomas, in a paper on form and function, thought it 'hard to imagine many objections to a bracket of *c.* 750–850'.[7] Henderson, pointing out the numerous stylistic differences between the sarcophagus and the Dupplin Cross, dated to 820, suggests that there could easily be as much as a generation between them and concludes that 'the date of the sarcophagus is on balance likely to fall in the second half of the eighth century'.[8]

It is not immediately apparent why the sarcophagus could not equally well be a generation later than the Dupplin cross, which would give it a date in the middle of the ninth century. The dated Class II symbol stones listed earlier in this chapter have an immediate relevance to the problem. Meigle 1 (Nechtan son of Derile, d. 732), Glamis 2 (Talorgan son of Fergus, d. 750), Aberlemno 2 (Oengus son of Fergus, d. 761), Meigle 6 (Kenneth son of Ferat, d. 843) and St Vigeans 1 (Drust son of Ferat, d. 848), with dates extending across more than a hundred years, are all characterized by rather flat relief figures. It is difficult to see any reason for placing the sarcophagus anywhere in this sequence. The dating of these symbol stones, whose sculptural technique differs so markedly from that of the sarcophagus, demonstrates very clearly that it must be later than the middle of the ninth century. The problem now is to find examples of sculptural work which can be more closely compared with the sarcophagus.

Breedon-on-the-Hill, Leicestershire: carving of an angel. Compare with David on the St Andrews sarcophagus. (Photo: Stephen J. Plunkett)

A sculptured stone fragment from Kinneddar near Elgin, possibly from a sarcophagus panel, shows a lion with its jaws being wrenched open. Its similarities to the same part of the St Andrews scene are so close at to 'suggest strongly that the Kinneddar fragment is contemporary with the sarcophagus'.[9] Unfortunately, this does not help to date either; it simply means that whatever date you give to the one is automatically carried over to the other. A possibly more interesting comparison is with the carving of an angel framed in an archway at Breedon-on-the-Hill, Leicestershire, in far-away Mercia. The beautiful calm of the angel is a far remove from the raw strength of David grappling with the lion, but the two figures do show a remarkable similarity of posture and treatment. A tenth-century date has been proposed for the Breedon angel but this has not been generally accepted, a date in the late eighth or early ninth seeming to be more popular.[10] Once again, the dating of comparable sculpture is not sufficiently reliable to give a firm date to the sarcophagus.

Two basic questions remain to be answered. First, who in the second half of the ninth century (or later) was of sufficient importance, wealth or influence to have had such a monument made for him? Secondly, when was direct cultural contact likely to have extended beyond Northumbria as far as Mercia? The second half of the ninth century, in Scotland and England, was dominated by the Danish invasions. Kenneth mac Alpin and the Picto-Scottish kings who followed him managed to retain most of the old Pictish kingdom with the exception of Shetland, Orkney and Caithness. The English kings were less fortunate, particularly in the east, and from the Scottish point of view, the most significant effect was the break-up of the old Northumbrian kingdom. From the English point of view, the most significant change was the rise of Wessex.[11] This began with Alfred's effective resistance against the Danes, particularly at the battle of Edington in Wiltshire in 878. Alfred's progress was continued by his son Edward (899–924) and his grandson Athelstan (924–940). In Scotland, the first half of the tenth century was dominated by one king, Constantine son of Aed and grandson of Kenneth mac Alpin. During his long reign (900–943), he was one of the four most powerful people in Britain. The others were the kings of England (Wessex), the kings of the Strathclyde Britons and the Danish kings of York and Dublin. Constantine signed a treaty with Edward of England at Bakewell in Derbyshire in 920 and another with Athelstan at Eamont near Penrith in 927. His neighbours, the Kings of England, ruled the whole country as far south as the English Channel. Never before had the cultural contacts of the Picts or Scots extended so far.

Constantine son of Aed would seem to be the ideal choice as owner and occupant of the St Andrews sarcophagus. To add to his general suitability as a great king with wide political and cultural contacts, he abdicated in 943 and retired to St Andrews (Kinrymont), where he ended his days as a monk and is even said to have been abbot for five years. He died in 952. To suggest that the sarcophagus was made for Constantine son of Aed may worry some Pictophiles. Constantine son of Aed is known as Constantine II of a Scottish dynasty beginning with the reign of Kenneth mac Alpin (Kenneth had an elder son who became Constantine I). In answer to this I can do no better than quote from *The Age of the Picts*. Constantine son of Aed 'was son of the last recorded King of the Picts, and was himself known as King of Alban by the Irish and as King of the Scots by the English. If anyone deserved the title of first King of the Scots, that person was surely Constantine son of Aed. Earlier kings, Constantine's grandfather Kenneth mac Alpin included, were only known as Kings of the Scots retrospectively. With Constantine's long life, the age of the Picts came to an end and the age of the Scots began.'[12] We might indeed suggest with some justification that the age of the Picts ended in the St Andrews sarcophagus in 952!

Expanded Symbol List

This list includes the possible additional symbols mentioned in Chapter 3 as well as some extra symbols not yet found on symbol stones. Suggested interpretations are given where possible. Chapter references are given for the interpretations and for the occurrence of symbols not listed or mentioned in Chapter 3.

Pair-forming symbols		Name	Chapter
1	Crescent and V-rod	Brude	8
2	Double disc and Z-rod	Drust	7
3	Pictish elephant	Edern	6
4	Double disc	Kenneth	10
5	Notched double disc		
6	Horseshoe		
7	Arch		
8	Mirror case		
9	Notched mirror case		
10	Fish	Nechtan	6
11	Rectangle		
12	Vertical rectangle		14
13	Eagle	Dunodnat	6
14	Raven		
15	Serpent and Z-rod	Derile	10
16	Serpent and straight rod		
17	Triple disc	Fergus	9
18	Divided rectangle and Z-rod	Oengus	9
19	Serpent		
20	Extended serpent		
21	Tuning fork	Erip	11
22	Flower		
23	Disc		
24	Crescent	Ferat	10
25	Notched crescent		
26	Divided rectangle		
27	Step		
28	Step with handles		
29	L-shaped figure		
30	Deer's head	Talorgan	10
31	Triple oval		

32	Ogee	Gartnait	8
33	Fish monster	The Briton	11
34	Extended fish monster		
35	Double crescent		
36	Goose facing backwards		
37	Goose facing forwards		
38	Boar		
39	Beast		
40	Twin discs		
41	Helmet		
42	Stag		
43	Wolf		
44	Horse		
45	Bull's head		
46	Dog's head	Erp	8
47	Square		
48	Arch and 'V-rod'		
49	Twin triangles		8
50	Crescent on triangle		14

Supplementary symbols

51, 52	Mirror and comb	RIP, etc.	12
53, 54, 55	Hammer, anvil, tongs	Manufacture, etc.	11
56	Crosier	Priest, Bishop	11

APPENDIX 2

Bilingual Ogham–Latin Inscriptions in Wales

The numbers are those given to the monuments in Nash-Williams, *Early Christian Monuments of Wales* (University of Wales Press, 1950)

43 TURPIL[LI MAQI(?) TRIL]LUNI
   TVRPILLI (h)IC IACIT PVVERI TRILVNI DVNOCATI

70 CVNACENNIVI ILVVETO
   CVNOCENNI FILIV[S] CVNOGENI HIC IACET

71 MAQUTRENI SALICIDUNI
   [M]ACCVTRENI SALICIDVNI

84 ICORIGAS
   ICORI(x) FILIVS POTENTINI

127 TRENACCATLO
   TRENACATVS (h)IC IACIT FILIUS MAGLAGNI

138 VOTECORIGAS
   MEMORIA VOTEPORIGIS PROTICTORIS

142 INIGENA CUNIGNI AUITTORIGES
   AVITORIA FILIA CVNIGNI

150 DUMELEDONAS MAQI M[UCOI]
   BARRIVEND- FILIVS VENDVBARI HIC IACIT

160 DECCAIBAR VUGLOB DISI
   DE[CAB]ARBALOM FI[L]IVS BROCAGN

169 BIVVA[IDONA(s)] AVVI BODDIB[EVVA(s)]
   BIVAD- FILI BODIBEV-

176 S[I]B[I]L[I]N[I] [TO]VISACI
   SIMILINI TOVISACI

198 POPIA[S] ROL[IO]N M[AQ]I LL[E]NA
   PVMPEIVS CARANTORIVS

298 VENDOGNI
   VENDAGNI FILI V[ ]NI

301 MAGL[IA(?)] DUBR[ACUNAS (?) MAQI]INB
   ET SINGNO CRUCIS IN ILLAM FINGSI ROGO OMNIBUS AMMULANTIBUS IBI EXORENT
   PRO ANIME CATUOCONI

305 TRENAGUSU MAQI MAQITRENI
   TRENEGUSSI FILI MACUTRENI HIC IACIT

306 ETTERN[I MAQI VIC]TOR
   ETTERN-FILI VICTOR(is)

308   D[O]V[A]TUCEAS
       DOB[I]TVCI FILIUS EVOLENG[I]
312   DOVAGNI
       TIGERNACI DOBAGNI
313   [A]NDAGELLI MACU CAV[ETI(?)]
       ANDAGELL- IACIT FILI CAVET
353   MAGLICUNAS MAQI CLUTAR[I]
       MAGLOCVN(i) FILI CLVTOR-
354   VITALIANI
       VITALIANI EMERETO
384   SAGRAGNI MAQI CUNATAMI
       SAGRANI FILI CVNOTAMI
390   OGTENLO(?)
       HOGTIVIS FILI DEMETI
404   GENDILI
       GE[NDILI]

APPENDIX 3
Some Unsolved Symbols

In the preceding chapters, interpretations have been suggested for nearly half the symbols listed in Mack's *Field Guide to the Pictish Symbol Stones*. Of the ten most abundant pair-forming symbols, we have interpretations for seven; from the next ten, we have identifications for five; and from the remaining sixteen we have identifications for only two. This is just the sort of pattern we might expect, with fewer clues being available for the less abundant symbols. But what of the relatively abundant symbols that we have failed to interpret? The following table lists these in order of decreasing abundance, with the numbers on Class I and Class II stones indicated.

Symbol	Number	Class I	Class II
Arch	20	19	1
Mirror case	20	18	2
Rectangle	17	16	1
Serpent	9	7	2
Disc	8	8	0
Flower	8	4	4
Step	6	1	5
Divided rectangle	6	6	0

One reason why these symbols have not been interpreted so far is that nearly all of them occur predominantly on Class I stones, whereas most of our discussion has been concentrated on Class II stones. Class II stones contain a wealth of supplementary information, which has enabled us to identify the memorials to four Pictish kings and to work out three- or four-generation pedigrees for several Pictish families. Is there any possibility of extending this sort of investigation back into the period of the Class I stones?

Assuming that the Class I and Class II stones commemorate similar sections of the population, we should be able to form a rough idea of how many kings we might expect to find among the Class I stones. Four kings in a sample of sixty-one Class II stones is a ratio of 1 to 15. At this rate, we might expect to find memorials to eleven kings among the 165 Class I stones. Looked at another way, we might say that during the likely period of the Class II stones, roughly 711 to 848, we have memorials to four out of a possible twenty-one kings, that is a ratio of 1 to 5. In the possible period for the erection of Class I stones, maybe 450 to 711, we might therefore expect to have memorials to five out of the possible twenty-five kings. Taking these two estimates together, we might expect Class I memorials to eight kings, give or take a few. The question is: Would we be able to recognize them?

Assuming that all the symbol interpretations suggested in earlier chapters are correct, there are three Class I stones which provide name matches with kings of the appropriate period. These are Rhynie 5, with a double disc and Z-rod beside, but slightly higher than, a beast's head, for Drust son of Erp; Dunrobin 1, with a fish above a tuning fork, for Nechtan son of Erip; and Brandsbutt, with a crescent and V-rod above a serpent and Z-rod, for Brude son of Derile. The probability that these stones do indeed commemorate the kings whose names they match has been discussed in Chapter 16.

Any other possible kings among the Class I symbol stones must have one or both their symbols as yet unidentified. An examination of the list of kings for the appropriate period, from the middle of the fifth century to the beginning of the eighth, shows how we may reduce the number of potentially royal symbol stones to manageable proportions.

It will be noticed that none of the kings listed is a son of Brude or Drust or Nechtan, and the name Edern is not mentioned at all. Thus out of the 165 Class I stones, we can exclude all those with crescent and V-rod (Brude), double disc and Z-rod (Drust) or fish (Nechtan) in the lower position, and all those with the Pictish elephant (Edern) in either position. Taking these and a few other similar observations into account, we can reduce the list of possible royal Class I stones from 165 to 19. Some of these nineteen stones are likely to be royal memorials, but unfortunately we have no means of saying which.

The commonest symbol in this reduced list is the mirror case, with five examples in the lower position. The upper symbols on these five stones are the crescent and V-rod (two examples), the ogee, the triple oval and the goose. It would seem reasonable to start by equating the mirror case with either Girom or Wid, each the father of three successive kings, any one of whom might have left a surviving Class I memorial. The sons of Girom were Drust, Gartnait and Cailtran. There is no stone with a double disc and Z-rod (for Drust) above the mirror case. The ogee has already been associated with Gartnait (see Chapter 8), thus leaving the triple oval or the goose for Cailtran. The sons of Wid were Gartnait, Brude and Talorgan. Gartnait is represented by the ogee and Brude could be commemorated on one of the two stones with the crescent and V-rod. There is no stone with a deer's head (for Talorgan) above the mirror case. Since the mirror case is one of the symbols which might be subdivided, it is worth pointing out that on Kintradwell 1, the ogee is above a notched mirror case, whereas on both Inverurie 1 and Advie, the crescent and V-rod is above a mirror case without a notch. The case for identifying the mirror case, with or without a notch, with either Girom or Wid is far from convincing. After all, the mirror case might not represent either Girom or Wid. Then we could try to work it the other way round. There are four kings called Drust in this period, the sons of Girom, Wdrost, Munait and Donnel. The only symbol stone in our reduced list which could be identified with one of these is Congash 2, with a double disc and Z-rod above the unique helmet symbol. If this is a royal stone, the helmet could represent Girom, Wdrost, Munait or Donnel, but we have no means of telling which and no means of knowing whether Drust son of *Helmet* was indeed a king. It is frustrating to think that maybe four of these nineteen symbol stones relate to kings whose names we know and yet there seems to be no possible way of knowing which they are. There are just too many unknowns and not enough equations. The result is disappointing, but the attempt had to be made, just on the off-chance that something more definite might have emerged.

For the benefit of anyone tempted to tackle the problem, the relevant stones are listed below with their symbols. For further information, consult Alastair Mack's *Field Guide to the Pictish Symbol Stones*.

Class I Stone	Upper Symbol	Lower Symbol
Congash 2	Double disc and Z-rod	Helmet
Newton of Lewesk	Mirror case	Double crescent
Sandside	Triple oval	Mirror case
Kintradwell 1	Ogee	Mirror case
Rothiebrisbane	Horseshoe	Disc
Dun Osdale	Crescent and V-rod	Disc
Benbecula	Rectangle	Disc
Newbigging Leslie	Rectangle	Wolf
Grantown	Stag	Rectangle
Tillytarmont 1	Goose	Mirror case
Peterhead	Goose	Rectangle
Knocknagael	Mirror case	Boar

Glamis 1	Beast	Serpent
Craigmyle	Divided rectangle	Serpent
Clynekirkton 1	Crescent and V-rod	Rectangle
Sandness	Rectangle	Horseshoe
Crosskirk	Crescent and V-rod	Horseshoe
Inverurie 1	Crescent and V-rod	Mirror case
Advie	Crescent and V-rod	Mirror case

The kings of the relevant period, who might be matched with some of these symbol stones, are listed below. The list is based on the Group A version of the *Pictish Chronicle* and the spelling has been standardized. For some of these kings the name of the father is not known. The few symbol stones which have already been identified with kings of this period are indicated in the final column.

King	Son of	Date of Death	Symbol stone
Drust	Erp	478	Rhynie 5
Talorgan	Aniel	482	
Nechtan	Erip	506	Dunrobin 1
Drust	–	536	
Galanan	–	548	
Drust	Wdrost	553	
Drust	Girom	558	
Gartnait	Girom	565	
Cailtran	Girom	566	
Talorgan	Muirocholaich	577	
Drust	Munait	578	
Galam	–	580	
Brude	Maelchon	584	
Gartnait	Domnach	599	
Nechtan	–	615	
Kenneth	Lutrin	631	
Gartnait	Wid	635	
Brude	Wid	641	
Talorgan	Wid	653	
Talorgan	Enfret	657	
Gartnait	Donnel	663	
Drust	Donnel	672	
Brude	Bile	693	
Taran	Entifidich	697	
Brude	Derile	706	Brandsbutt

Notes

Chapter 1

1. Genesis 31: 45.
2. Joshua 15: 6 and 18: 17.
3. 1 Samuel 7: 12.
4. Joussaume, Roger, 1988, *Dolmens for the Dead: Megalith-Building throughout the World*, English trans., B.T. Batsford Ltd, p.250.
5. *Ibid*, p. 249.
6. Parts of two incised circles can be seen on the side facing the road, a larger one above and a smaller one below. The surface of the stone is badly scored by chisel marks, but it may have been a Class I symbol stone rather then a plain prehistoric standing stone.
7. Wainwright, F.T. (ed.), 1956, *The Problem of the Picts*, Thomas Nelson.
8. Chadwick, John, 1967, *The Decipherment of Linear B*, 2nd edn, Cambridge University Press.
9. Forsyth, Katherine, 1997, 'Some thoughts on Pictish Symbols as a Formal Writing System', in David Henry (ed.), *The Worm, the Germ and the Thorn*, Pinkfoot Press.
10. Budge, Sir E.A. Wallis, 1910, *Egyptian Language: Early Lessons in Egyptian Hieroglyphs with Sign List*, Routledge & Kegan Paul.

Chapter 2

1. Spearman, Michael, R. and John Higgitt (eds), 1993, *The Age of Migrating Ideas: Early Medieval Art in Northern Britain*, Alan Sutton Publishing Ltd.
2. Sherley-Price, L. (trans), *Bede, Ecclesiastical History of the English People*, Penguin, 1990, p. 45.
3. Cramp, Rosemary, 1984, *Corpus of Anglo-Saxon Stone Sculpture, Vol. 1, County Durham and Northumberland*, Oxford University Press, Monkwearmouth 8a–b, Plates 112–15; Kitzinger, Ernst, 1993, 'Interlace and Icons: Form and Function in Early Insular Art', pp. 3–15, in Spearman and Higgitt, *op. cit.*
4. Cramp, *op. cit.*, Monkwearmouth 9, 17, 18, 19, 21.
5. Cramp, *op. cit.*, Monkwearmouth 5, Jarrow 10, 11, 12, 16.
6. Kitzinger *op. cit.*
7. Foster, Sally M. (ed.), 1998, *The St Andrew's Sarcophagus*, Four Courts Press.
8. Gilbert, Inga, 1995, *The Symbolism of the Pictish Stones in Scotland: A Study of Origins*, Speedwell Books.
9. Laing, Lloyd and Laing, Jennifer, 1984, 'The Date and Origin of the Pictish Symbols', *Proceedings of the Society of Antiquaries of Scotland*, 114, 261–76.
10. Peterson, Edward, 1996, *The Message of Scotland's Symbol Stones*, PCD Ruthven Books, Aberuthven.

Chapter 3

1. Jackson, Anthony, 1984, *The Symbol Stones of Scotland: A Social Anthropological Resolution of the Problem of the Picts*, Orkney Press, p. 60.
2. There is one occurrence of a solitary Z-rod on the back of the head of a silver hand-pin from Norrie's Law (see Chapter 8) but the middle limb of the Z is missing. If it was ever intended as a Z-rod, with or without a double disc, it was never completed.

3. Fox-Davies, A.C., 1969, *A Complete Guide to Heraldry*, 2nd edn, Thomas Nelson and Sons Ltd.
4. Forsyth, *op. cit.*
5. Peterson, *op. cit.*
6. Thomas, Charles, 1963, 'The Interpretation of the Pictish Symbols', *Archaeological Journal*, 120, 31–97.
7. Laing and Laing, *op. cit.*
8. Peterson *op. cit.*, p. 88.
9. Fox, Sir Cyril, 1949, 'Celtic Mirror Handles in Britain', *Archaeologia Cambrensis*, vol. 100, pp. 24–44; Lloyd-Morgan, G., 1980, 'Roman Mirrors and Pictish Symbol: A Note on Trade and Contact', in W.S. Hanson and L.J.F. Keppie (eds), *Roman Frontier Studies*, BAR International Series, 71(i), pp. 97–106. Lloyd-Morgan's suggestion that the mirror case symbol (circular disc and rectangle with or without square indentation) might be a hinged or lid mirror in the closed position, while the double disc might be a similar mirror in the opened position, is belied by the bronze statuette from the Thames at London Bridge (Lloyd-Morgan, G., 1974, 'A Bronze Statuette from London Bridge', *Antiquaries Journal*, 54, 85–6), holding just such a mirror in his right hand, which indicates that the hinge between the two discs would be so close as to leave no room for the 'rectangle' of the Pictish symbols.
10. Foster, Sally M., 1990, 'Pins, Combs and the Chronology of Later Atlantic Iron Age Settlement', in Ian Armit (ed.), *Beyond the Brochs: Changing Perspectives on the Late Iron Age in Atlantic Scotland*, Edinburgh University Press. Some of the more elaborate comb symbols are unlikely to be exact representations of actual combs and simply reflect the Pictish artists' delight in adding little curly bits to their drawings!
11. Jackson, *op. cit.*, chap. 4, pp. 60–79.

Chapter 4

1. Allen, J. Romilly and Anderson, J. *The Early Christian Monuments of Scotland*, reprinted 1993, Pinkfoot Press, vol. 2, p. 125.
2. Jackson, *op. cit.*, p. 18.

Chapter 5

1. Skene W.F. (ed.), 1867, *Chronicles of the Picts, Chronicles of the Scots, and other Early Memorials of Scottish History*, HM General Register House, pp. 4–10, 24–30, 149–52, 172–6, 200–8, 285–90, 396–400.
2. *Annals of Tighernach* (extracts from), Skene, *op. cit.*, pp. 66–78; *Annals of Ulster* (extracts from), Skene, *op. cit.*, pp. 343–74.
3. Nash-Williams, V.E., 1950, *The Early Christian Monuments of Wales*, University of Wales Press.
4. Samson, Ross, 1992, 'The Reinterpretation of the Pictish Symbols', *Journal of the British Archaeological Association*, 145, 29–65.
5. Hall, Hubert (ed.), 1896, *Red Book of the Exchequer, Rerum Britanni Medii Aevi Scriptores*, vol. 99, Part 1, p. 3. Pedigree, in Latin, set out as continuous text.
6. Moor, Charles, *Knights of Edward I, The Publication of the Harleian Society*, vols 80–4, 1929–1932.
7. Samson, *op. cit.*

Chapter 6

1. Macalister, R.A.S., 1949, *The Archaeology of Ireland*, Methuen and Co. Ltd.
2. Nash-Williams, *op. cit.*
3. Jackson, *op. cit.*, p. 182, based on Padel, O.J., 1972, *Inscriptions of Pictland*, unpublished MLitt thesis, University of Edinburgh.
4. Stevenson, Robert B.K., 1959, 'The Inchyra Stone and some other Unpublished Early Christian Monuments', *Proceedings of the Society of Antiquaries of Scotland*, vol. 92, 33–55.
5. Williams, A.H., 1969, *An Introduction to the History of Wales*, University of Wales Press, vol. 1, p. 70.
6. Alcock, Leslie, 1971, *Arthur's Britain*, Allen Lane, pp. 128–9.
7. Yeoman, Peter, 1999, *Pilgrimage in Medieval Scotland*, Batsford, pp. 62–4.

Chapter 7

1. Clancey, O.C., 1993, 'The Drosten Stone: a new reading', *Proceedings of the Society of Antiquaries of Scotland*, vol. 123, pp. 345–53.

2. *Ibid.*
3. Sherley-Price, *op. cit.*, p. 148.
4. Skene, *op. cit.*, pp. 8–10.
5. Winterbottom, Michael, 1978, *Gildas: The Ruin of Britain and Other Works*, Phillimore.
6. Higham, N.J., 1994, *The English Conquest: Gildas and Britain in the Fifth Century*, Manchester University Press, chap. 5, pp. 118–45; O'Sullivan, Thomas D., 1978, *The 'De Excidio' of Gildas: Its Authentication and Date*, E.J. Brill, Leiden.
7. Winterbottom, *op. cit.*, p. 21.
8. Sherley-Price, *op. cit.*, p. 97.
9. Cummins, W.A., *The Age of the Picts*, Alan Sutton Publishing Ltd, chap. 4, pp. 22–6.

Chapter 8

1. Curle, A.O., 1920, 'Report of the Excavations on Traprain Law in the Summer of 1919', *Proceedings of the Society of Antiquaries of Scotland*, vol. 54, pp. 95–7.
2. Henderson, Isabel, 1979, 'The Silver Chain from Whitecleugh, Shieldholm, Crawfordjohn, Lanarkshire', *Transactions of the Dumfriesshire and Galloway Natural History and Antiquarian Society*, vol. 54, pp. 20–8.
3. *Ibid.*
4. Graham-Campbell, James, 1991, 'Norrie's Law, Fife: On the Nature and Dating of the Silver Hoard', *Proceedings of the Society of Antiquaries of Scotland*, vol. 121, pp. 241–59; Graham-Campbell, James, 1993, 'The Norrie's Law Hoard and the Dating of Pictish Silver', pp. 115–17, in Spearman and Higgitt, *op. cit.*
5. Anderson, A.O. and Anderson, M.O., (eds and trs), 1961, *Adomnan's Life of Columba*, London, Thomas Nelson.
6. Frere, S.S., 1987, *Britannia: A History of Roman Britain*, 3rd edn, Routledge and Kegan Paul, pp. 339–42, 354–5.
7. Benton, Sylvia, 1930, 'The Excavations of the Sculptor's Cave, Covesea, Morayshire', *Proceedings of the Society of Antiquaries of Scotland*, vol. 65, pp. 177–216.
8. Stevenson, Robert B.K. and Emery, John, 1964, 'The Gaulcross Hoard of Pictish Silver', *Proceedings of the Society of Antiquaries of Scotland*, vol. 97, pp. 206–11.

Chapter 9

1. Skene, *op. cit.*, pp. 66–78, 343–74.
2. Skene, *op. cit.*, p. 8.

Chapter 10

1. This and other possible artists' signatures could not possibly have been recognized without the aid of that splendid illustrated publication dating back to the beginning of the century, known to generations as ECMS and recently reprinted: J. Romilly Allen and Joseph Anderson, *The Early Christian Monuments of Scotland*, reprinted, 1993, Pinkfoot Press, two volumes.
2. Restoration of this stone has resulted in the loss of about six inches near the top – the damaged part of the stone which formerly displayed the Pictish elephant. The nature of the loss can most easily be appreciated by looking at the front of the stone, where the proportions of the cross are wrong, the top being too short.
3. Sherley-Price, *op. cit.*, p. 309.
4. Simpson, W. Douglas, 1935, *The Celtic Church in Scotland: A Study of its Penetration Lines and Art Relations*, Aberdeen University Press, chap. 9; Simpson, W. Douglas, 1963, 'The Early Romanesque Tower at Restenneth Priory, Angus', *Antiquaries Journal*, vol. 43, pp. 269–83.

Chapter 11

1. Cummins, *op. cit.*, p. 136.
2. *Ibid*, p. 132.
3. ECMS, Part 3, p. 42.
4. James, Edward, 1998, 'The Continental Context', in Sally M. Foster (ed.), *The St Andrews Sarcophagus*, Four Courts Press, p. 246.
5. Thomas, A.C., 1994, 'A Black Cat among the Pictish Beasts? Some Ideas from Recent Cryptozoology', *Pictish Arts Society Journal*, vol. 6, pp. 1–8.
6. Nash-Williams, *op. cit.*, p. 102.
7. Ritchie, Anna, *Picts*, HMSO.
8. Nash-Williams, *op. cit.*, p. 84.
9. Close-Brookes, Joanna, 1989, *Pictish Stones in Dunrobin Castle Museum*, Pilgrim Press.

10. Crouch, David, 1990, *William Marshall*, Longman.
11. Christison, Dr, 1905, 'Report on the Society's Excavations on the Portalloch Estate, Argyll, in 1904–5', *Proceedings of the Society of Antiquaries of Scotland*, series 4, vol. 3, pp. 259–322.
12. Winterbottom, *op. cit.*
13. Frere, *op. cit.*, p. 339.

Chapter 12

1. Mack, Alastair, 1997, *Field Guide to the Pictish Symbol Stones*, Pinkfoot Press, p. 5.
2. Macalister, R.A.S., 1945, *Corpus Inscriptionum Insularum Celticarum*, Stationery Office, Dublin, vol. I.
3. Nash-Williams, *op. cit.*
4. Collingwood, R.G. and Wright, R.P., 1965, *The Roman Inscriptions of Britain*, vol. I, *Inscriptions on Stone*.
5. *Ibid*, p. xvi; pers. comm. from Professor A.D. Nock.
6. Nash-Williams, *op. cit.*
7. Macalister, R.A.S., 1949, *Corpus Inscriptionum Insularum Celticarum*, Stationery Office, Dublin, vol. II.

Chapter 13

1. Carrington, Anne, 1996, 'The Horseman and the Falcon: Mounted Falconers in Pictish Sculpture', *Proceedings of the Society of Antiquaries of Scotland*, 126, pp. 459–68.
2. Coss, Peter, 1993, *The Knight in Medieval England, 1000–1400*, Alan Sutton Publishing, p. 24.
3. Ashmore, P.J., 1980, 'Low Cairns, Long Cists and Symbol Stones', *Proceedings of the Society of Antiquaries of Scotland*, 110, 346–55.
4. MacLagan Wedderburn, Laurie M. and Grime, Dorothy M., 1984, 'The Cairn Cemetery at Garbeg, Drumnadrochit', in J.G.P. Friell and W.G. Watson (eds), *Pictish Studies: Settlement, Burial and Art in Dark Age Northern Britain*, BAR British Series, 125, pp. 151–67.
5. Close Brookes, Joanna, 1980, 'Excavations in the Dairy Farm Park, Dunrobin, Sutherland', *Proceedings of the Society of Antiquaries of Scotland*, 110, 328–45.

6. Gourlay, Robert, 1984, 'A Symbol Stone and Cairn at Watenan, Caithness', in Friell and Watson, *op. cit.*, pp. 131–3.
7. Proudfoot, Edwina, 1996, 'Excavations at the Long Cist Cemetery on Hallow Hill, St Andrews, Fife', *Proceedings of the Society of Antiquaries of Scotland*, 126, 387–454.
8. Kaland, Sigrid H.H., 1993, 'The Settlement of Westness, Rousay', in Colleeen E. Batey, Judith Jesch and Christopher D. Morris, *The Viking Age in Caithness, Orkney and the North Atlantic*, pp. 308–17.
9. Dalland, Magnar, 1992, 'Long Cist Burials at Four Winds, Longniddry, East Lothian', *Proceedings of the Society of Antiquaries of Scotland*, 122, 197–206.
10. Cowie, T., 1978, 'Excavations at the Catstane, Midlothian', *Proceedings of the Society of Antiquaries of Scotland*, 109, 166–201.
11. Dalland, Magnar, 1993, 'The Excavation of a Group of Long Cists at Avonmill Road, Linlithgow, West Lothian', *Proceedings of the Society of Antiquaries of Scotland*, 123, 337–44.
12. Sherley-Price, *op. cit.*, p. 59.
13. *Ibid*, pp. 225, 255.
14. Rutherford, Anthony and Ritchie, Graham, 1975, 'The Catstane', *Proceedings of the Society of Antiquaries of Scotland*, 105, 183–8.
15. Sherley-Price, *op. cit.*, p. 148.
16. Alcock, Leslie and Alcock, Elizabeth A., 1992, 'Reconnaissance Excavations and other Fieldwork at Forteviot, Perthshire, 1981', *Proceedings of the Society of Antiquaries of Scotland*, 122.
17. Coss, *op. cit.*, p. 13.

Chapter 14

1. The symbols from this cave have been illustrated in ECMS Part III (volume 2 of the new edition), p. 130 and in Laing, L. and Laing, J., 1993, *The Picts and the Scots*, Alan Sutton, p. 107.
2. Ritchie, J.N.G. and Stevenson, J.N., 1993, 'Pictish Cave Art at East Wemyss, Fife', pp. 203–8, in Spearman and Higgitt, *op. cit.*
3. Sutherland, Elizabeth, 1994, *In Search of the Picts*, Constable, p. 232.

4. ECMS, Part III (volume 2 of new edition), pp. 370–3.
5. Barnes, M.P., 1993, 'The Interpretation of the Runic Inscriptions of Maeshowe', in Batey, Jesh and Morris, *The Viking Age in Caithness, Orkney and the North Atlantic*, pp. 349–69.
6. Benton, *op. cit.*
7. Barnes, *op. cit.*
8. Hedges, J.W., 1987, *Bu, Gurness and the Brochs of Orkney*, British Archaeological Reports, British Series.
9. Hunter, J.R., 1990, 'Pool, Sanday: a Case Study for the Late Iron Age and Viking Periods', in Ian Armit (ed.), *Beyond the Brochs*, pp. 175–93.
10. McGregor, Arthur, 1974, 'The Broch of Burrian, North Ronaldsay', *Proceedings of the Society of Antiquaries of Scotland*, 105, 63–118.
11. Curle, A.O., 1934, 'An Account of Further Excavations at Jarlshof, Sumburgh, Shetland in 1932 and 1934', *Proceedings of the Society of Antiquaries of Scotland*, 68, 224–319.
12. Bruce, J., 1907, 'Notice of the Excavation of a Broch at Jarlshof, Sumburgh, Shetland', *Proceedings of the Society of Antiquaries of Scotland*, 41, 11–33.
13. Smith, J.A., 1883, 'Notes on some Stone Implements, etc. from Shetland, now presented to the Museum', *Proceedings of the Society of Antiquaries of Scotland*, 17, 291–9.
14. McGregor, *op. cit.*
15. Page, R.I., 1973, 'The Runic Inscriptions from N 59', in J.N.L. Myres and Barbara Green, 'The Anglo-Saxon Cemeteries of Caistor-by-Norwich and Markshall, Norfolk', *Report of the Research Committee of the Society of Antiquaries of London*, no. XXX, pp. 114–17.
16. *Ibid.*
17. *Ibid.*
18. Addyman, P.V. and Hill, D.H., 1969, 'Saxon Southampton: A Review of the Evidence, Part II: Industry, Trade and Everyday Life', *Proceedings of the Hampshire Field Club Archaeological Society*, 26, 61–96.

Chapter 15

1. 'Legend of St Andrew', Skene, *op. cit.*, p. 187.
2. Forsyth, Katherine, 1996, 'The Inscriptions on the Dupplin Cross', in C. Bourke (ed.), *From the Isles of the North: Early Medieval Art in Ireland and Britain*, pp. 237–44.
3. Skene, *op. cit.*, p. 8.
4. ECMS, Part III (vol. 2 in new edition), p. 297.
5. Ritchie, J.N.G., 1997, 'Recording Early Christian Monuments in Scotland', in D. Henry (ed.), *The Worm, the Germ and the Thorn*, Pinkfoot Press, pp. 119–28.
6. 'Legend of St Andrew', Skene, *op. cit.*, p. 188.

Chapter 16

1. Forsyth, Katherine, 1996, 'The Inscriptions on the Dupplin Cross', in C. Bourke (ed.), *From the Isles of the North: Early Medieval Art in Ireland and Britain*, pp. 237–44.
2. Henderson, Isabel, 1998, '*Primus inter Pares*: The St Andrews Sarcophagus and Pictish Sculpture', in Sally M. Foster (ed.), *The St Andrews Sarcophagus*, p. 154.
3. Cummins, *op. cit.*
4. Skene, *op. cit.*, p. 183.
5. For a thorough discussion of the problem see Ursula Hall, 1994, *St Andrew and Scotland*, St Andrews University, chap. 4, pp. 46–77.
6. Skene, *op. cit.*, p. 188.
7. Thomas, A.C., 1998, 'Form and Function', in Sally M. Foster (ed.), *The St Andrews Sarcophagus*, p. 95.
8. Henderson, *op. cit.*, p. 154.
9. *Ibid*, p. 130.
10. Plunkett, Steven J., 1998, 'The Mercian Perspective', in Sally M. Foster (ed.), *The St Andrews Sarcophagus*, p. 219.
11. For a general account of the history of this period see F.M. Stenton, *Anglo-Saxon England*, Clarendon Press, chaps VIII and X.
12. Cummins, *op. cit.*, p. 143.

Bibliography

Addyman, P.V. and Hill, D.H., 1969, 'Saxon Southampton: A Review of the Evidence Part II: Industry, Trade and Everyday Life', *Proceedings of the Hampshire Field Club Archaeological Society*, 26, 61–96

Alcock, Leslie, 1971, *Arthur's Britain: History and Archaeology, AD 367–634*, London, Allen Lane

—— and Alcock, Elizabeth A., 1992, 'Reconnaissance excavations on Early Historic fortifications and other royal sites in Scotland, 1974–84; 5: A, Excavations and other fieldwork at Forteviot, Perthshire, 1981; B, Excavations at Urquhart Castle, Inverness-shire, 1983; C, Excavations at Dunottar, Kincardineshire, 1984', *Proceedings of the Society of Antiquaries of Scotland*, 122, 215–93

Allen, J. Romilly and Anderson, Joseph, 1903, *The Early Christian Monuments of Scotland*, with an Introduction by Isabel Henderson, Balgavies, Angus, Pinkfoot Press, two vols, 1993

Anderson, A.O. and Anderson, M.O., (eds and trs), *Adomnan's Life of Columba*, London, Thomas Nelson, 1961

Armit, Ian (ed.), 1990, *Beyond the Brochs: Changing Perspectives on the Late Iron Age in Atlantic Scotland*, Edinburgh, Edinburgh University Press

Ashmore, P.J., 1980, 'Low Cairns, Long Cists and Symbol Stones', *Proceedings of the Society of Antiquaries of Scotland*, 110, 346–55

Barnes, Michael P., 1993, 'The Interpretation of the Runic Insciptions of Maeshowe', in Colleen E. Batey, Judith Jesch and Christopher D. Morris, *The Viking Age in Caithness, Orkney and the North Atlantic*, Select Papers from the Proceedings of the Eleventh Viking Congress, Thurso and Kirkwall, 1989, pp. 349–69

Batey, Colleen E., Jesch, Judith and Morris, Christopher D. (eds). 1993, *The Viking Age in Caithness, Orkney and the North Atlantic*, Edinburgh, Edinburgh University Press

Benton, Sylvia, 1930, 'The Excavations of the Sculptor's Cave, Covesea, Morayshire', *Proceedings of the Society of Antiquaries of Scotland*, 65, 177–216

Bourke, C. (ed.), *From the Isles of the North: Early Medieval Art in Ireland and Britain*, Proceedings of the Third International Conference on Insular Art, Belfast, 1994

Bruce, John, 1907, 'Notice of the excavation of a broch at Jarlshof, Sumburgh, Shetland', *Proceedings of the Society of Antiquaries of Scotland*, 41, 11–33

Budge, Sir E.A. Wallis, 1910, *Egyptian Language: Early Lessons in Egyptian Hieroglyphs with Sign List*, London, Routledge and Kegan Paul Ltd

Carrington, Ann, 1996, 'The horseman and the falcon: mounted falconers in Pictish sculpture', *Proceedings of the Society of Antiquaries of Scotland*, 126, 459–68

Chadwick, John, *The Decipherment of Linear B*, 2nd edn, Cambridge, Cambridge University Press, 1967

Christison, Dr, 1905, 'Report on the Society's Excavations on the Poltalloch Estate, Argyll, in 1904–5', *Proceedings of the Society of Antiquaries of Scotland*, Series 4, Vol. 3, pp. 259–322

Clancey, O.C., 1993, 'The Drosten Stone: a new reading', *Proceedings of the Society of Antiquaries of Scotland*, 123, 345–53

Close-Brookes, Joanna, 1980, 'Excavations in the Dairy Park, Dunrobin, Sutherland, 1977', *Proceedings of the Society of Antiquaries of Scotland*, 110, 328–45

——, 1989, *Pictish Stones in Dunrobin Castle Museum*, Derby, Pilgrim Press

Collingwood, R.G. and Wright, R.P., 1965, *The Roman Inscriptions of Britain*, vol. I, *Inscriptions on Stone*, Oxford, Clarendon Press

Coss, Peter, 1993, *The Knight in Medieval England, 1000–1400*, Stroud, Alan Sutton Publishing Ltd

Cowie, T., 1978, 'Excavations at the Catstane, Midlothian, 1977', *Proceedings of the Society of Antiquaries of Scotland*, 109, 166–201

Cramp, Rosemary, 1984, *Corpus of Anglo-Saxon Stone Sculpture, vol. 1: County Durham and Northumberland*, two parts, Oxford, Oxford University Press for British Academy

Crouch, David, 1990, *William Marshall: Court, Career and Chivalry in the Angevin Empire, 1147–1219*, London, Longman

Cummins, W.A., 1995, *The Age of the Picts*, Stroud, Alan Sutton Publishing Ltd

Curle, A.O., 1920, 'Report on the excavations on Traprain Law in the summer of 1919', *Proceedings of the Society of Antiquaries of Scotland*, 54.

Curle, Alexander O., 1934, 'An Account of Further Excavations at Jarlshof, Sumburgh, Shetland in 1932 and 1934', *Proceedings of the Society of Antiquaries of Scotland*, 68, 224–319

Dalland, Magnar, 1992, 'Long Cist Burials at Four Winds, Longniddry, East Lothian', *Proceedings of the Society of Antiquaries of Scotland*, 122, 197–206

——, 1993, 'The excavation of a group of long cists at Avonmill Road, Linlithgow, West Lothian', *Proceedings of the Society of Antiquaries of Scotland*, 123, 337–44

Forsyth, Katherine, 1996, 'The Inscriptions on the Dupplin Cross', in C. Bourke (ed.), *From the Isles of the North: Early Medieval Art in Ireland and Britain*, Proceedings of the Third International Conference on Insular Art, Belfast, 1994, pp. 237–44

——, 1997, 'Some thoughts on Pictish symbols as a formal Writing System', in David Henry (ed.), *The Worm, the Germ and the Thorn: Pictish and Related Studies Presented to Isabel Henderson*, Balgavies, Angus, Pinkfoot Press

Foster, Sally M., 1990, 'Pins, Combs and the Chronology of Later Atlantic Iron Age Settlement', in Ian Armit (ed.), *Beyond the Brochs: Changing Perspectives on the Late Iron Age in Atlantic Scotland*, Edinburgh, Edinburgh University Press, pp. 143–74

—— (ed.), 1998, *The St Andrews Sarcophagus: A Pictish Masterpiece and its International Connections*, Dublin, Four Courts Press

Fox, Sir Cyril, 1949, 'Celtic Mirror handles in Britain, with special reference to the Colchester Handle', *Archaeologia Cambrensis*, 100, 24–44.

Fox-Davies, A.C., *A Complete Guide to Heraldry*, 2nd edn, revised and annotated by J.P. Brooke-Little, London, Thomas Nelson and Sons Ltd, 1969

Frere, S.S., *Britannia: A History of Roman Britain*, London, Routledge and Kegan Paul, 3rd edn, 1987

Friell, J.G.P. and Watson, W.G. (eds), 1984, *Pictish Studies: Settlement, Burial and Art in Dark Age Northern Britain*, BAR British Series, 125

Gilbert, Inga, 1995, *The Symbolism of the Pictish Stones in Scotland: A Study of Origins*, Edinburgh and Dorset, Speedwell Books

Gourlay, Robert, 1984, 'A Symbol Stone and Cairn at Watenan, Caithness', in J.G.P. Friell and W.G. Watson (eds), *Pictish Studies: Settlement, Burial and Art in Dark Age Northern Britain*, Oxford, BAR British Series, 125, pp. 131–3

Graham-Campbell, James, 1991, 'Norrie's Law, Fife: On the Nature and Dating of the Silver Hoard', *Proceedings of the Society of Antiquaries of Scotland*, 121, 241–59

——, 1993, 'The Norrie's Law Hoard and the Dating of Pictish Silver', pp. 115–17, in Michael Spearman and John Higgitt (eds), *The Age of Migrating Ideas: Early Medieval Art in Northern Britain and Ireland*, Proceedings of the Second International Conference on Insular Art, Stroud, Alan Sutton Publishing Ltd

Hall, Hubert (ed.), 1896, *Red Book of the Exchequer, Rerum Britannicarum Medii Aevi Scriptores*, vol. 99

Hall, Ursula, 1994, *St Andrew and Scotland*, St Andrews, St Andrews University Library

Hedges, John W., 1983, *Bu, Gurness and the Brochs of Orkney*, Oxford, British Archaeological Reports, British Series, vols 163–5

Henderson, Isabel, 1979, 'The Silver Chain from Whitecleugh, Shieldholm, Crawfordjohn, Lanarkshire', *Transactions of the Dumfriesshire and Galloway Natural History and Antiquarian Society, Wanlockhead and Leadhills Volume*, vol. 54, pp. 20–8

——, 1998, '*Primus inter Pares*: The St Andrews Sarcophagus and Pictish Sculpture', in Sally M. Foster (ed.), *The St Andrews Sarcophagus: A Pictish Masterpiece and its International Connections*, Dublin, Four Courts Press, pp. 97–167

Henry, David (ed.), 1997, *The Worm, the Germ and the Thorn: Pictish and Related Studies Presented to Isabel Henderson*, Balgavies, Angus, Pinkfoot Press

Higham, N.J., 1994, *The English Conquest: Gildas and Britain in the Fifth Century*, Manchester, Manchester University Press

Hunter, J.R., 1990, 'Pool, Sanday: A Case Study for the Late Iron Age and Viking Periods', in Ian Armit (ed.), *Beyond the Brochs: Changing Perspectives on the Late Iron Age in Atlantic Scotland*, Edinburgh, Edinburgh University Press, 1994

Jackson, Anthony, *The Symbol Stones of Scotland: A Social Anthropological Resolution of the Problem of the Picts*, Orkney, Orkney Press, 1984

James, Edward, 1998, 'The Continental Context', in Sally M. Foster, 1998 *The St Andrews Sarcophagus: A Pictish Masterpiece and its International Connections*, Dublin, Four Courts Press, pp. 240–9

Joussaume, Roger, 1988, *Dolmens for the Dead: Megalith-Building throughout the World*, English trans., London, B.T. Batsford Ltd

Kaland, Sigrid H.H., 1993, 'The Settlement of Westness, Rousay', in Colleeen E. Batey, Judith Jesch and Christopher D. Morris, *The Viking Age in Caithness, Orkney and the North Atlantic*, Select Papers from the Proceedings of the Eleventh Viking Congress, Thurso and Kirkwall, 1989, pp. 308–17

Kitzinger, Ernst, 1993, 'Interlace and Icons: Form and Function in Early Insular Art', pp. 3–15, in Michael Spearman, R. and John Higgitt (eds), *The Age of Migrating Ideas: Early Medieval Art in Northern Britain and Ireland*, Proceedings of the Second International Conference on Insular Art, Stroud, Alan Sutton Publishing Ltd

Laing, Lloyd R. and Laing, Jennifer, 1984, 'The Date and Origin of the Pictish Symbols', *Proceedings of the Society of Antiquaries of Scotland*, 114, 261–76

——, 1993, *The Picts and the Scots*, Stroud, Alan Sutton Publishing Ltd

Lloyd-Morgan, G., 1974, 'A Bronze Statuette from London Bridge', *Antiquaries Journal*, 54, 85–6

——, 1980, 'Roman mirrors and Pictish symbol: a note on trade and contact', in W.S. Hanson and L.J.F. Keppie (eds), *Roman Frontier Studies*, Oxford, BAR International Series, 71(i), pp. 97–106

Macalister, R.A.S., 1945, 1949, *Corpus Inscriptionum Insularum Celticarum*, vols I and II, Stationery Office, Dublin

——, 1949, *The Archaeology of Ireland*, London, Methuen and Co. Ltd

Mack, Alastair, 1997, *Field Guide to the Pictish Symbol Stones*, Balgavies, Angus, Pinkfoot Press

MacLagan Wedderburn, Laurie, M. and Grime, Dorothy M., 1984, 'The Cairn Cemetery at Garbeg, Drumnadrochit', in J.G.P. Friell and W.G. Watson (eds) *Pictish Studies: Settlement, Burial and Art in Dark Age Northern Britain*, Oxford, BAR British Series, 125, pp. 151–67

Mac Lean, Douglas, 1997, 'Maelrubai, Applecross and the Late Pictish Contribution West of Drumalban', in Henry, David (ed.), *The Worm, the Germ and the Thorn: Pictish and Related Studies Presented to Isabel Henderson*, Balgavies, Angus, Pinkfoot Press, pp. 173–87

McGregor, Arthur, 1974, 'The Broch of Burrian, North Ronaldsay', *Proceedings of the Society of Antiquaries of Scotland*, 105, 63–118

Moor, Charles, 1929–1932, *Knights of Edward I*, Harleian Society, vols 80–4

Nash-Williams, 1950, *The Early Christian Monuments of Wales*, Cardiff, University of Wales Press

O'Sullivan, Thomas D., 1978, *The De Excidio of Gildas: Its Authentication and Date*, Leiden, E.J. Brill

Page, R.I., 1973, 'The Runic Inscriptions from N 59', in J.N.L. Myres and Barbara Green, 'The

Anglo-Saxon Cemeteries of Caistor-by-Norwich and Markshall, Norfolk', *Report of the Research Committee of the Society of Antiquaries of London*, no. XXX, pp. 114–17

Peterson, Edward, 1996, *The Message of Scotland's Symbol Stones*, Aberuthven, PCD Ruthven Books

Plunkett, Steven J., 1998, 'The Mercian Perspective', in Sally M. Foster (ed.), *The St Andrews Sarcophagus: A Pictish Masterpiece and its International Connections*, Dublin, Four Courts Press, p. 202–26

Proudfoot, Edwina (with contributions by others), 1996, 'Excavations at the long cist cemetery on Hallow Hill, St Andrews, Fife, 1975–7', *Proceedings of the Society of Antiquaries of Scotland*, 126, 387–454

Ritchie, Anna, 1989, *Picts: An Introduction to the Life of the Picts and the Carved Stones in the care of the Secretary of State for Scotland*, HMSO

Ritchie, J.N. Graham and Stevenson, John N., 1993, 'Pictish Cave Art at East Wemyss, Fife', pp. 203–8, in Michael Spearman and John Higgitt (eds), *The Age of Migrating Ideas: Early Medieval Art in Northern Britain and Ireland*, Proceedings of the Second International Conference on Insular Art, Stroud, Alan Sutton Publishing Ltd

Ritchie, J.N.G., 1997, 'Recording Early Christian Monuments in Scotland', in D. Henry (ed.), *The Worm, the Germ and the Thorn: Pictish and Related Studies Presented to Isabel Henderson*, Balgavies, Angus, Pinkfoot Press, 119–128

Rutherford, Anthony and Ritchie, Graham, 1975, 'The Catstane', *Proceedings of the Society of Antiquaries of Scotland*, vol. 105, pp. 183–8

Samson, Ross, 1992, 'The Reinterpretation of the Pictish Symbols', *Journal of the British Archaeological Association*, 145, 29–65

Sherley-Price, L. (trans.) Bede, *Ecclesiastical History of the English People with Bede's Letter to Egbert and Cuthbert's Letter on the Death of Bede*, rev. edn, Harmondsworth, Penguin, 1990

Simpson, W. Douglas, 1935, *The Celtic Church in Scotland: A Study of its Penetration Lines and Art Relations*, Aberdeen, Aberdeen University Press

——, 1963, 'The Early Romanesque Tower at Restenneth Priory, Angus', *Antiquaries Journal*, 43, 269–83

Skene, W.F., 1867, *Chronicles of the Picts, Chronicles of the Scots, and other Early Memorials of Scottish History*, Edinburgh, HM General Register House

Smith, John Alexander, 1883, 'Notes on some stone implements, etc. from Shetland, now presented to the Museum', *Proceedings of the Society of Antiquaries of Scotland*, 17, 291–9

Spearman, R. Michael and John Higgitt (eds), 1993, *The Age of Migrating Ideas: Early Medieval Art in Northern Britain and Ireland*, Proceedings of the Second International Conference on Insular Art, Stroud, Alan Sutton Publishing Ltd

Stenton, F.M., *Anglo-Saxon England*, Oxford, Clarendon Press

Stevenson, Robert B.K., 1959, 'The Inchyra Stone and some other Unpublished Early Christian Monuments', *Proceedings of the Society of Antiquaries of Scotland*, vol. 92, 33–55

—— and Emery, John, 1964, 'The Gaulcross Hoard of Pictish Silver', *Proceedings of the Society of Antiquaries of Scotland*, vol. 97, pp. 206–11

Sutherland, Elizabeth, 1963, *In Search of the Picts*, London, Constable

Thomas, A. Charles, 1963, 'The Interpretation of the Pictish Symbols', *Archaeological Journal*, 120, 31–97

——, 1994, 'A Black Cat among the Pictish Beasts? Some Ideas from Recent Cryptozoology', *Pictish Arts Society Journal*, vol. 6, 1–8

——, 1998, 'Form and Function', in Sally M. Foster (ed.), *The St Andrews Sarcophagus: a Pictish Masterpiece and its International Connections*, Dublin, Four Courts Press, pp. 84–96

Wainwright, F.T. (ed.), 1956, *The Problem of the Picts*, Edinburgh, Thomas Nelson

Williams, A.H., 1959, *An Introduction to the History of Wales*, vol. I, *Prehistoric Times to 1063 AD*, Cardiff, University of Wales Press

Winterbottom, Michael, 1978, *Gildas: The Ruin of Britain and Other Works*, Chichester, Phillimore

Yeoman, Peter, 1999, *Pilgrimage in Medieval Scotland*, London, B.T. Batsford Ltd/Historic Scotland

Index

Individual symbol stones, symbols and their interpretation are all indexed under symbol. Entries in *italics* indicate illustrations.